Empire
for Liberty

Empire
for Liberty

◆   ◆   ◆   ◆   ◆   ◆

MELVILLE AND THE POETICS

OF INDIVIDUALISM

Wai-chee Dimock

PRINCETON UNIVERSITY PRESS

PRINCETON, NEW JERSEY

Copyright © 1989 by Princeton University Press
Published by Princeton University Press, 41 William Street,
Princeton, New Jersey 08540
In the United Kingdom: Princeton University Press, Guildford, Surrey

Library of Congress Cataloging-in-Publication Data
Dimock, Wai-Chee, 1953–
Empire for liberty : Melville and the poetics of individualism / Wai-Chee
Dimock.
p.   cm.
Bibliography: p.
Includes index.
ISBN 0-691-06758-9 (alk. paper)
1. Melville, Herman, 1819–1891—Criticism and Interpretation.
I. Title.
PS2387.D55   1988
813'.3—dc19   88-19680

This book has been composed in Goudy Old Style

Clothbound editions of Princeton University Press books are printed
on acid-free paper, and binding materials are chosen
for strength and durability. Paperbacks, although satisfactory
for personal collections, are not usually suitable for library rebinding

Printed in the United States of America by Princeton University Press,
Princeton, New Jersey

For my parents

Contents

◆   ◆   ◆

Acknowledgments

◆   ◆   ◆

A FELLOWSHIP from the American Council of Learned Societies enabled me to begin this book, and a Henry Rutgers Research Fellowship from Rutgers University enabled me to finish it. I am grateful to the National Endowment for the Humanities for a stipend to attend a Summer Institute at Berkeley in 1985. For his patience and goodwill, I am indebted to Robert E. Brown, my editor at Princeton University Press. For his careful copyediting, I want to thank Brian R. Mac-Donald.

Since this book is an implicit argument against the idea of originality, it is a special pleasure for me to acknowledge, on this occasion, a number of people who, in being so formidably and generously present, not only prove my point but make it a bearable reality: Jean-Christophe Agnew, Sacvan Bercovitch, Richard Brodhead, Peter Dimock, Susan Eilenberg, Charles Feidelson, Walter Herbert, Myra Jehlen, Laura Kendrick, David Leverenz, R.W.B. Lewis, Walter Benn Michaels, Toni Morrison, Donald Pease, Richard Poirier, Mary Poovey, Barry Qualls, Peter Schmidt, Fred See, Mark Seltzer, Alan Trachtenberg, Lynn Wardley. My dog, Ishi, who keeps everything in perspective, has left his mark here as well.

Empire
for Liberty

1. Nation, Self, and Personification

"YOU MUST have plenty of sea-room to tell the Truth in," Melville said in an inspired though not usually remarked moment in "Hawthorne and His Mosses."[1] He was thinking, perhaps, less of *Mosses from an Old Manse*, the slim volume under review, than of the "imperial folio" he himself happened to be writing at the moment. *Moby-Dick* was a "mighty book" imaged after the "mighty bulk" of the whale, Melville explained. Its "outreaching comprehensiveness of sweep" was to encompass "the whole circle of the sciences, and all the generations of whales, and men, and mastodons, past, present, and to come, with all the revolving panoramas of empire on earth."[2]

Truth had its spatial appetites, Melville seemed to suggest. For its proper accommodation one needed a vast theater—indeed, nothing short of an empire would do. Melville was by no means the only one to make "sea-room" such a cardinal virtue, and such a cardinal necessity. Jefferson, in his 1805 inaugural address, had entertained a similar premise. "The larger our association," he said, "the less will it be shaken by local passions."[3] Jefferson was speaking in the wake of the Louisiana Purchase (1803), an event which rapidly put to rest the fear that space might be a liability for republican government. Far from being a liability, territorial expansion had come to be seen, by the 1830s, as a basic requirement for the nation's well-being, so basic that it became practically an alimentary need. Major Davezac, a speaker at the 1844 New Jersey Democratic State Convention, proceeded from just that premise when he alluded to America's "pasture grounds"—invoking, in his zeal, if not the "mighty bulk" of the whale, then something almost as bulky:

> Make way, I say, for the young American Buffalo—he has not yet got land enough; he wants more land as his cool shelter in summer—he wants more land for his beautiful pasture grounds. I tell you, we will give him Oregon for his summer shade, and the region of Texas as his winter pasture. (Applause.) Like all of his race, he wants salt, too. Well, he shall have the use of two oceans—the mighty Pacific and turbulent Atlantic shall be his.[4]

Melville's love of "sea-room" was perhaps more widely shared than we might think. He could not have known about a speech at the New Jersey convention, and the point here is not to trace any "influence" from that quarter. Yet, in a broader, less determinate fashion, Melville and Major Davezac do seem to occupy some common ground—a domain of cultural inscription shadowed forth in authorial pronouncements no less than in expansionist rhetoric. What brings them together, in their respective plea for authorial "sea-room" and bovine "pasture grounds," is a shared convention of ideas—a convention that, even as it entertains the diversity of individual utterances, is nonetheless regulative in the constitution of that individuality. The relation between Melville and Davezac then, between the enshrined writer and the forgotten speaker, is the relation between two voices inhabiting a historical moment: they are conditioned by that moment, circumscribed by it, and differentiated within it. At once parallel and separate, they map forth a kinship in difference.

It is the difference, of course, to which we have customarily attended: we have taken that difference for granted, embraced it as an article of faith, developed elaborate arguments from this central premise. Yet something surely ought to be said about the kinship as well. To do so is not to make a Davezac out of Melville, or even to uncover a Davezac in him, but to restore a measure of historical contingency to such categories as "authorship," "textuality," and indeed "literature" itself. If we are to think of authorship as an articulation of the author's selfhood, and if that selfhood is itself a contingent term within a historical process, then literature too must be understood to be contingent. There is no transcendent ground, ultimately, for its formal authority—its assembly of shape and meaning—because the "author" who authorizes that form is himself historically constituted. And if by literature we still refer to a collection of honored texts, the "text" too must be understood to be an expedient (rather than absolute) term, pressed into service only by fiat and for the sake of convenience. For the "text" and its "context" are in every case inseparable, the latter being not so much external to the former as constitutive of it, encompassing it and permeating it as the condition of its textuality.

And so, obscure as he once was and discredited as he has since become, Major Davezac is nonetheless a phenomenon worth recalling—not only to be studied independently, but also to help us contextualize what might otherwise have appeared discrete and contextless. In the presence of such a figure, whose historicity is manifest, we can begin to imagine Melville's own historicity in all its filiations and correspondences. The emphasis on kinship, then, is hardly an attempt to demote the author. It is, rather, an attempt to disseminate within him a network of associations and, in so doing, to ask again what constitutes an "author," what constitutes a "text," and what constitutes the "subject" of literary studies. Such an approach necessarily shifts the emphasis away from the achievements of individual authors to the relational matrix they inhabit. If this seems a disservice to the author in one sense, the disservice, I hope, will simultaneously be a tribute.

For to the extent that the text is seen not as a reified entity—not a monument of individual achievement, but a field of permutating relations—the author too is saved from the fate of reification.[5] He is saved, in Melville's case, from the fate of being always and only a "great author." Excused momentarily from that imposing charge, he takes on a more interesting contour: he is not so much a given as a problematic, produced and reproduced by the relations that engage him. If he sometimes exemplifies a "poetics of individualism" (as he does in my account), he is nonetheless not reducible to that poetics, because he is neither enclosed by it nor exhausted within it. Other poetics, other modes of human meaning and legitimacy, will find a voice in him as well, as other critics will testify. To focus on the context of authorship, then, is not only to resist a reified notion of that activity; it is also to reflect on the inescapably contextual character of literary criticism itself, and to resist *its* tendency to reify its own procedures. For that reason, this study will not aim to be a "definitive study." Embedded in its own context—in the current debate about individualism—it is necessarily partial, partisan, provisional. If this makes for a more limited project, it also makes for a somewhat different kind of criticism—one that insists, I hope, on the contingency of author and critic both.

In any case, as the exemplar of a "poetics of individualism," Melville will emerge, in my account, as something of a representative author, a man who speaks for and with his contemporaries, speaking for them and with them, most of all, when he imagines himself to be above them, apart from them, opposed to them. He belongs, in this sense, to the company of those whom Sacvan Bercovitch has called "prophets of probation": "historian-seers whose representative qualities were enhanced by their hostility toward those they represented," in whom "alienation and engagement" were, "by their very contradictions . . . made to correspond."[6] Given such a premise, my goal obviously is not to uncover a timeless meaning in Melville's writings, but to multiply within them some measure of their density of reference: to examine them, in short, not in their didactic relation to the twentieth century, but in their dialogic relation to the nineteenth.

Two recent studies, Michael Rogin's *Subversive Genealogy: The Politics and Art of Herman Melville*, and James Duban's *Melville's Major Fiction: Politics, Theology, and Imagination*, have done much to invoke just that sense of cultural dialogue in Melville.[7] This study differs from both in locating that dialogue not in thematic representation, but in what I call "textual governance"—the formal logic by which Melville executes his authorial dictates, supervises and legitimizes, affixes meanings and assigns destinies. This textual governance, I believe, cannot be divorced from the social governance of antebellum America, for the terms of Melville's authorial sovereignty, by which he fashions his textual universe into a textual given, are ultimately analogous to the terms of America's national sovereignty, by which the social universe is fashioned into a social given. From this perspective, Melville's authorial practices are neither strictly private nor even strictly literary, for what they adumbrate, in their controlling logic of form, is something like a controlling "logic of culture."[8]

Melville, of course, would not be happy with such an account. Authorship, for him, is almost exclusively an exercise in freedom, an attempt to proclaim the self's sovereignty over and against the world's. To be worthy of its name, authorship must wrest itself free of what he calls the world's "dull common places"; it must indulge in its own "play of freedom and invention"; it must bring forth "those deep far-away things in [itself]." Indeed, the art of authorship, as he describes it in a celebrated moment in "Hawthorne and His Mosses," is none other than the art of escape: "in this world of lies, Truth is forced to fly like a scared white doe in the woodlands."[9] Truth here assumes its characteristic Melvillean pose as the persecuted object. But it has other poses as well, as we can see (in a less celebrated passage) in a letter to Hawthorne:

> By visible truth, we mean the apprehension of the absolute condition of present things as they strike the eye of the man who fears them not, though they do their worst to him,—the man who, like Russia or the British Empire, declares himself a sovereign nature (in himself) amid the powers of heaven, hell, and earth.[10]

Truth here belongs to individuals of a very special kind, individuals who have every right to call themselves "imperial selves." Unlike the ones Quentin Anderson describes, however, these selves are "imperial" not only in consciousness but also in conduct: indeed, their very mode of existence seems to have something in common with the Russian and British empires.[11] At once autonomous and impregnable, "a sovereign nature (in himself)," the imperial self is quite literally empire-like, his province of selfhood akin to a national polity. The mutuality between self and nation here is no accident, for it was just such a mutuality (as I will try to show) that consti-tuted both the self and the nation in antebellum America. In Melville's context, the mutuality between self and nation pro-duces an individual who, being empirelike, can finally have at his disposal the "sea-room" that Truth demands. In short, the spatial appetites of Truth make the author an "imperial" self almost by necessity—imperial, not only because he writes freely, in sovereign autonomy, but also because he writes ap-propriatively, like an empire. His authorship enlists the sov-ereignty of both self and nation—both the freedom of the for-mer and the dominion of the latter—to bring forth a new sovereign, an authorial variety, a figure whose literary individ-ualism is always imperially articulated. This logic suggests to Melville, in *Mardi*, that, "like many a monarch, I am less to be envied, than the veriest hind in the land." The same logic inspires him to produce an "imperial folio" in *Moby-Dick*, and to complain, in *Pierre*, that "the Empire of Human Knowledge can never be lasting in any one dynasty, since Truth still gives new Emperors to the earth."[12]

Lasting or not, Melville clearly thinks of himself as one of Truth's "Emperors." To Hawthorne, for instance, he depicts himself as the "lord of a little vale in the solitary Crimea" (adding, in a burst of elation, that Hawthorne's approval of *Moby-Dick* has "now given me the crown of India").[13] Imperial sovereignty in such remote regions would presumably give him the privilege he had wishfully attributed to the whale in *Moby-Dick*, that of "liv[ing] in this world without being of it."[14] Such are the terms of authorial freedom for Melville. And yet, even as he lays claim to that freedom, the very idiom of his claim already suggests a bond between him and the world from which he wishes to be free. For Melville, as it turns out, is hardly the only one to speak of personal freedom in imperial terms. Blackstone had resorted to the same idiom when he characterized the basis of individual freedom—"the right of property"—as "that sole and despotic dominion which one man claims and exercises over the external things of the world."[15] Even more famously, and closer to home, Jefferson had immortalized the same idiom, the same conjunction of freedom and dominion, in his striking (and not altogether oxymoronic) praise of America: as an "empire for liberty."[16]

If Melville's language of freedom resonated with Jefferson's, it resonated, just as surely, with the language of freedom in antebellum expansionist discourse. The idea that America was an "asylum for those who love liberty" had been a commonplace, of course, since the eighteenth century.[17] In the 1840s, however, the phrase "extending the area of freedom" came to have many useful new meanings. Andrew Jackson had coined that phrase to justify the annexation of Texas, and, in one form or another, the word "freedom" came to be a code word for America's continental expansionism.[18] John L. O'Sullivan (in an editorial that launched the phrase "Manifest Destiny") suggested, for instance, that America's claims to Oregon were justified by the "great experiment of liberty" to which Providence had appointed it.[19] Less providentially minded, Representative Duncan put the cause of liberty even more bluntly. "Personal liberty is incompatible with a crowded population," he said, and the "possession and occupation of Oregon" thus have "the love of liberty for its means, liberty itself for its reward, and the spread of free principles and republican institutions for its end."[20] The *United States Magazine and Democratic Review* summed it up best of all. Whereas European powers "conquer only to enslave," it reasoned, America, being "a free nation," "conquers only to bestow freedom."[21]

Far from being antagonistic, "empire" and "liberty" are instrumentally conjoined. If the former stands to safeguard the latter, the latter, in turn, serves to justify the former. Indeed, the conjunction of the two, of freedom and dominion, gives America its sovereign place in history—its Manifest Destiny, as its advocates so aptly called it. Within this context, Melville's terms of authorial sovereignty—his particular conjunction of freedom and dominion—would seem exactly to replicate the terms of national sovereignty. That he should evoke the nation's territorial acquisitions to image forth a writer's literary achievements is no accident. Hawthorne is to be admired, Melville thinks, because his authorial geography mirrors the nation's: "The smell of your beeches and hemlocks is upon him; your own broad prairies are in his soul; and if you travel away inland into his deep and noble nature, you will hear the far roar of his Niagara."[22]

Majestic in sweep, replete with "sea-room," the authorial geography here perhaps says less about Hawthorne than about Melville. It makes sense that America should strike Melville as the ultimate model for authorship, for what the nation has to offer is what the author needs to learn: a form of governance, a form of legitimation and subordination, license and control. Melville's authorial enterprise can be seen, in this regard, as a miniature version of the national enterprise. It can be seen, more specifically, as a miniature version of Manifest Destiny—understood here not as a specific set of events, but as an informing logic of freedom and dominion, a logic that underwrites not only what Michael Rogin calls the "internal imperialism" of an expansionist nation, but also what (following John L. O'Sullivan) we might call the "great experiment of liberty" of the literary self.[23]

Beginning with *Mardi*, Melville's first attempt at "serious" authorship, each of his novels seems to embody, in its textual governance, a principle of "empire for liberty." The novels differ enormously, of course, but even in their divergence—from the chartless extravagance in *Mardi* to the charted normality in *Redburn* and *White-Jacket*, through the relentless narratives of doom in *Moby-Dick* and *Pierre*, and closing with the systematic unaccountability of *The Confidence-Man*—what each book invokes, affirms, and defends is always the principle of imperial freedom, a principle of authorial license embedded in a technology of control. In that regard, Melville dramatizes the very juncture where the logic of freedom dovetails into the logic of empire, or (which is the same thing) where the imperial self of Jacksonian individualism recapitulates the logic of Jacksonian imperialism. Indeed, it is through Melville, through his authorial exercises in freedom and dominion, that we are able to see Manifest Destiny—not as most of us see it now, as a quaint idea, but as innumerable antebellum Americans saw it, as a powerful account of national and individual destiny, an account that conferred on both the nation and the self a sense of corporeal autonomy in space, and teleological ascendancy in time. Given the historical assumptions of this study, I will discuss at the outset, and beyond the confines of Melville's writings, the twin phenomena I claim he elucidates: Jacksonian imperialism and Jacksonian individualism, the building of an imperial nation and the making of a sovereign self. What follows then, will be a general account not only of those historical developments, but also of the way they converge in a distinctive mode of discourse—what I call the "narrative of personification"—a mode especially congenial to an "empire for liberty."

Antebellum America, the age of individualism, was also a period of sharpening tensions and polarities. The economic revolutions that promoted massive migrations westward and southward, and from rural areas to industrial centers, also resulted in the destruction of the self-sufficient farm economy, the collapse of the artisan and apprenticeship system, and the breakdown of traditional familial and communal ties.[24] Even as it generated new social and labor relations, industrial capitalism also generated new areas of conflict: actual conflict between whites and Indians on the frontier and, in the urban centers, the specter of "Capital against Labor," a horror presaged by the growing extremes of wealth and poverty and the progressive consolidation of class boundaries.[25] By 1860 more than half the nation's wealth was owned by five percent of the population; in Philadelphia the lower eighty percent of the population owned no more than three percent of the wealth.[26] Such "fatal extremes of overgrown wealth and desperate poverty" (to use Horace Mann's emphatic words)[27] were exacerbated by the arrival and congregation of immigrants in cities. During the 1830s around 600,000 immigrants came to the United States, a fourfold increase over the 1820s. In the next decade the figure rose to 1,700,000, and to 2,600,000 in the 1850s.[28] These new arrivals, indigent and primarily Catholic, provoked not only Know-Nothing nativism and anti-Catholic violence but also fearful visions of a permanent (and ultimately insurgent) underclass.

Jacksonian America, in short, was an America newly confronted with class difference, which explains why "prosperity" became a damning word in the period's public oratory, and why the poor suddenly appeared as "a race of famished, infuriated animals, goaded by instinct, and unrestrained by prospective hopes and fears." Such animals, "looking up with green eyed envy upon all the happy fruits of virtue" in the "orders of society above," were "like so many sparks falling upon a train already prepared for an explosion."[29] When "all the capital is in the hands of one class, and all the labor is thrown upon another," Horace Mann dolefully predicted, the most "hideous evils . . . are always engendered between capital and labor."[30] His sentiments were exactly echoed, if from a somewhat different political perspective, by Theophilus Fisk, in a speech menacingly titled "Capital Against Labor":

> Though the power of wealth in the hands of the few may for a time keep down the industrious many, yet the hazard of experimenting too far with those who have suffered so much and so long had better be taken into the calculation before a system of continued, permanent robbery be determined upon. . . . Beneath their feet an earthquake slumbers. There is a period in the affairs of men when forbearance ceases to be a virtue, when patient endurance becomes criminal.[31]

Images of earthquakes, volcanic eruptions, and other catastrophic violence dominated antebellum discourse on labor relations and class divisions. In this instance, the allusion to *Julius Caesar* ("There is a tide in the affairs of men") is especially interesting, for if Fisk was directly threatening an industrial calamity—the calamity of Capital against Labor—what he seemed also to be threatening, somewhat more allusively, was an imperial calamity, something like the fate of empire. It was a fate that Jacksonian America, committed as it was to territorial conquests, could hardly afford to ignore.

Empires, even to their most ardent defenders, had always

seemed to exhibit a lamentable and seemingly inescapable cycle of rise and fall. Thomas Cole had dramatized that cycle, for instance, in *The Course of Empire*. Even earlier, the knowledge of that imperial cycle had given a nervous edge to an otherwise jubilant oration, William Henry Drayton's *A Charge on the Rise of the American Empire*:

> Empires have their zenith—and their descension to a dissolution. . . . Three and thirty years numbered the illustrious Days of the Roman greatness—Eight Years measure the Duration of the British grandeur in meridian Lustre! How few are the Days of true Glory! . . . The Almighty . . . has made choice of the present generation to erect the American Empire. . . . An Empire that as soon as started into Existence, attracts the Attention of the Rest of the Universe; and bids fair, by the blessing of God, to be the most glorious of any upon Record.[32]

If the tone here was rapturous, the implication was not. For all his desire to extol the glory of the American Empire, what Drayton dramatized instead was the fearful ephemerality of that empire, its imminent danger of being usurped, surpassed, consigned to oblivion. The very word "empire" engendered not only pride but also anxiety, not only America's hope of unexampled greatness but also its fear of exampled decline. For to call America an "Empire" (even "the most glorious of any upon Record") was to invite comparisons with other empires, to invoke a common profile and a common fate—in short, it was to position America in history, as a temporal and presumably temporary phenomenon.

It took some ingenuity to make an exception of America, and a perennial task for American historians, from John Winthrop on, was to claim for America a special dispensation, a sort of providential exemption from history. The American form of government, Madison explained, was one that had "no model on the face of the globe," and "no parallel in the annals of human society." The *United States Magazine and Democratic Review* agreed. America was "first in the history of mankind," it said even more succinctly.[33] And because America's institutions were "susceptible of infinite improvement," its tenure on earth was likewise infinite. "We fondly believe," said one orator in 1817, "that ours will endure unhurt by the ravages of time."[34] In other words, America marked not only the beginning of a "New Heaven and a New Earth" but also an absolute, atemporal order of truth and justice. It stood at once as the culmination of progress and end to progress, fulfillment of history and emancipation from history. Unfolding in time, America remained ultimately timeless.

America's timeless permanence seemed especially assured in the context of the nation's continental expansion. Its territorial acquisitions, many thought, would win it a place in eternity. How this worked was neatly spelled out by the *United States Magazine and Democratic Review*, in an 1838 essay celebrating America as "The Great Nation of Futurity":

> The far-reaching, the boundless future will be an era of American greatness. In its magnificent domain of space and time, the nation of many nations is destined to manifest to mankind the excellence of divine principles. . . . Its floor shall be a hemisphere—its roof the firmament of the star-studded heavens, and its congregation an Union of many Republics, comprising hundreds of happy millions.[35]

America's claims to being the "nation of futurity" had everything to do, apparently, with its geographical expanse, its territorial claims to an entire "hemisphere." Such an empire was to be one of both "space and time," for America's dominion in space would, in this formulation, ensure its dominion over time. Latitude and longevity were interchangeable as far as the *Democratic Review* was concerned, and because the former was fast becoming an established fact, the latter would seem a logical inference. This expansionist publication was by no means alone in equating the temporal and the spatial. Melville, for instance, was to make the same equation in *White-Jacket*, when he asserted America's title to "the Future" as a corollary to its "future inheritance" of "the broad domains of the political pagans."[36] A legendary Kentuckian put this even more dramatically. Working on the same equation of time and space—and the same inference of time from space—he explained that America was bounded "on the west by the Day of Judgment."[37]

"A perfectly closed system," Georg Lukács writes, "reduces space and time to a common denominator and degrades time to the dimension of space."[38] Lukács is speaking generally of the process of production in an industrial economy, but his insight would seem to apply, with uncanny aptness, to the economy of time and space in Jacksonian America, an economy that operated most particularly by the equation of time with space, by the degradation of time into space. The very phrase "Manifest Destiny" dramatizes this spatialization, for to be "manifest," America's future must become "destiny"— which is to say, it must be mapped on a spatial axis, turned into providential design. Only then would that future manifest itself, only then would it be immanent, legible, foreordained, and guaranteed. This spatialization of time characterized, I suggest, not only the expansionist social discourse of antebellum America but also its literary productions.[39] The "predestined" narrative of *Moby-Dick*, for instance, demonstrates just this spatialized economy. Such an economy, I further suggest, represented the empire's best defense, for if temporal decline remained an imperial fate, the subordination of time to space would put off that fate indefinitely. Expanding not only continentally but eventually to include the entire hemisphere, America would dispense space as a sort of temporal currency, buying its tenure in time with its extension in space.

Extension in space had other benefits as well. Quite aside from its salutary effect on the future of empires, it also had a more immediate effect on what was then afflicting the nation, the affliction of "Capital against Labor," the occasion for Theophilus Fisk's impassioned speech. Within that context, the nation's continental land mass was nothing if not an "appointed remedy." Those were Emerson's words. Ever elusive, he would only talk about the West's "commanding and increasing power on the citizen, [its] sanitive and Americanizing influence."[40] Speaking more bluntly, Horace Greeley identified the West as the nation's primary asset in labor management. "The public lands are the great regulator of the relations of Labor and Capital, the safety valve of our industrial and social engine," he announced.[41] His faith was widely shared—no less fervently by those who advocated the cause of labor. George Henry Evans, the chief journalistic spokesman for the New York Working Men's party, demanded, for instance, that "an outlet be formed that will carry off our superabundant labor to the salubrious and fertile West."[42]

Space offered the best solution to class conflict. Whether as "appointed remedy" or "safety valve," the salubrious and fertile West would solve the problem of "Labor and Capital": and it would do so mechanically, effortlessly, as a matter of course. Antebellum Americans, Harriet Martineau reported, looked to the "possession of land" as "the cure for all social evils."[43] What allowed them to be so hopeful, of course, was an implicit belief (or perhaps a need to believe) that conflict was something aberrant, ephemeral, something easily corrected by mechanical means. Class conflict and Indian extermination notwithstanding, the governing tenet of the age remained the doctrine of "harmony of interests," a doctrine promulgated in a variety of disciplines. Henry Carey, the leading political economist of the period, was confident, for instance, that the "interests of the capitalist and the laborer are . . . in perfect harmony with each other."[44] He popularized this idea in a book with a self-explanatory title, *The Harmony of Interests* (1848). At the other end of the social spectrum, Andrew Jackson Davis, the leading spiritualist of the age, was no less confident about the primacy of harmony. His even more popular book, *The Harmonial Man* (1853), argued for a "harmonial Republic" based on "organic Liberty."[45] Such a firm belief in "harmony" inspired visions of that happy state even in the most unlikely circumstances. One of the most cherished nineteenth-century paintings, *Peaceable Kingdom*, painted in almost a hundred versions by Edward Hicks, showed animals, both gentle and savage, mingling fondly with small children in the American wilderness—an appropriate image, Jacksonian Americans seemed to think, to commemorate William Penn's treaty with the Indians.

If Hicks's rhapsodic vision seemed wildly out of place in the face of the actual Jacksonian Indian policy, its very incongruity nonetheless suggests something about its logic of being. For what the painting embodied, in its fantasy of harmony, was finally a double logic and a double representation: a denial of conflict through the subordination of conflict, a denial of polarity through the regimentation of polarity. We might think of this as a "strategy of disavowal," a strategy that always entails, as Homi Bhabha suggests, a "process of splitting," whereby "the trace of what is disavowed is not repressed but repeated as something different."[46] Thus, within the doctrine of harmony, polarity is neither eliminated nor even repressed, but is simply transposed into a different set of terms, normalized as something analogous yet unrecognizable—something not only congruent with the doctrine of harmony but instrumental for its workings.

What this meant, more specifically, was the representation of polarity as a *sequential* phenomenon—as the genesis of difference through the teleology of time. The conflict between whites and Indians turned out to be no conflict at all, in this account, because the difference between them was just a matter of developmental discrepancy, not a matter of conflicting interests. Whites and Indians simply occupied two different stages in the story of human progress. This explained why Indians were systematically depicted as "children," creatures who had never gone beyond the first stage on the developmental chart. "The President views the Indians as the children of the Government," Secretary of War John H. Eaton reported (in a letter that also concluded that, should the Indians "refus[e] to comply, they must, necessarily, entail destruction upon their race").[47] This official view was echoed from less official quarters as well. "The Indian is a true child of the forest," Francis Parkman wrote, and because "barbarism is to civilization what childhood is to maturity," he went on logically to predict a sad end for those who had lingered in the "childhood" of mankind. Horace Greeley could not agree more. "The Indians are children," he announced. "Their arts, wars, treaties, alliances, habitations, crafts, properties, commerce, comforts, all belong to the very lowest and rudest ages of human existence"—not unlike the handiwork, in fact, of "any band of schoolboys from ten to fifteen years of age."[48]

If "Indian destruction generated . . . the major formulas of Jacksonian Democracy," as Michael Rogin argues,[49] one of those "formulas" was no doubt a strategy for representing conflict. Imaged in developmental terms, as the succession of "childhood" by "maturity," the conflict between whites and Indians over land possession ceased to appear as conflict, and became instead a painless story of growth. As James Hall explained, "Never was there an experiment of greater moral beauty, or more harmonious operation."[50] In short, to disperse polarity along the temporal axis—to depict it as sequence rather than opposition—was to obviate not only the idea of "conflict" but the idea of "victim." It was the Indians' destiny to die out, this formula went. Stuck in their anachronistic "childhood," they ended up being the victims of progress itself. And if they were the victims of progress, they were, by definition, nobody else's victims, certainly not the white man's. Antebellum Americans could accordingly rejoice in the primacy of harmony, for harmony was indeed a given in the narrative of progress, a narrative that admitted no warring polarity, only orderly succession.[51]

Orderly succession was the theme not only on the frontier but in the nation's cities as well. For the cities, too, turned out to be infested with savages, whose proper management necessitated yet another narrative of progress. These savages were the industrial variety, the working class, that "race of famished, infuriated animals," the mere thought of whom had filled Lyman Beecher with dread. With their congregation in the cities, barbarism seemed less an exotic threat than a metropolitan nightmare. For Horace Mann, the nightmare was all but imminent: only the utmost vigilance, he thought, could save "the race" from being plunged "at once into the weakness and helplessness of barbarism." Graphic accounts of that "barbarism" began appearing in such magazines as the *Atlantic.*[52] Even to a liberal reformer like Theodore Parker, there was a definite parallel between two forms of barbarism: on the frontier, the "Savages, the Inferior Races, the Perishing Classes of the world," and, "in the centre of civilization," the "Danger-ous classes of society."[53] The "barbarization" of the working class was a grave threat indeed, but if so, the representation of the danger was already a form of defense. For it was surely an exercise in labor management to depict laborers as "barbari-ans," since if class differences were no more than different stages in the progress from barbarism to civilization, all that one needed to do, to make the "dangerous classes" undanger-ous, was to civilize them. This accounts for the proliferation of those civilizing agencies, the "city missions," from the 1820s onward.[54] It also accounts for the use of another, per-haps even more powerful, civilizing instrument—the narrative of progress, known in this instance as the narrative of "self-improvement."

"Our paupers to-day, thanks to free labor, are our yeomen and merchants of tomorrow," the *New York Times* announced, offering one version of that narrative. Zachariah Chandler of-fered another version: "A young man goes out to service—to labor, if you please to call it so—for compensation until he acquires money enough to buy a farm . . . and soon he be-comes himself the employer of labor."[55] Chandler could afford to put both the laborer and the capitalist in the same picture, with no misgivings about "Capital against Labor," for in his narrative of self-improvement there was indeed no conflict, only progress, because the laborer was destined, in good time, to become himself the capitalist. It was Lincoln, however, who refined the narrative of progress to a programmatic clar-ity. Against Southern insinuations that wage earners in the North were "fatally fixed in that condition for life," he came up with the following chart of progress: "The man who labored for another last year, this year labors for himself, and next year he will hire others to labor for him."[56]

Individual progress, for Lincoln, was the surest sign of the North's superiority, the most powerful proof that it was "a so-ciety of equals." One might argue, of course, that to celebrate such "progress" at all was already to endorse a structure of in-equality, without which progress would have no meaning. Per-sonal advancement, even in Lincoln's example, could be demonstrated only if there were "others" to be employed by the one who could now afford to do the employing. Applauded as a laudable genesis of difference in time, the notion of self-improvement in effect sanctioned the hierarchical organization of difference at any given moment. Such considerations did not prevent Lincoln from depicting the North as a "society of equals"—but equality was perhaps not his primary concern.[57] His object rather was to suggest a conflict-free society, united in its harmony of interests—a society in significant contrast to the South. The North had nothing to fear from its industrial barbarians, after all. The narrative of self-improvement performed civilizing wonders.

The narrativization of conflict—the depiction of polarity as progress—was no doubt the most powerful use of fiction in antebellum America. As we can see, it worked just as well with the "dangerous classes" in the "centre of civilization" as it did with the savages on the frontier.[58] The narrative of Jacksonian individualism, the narrative of personal progress, was thus formally identical to the narrative of Jacksonian imperialism, the narrative of human progress. For our purposes, we might speak of both as narratives of "manifest destiny" (using that phrase once again generically), for what empowered both narratives, what made them such effective instruments of governance, was precisely their ability to fashion a "destiny" out of temporality, to impose a "manifest" harmony on what might otherwise appear naked conflict. Of course, the working class was depicted as the beneficiary of progress whereas the Indians were depicted as the victims of progress, but the difference in thematics ultimately mattered less than the identity of form in the two narratives. Both were overdetermined narratives whose outcome was at once inscribed and inevitable, whose temporal unfolding was no more than the unfolding of a spatial design.

What we are witnessing is, once again, the spatialization of time, but only here can we see the utility of such spatialization: what occasioned it, what energized its operations, what service it performed. Spatialized into developmental stages, time figured as a series of way stations—or, more crudely, as a series of dump sites—to accommodate the undesirable, the disaffected, the dangerous. The "childhood" of mankind, for example, provided a retrospective graveyard for the Indians, while Lincoln's "next year" offered itself as a promised land for the laborer who would soon "hire others to labor for him." In both cases, conflict and polarity vanished before a harmonizing narrative, a narrative that incorporated time only to harness it, only to remap its temporality into a spatialized field of progress.

The operative term I propose for these narratives of spatialized time is "allegory." My emphasis, ultimately, will be on personification, a procedure that encapsulates time within the spatial figure of the self-enclosed agent. It is useful at the outset, however, to discuss allegory somewhat more generally, to clarify my use of the term and indicate my indebtedness to (and divergence from) others who have contributed to its definitions. Maureen Quilligan, rejecting the traditional concern with the "levels" of meaning in allegory, has drawn attention instead to allegory as a particular kind of narrative, whose sequence is governed always by a signifying structure.[59] This emphasis, on the figural genesis of narrative, to some degree parallels my emphasis on the spatialization of narrative, on the inscription of temporality within a spatial design. I would like to examine allegory, however, beyond the semantic sphere (Quilligan's focus), and to locate it within a larger functional domain, where narratives might have uses other than those of the literary. In short, the figural imperative that Quilligan investigates as a linguistic function of allegory, I investigate as a social function. Indeed, if we are to think of the production of meaning as a social necessity—and if social meanings are produced primarily through figuration, as Clifford Geertz and others have suggested—it would be hard to imagine public discourse *without* allegory.[60]

The association of allegory with public discourse is rooted in the word's etymology (from the Greek *allos*, "other," and *agoreuein*, "to speak in the agora, or marketplace"). Although this is commonly recognized, most students of allegory have chosen to emphasize not its public character but its ability to "keep secret in the act of making public." According to J. Hillis Miller, for instance, allegory engages history only to "speak otherwise," only to dramatize the "eternal disjunction between the inscribed sign and its material embodiment."[61] This certainly makes allegory a paradigmatic text for deconstruction. Yet, even within this account, one might still wish to historicize the disjunction of reference Miller claims allegory exemplifies, to see it not as an "eternal" given but as a procedural effect. In other words, even if allegory represents a detachment from history and an ossification of history, even if it confronts us (as Walter Benjamin says) "with the *facies hippocratica* of history as a petrified, primordial landscape,"[62] the logic of "petrification" would seem no less interesting, and no less historical. For it is in that logic—in the conversion of "history" into "landscape," time into space—that allegory registers its own historical contingency, its own participation in what we might call a social economy of time and space.

The relation between allegory and time might turn out to be its defining feature as well as its controlling function. In a now classic essay, "The Rhetoric of Temporality," Paul de Man has argued that "in the world of allegory, time is the originary constitutive category." "It remains necessary," he says, "if there is to be allegory, that the allegorical sign refer to another sign that precedes it . . . a previous sign with which it can never coincide, since it is of the essence of this previous sign to be pure anteriority." Defined in those terms, temporality would seem to accrue to allegory strictly as a property of its *signifying* structure, as the inevitable temporal discrepancy between sign and referent. Extending this insight, however, de Man goes on to suggest that, as a property of its *narrative* structure, time in allegory is always "an ideal time that is never here and now but always a past or an endless future." Time is merely "ideal" here, because even though allegory represents "the tendency of the language toward narrative," the narrative nevertheless unfolds only in "an imaginary time [projected] in order to give duration to what is, in fact, simultaneous within the subject."[63] In other words, time exists in allegory strictly as a structural effect. It is generated by that structure, encompassed by it, and expressive of it. Its trajectory, being a matter of inscription, of teleological unfolding, is fixed and immanent at any given moment. To make de Man's point more explicit, we might say that time in allegory is no more than an emanation of its structure, no more than the temporal extension of a spatial design. In short, if time is "constitutive" of allegory, it is, in the same gesture, abstracted, reified, contained. This is what makes allegorical time "ideal" in de Man's sense, and what makes it appear, in Benjamin's description, as "a petrified, primordial landscape."

Commenting on the tyranny of structure, and the subordination of time, in allegory, Joel Fineman writes, "Allegory begins with structure, thinks itself through it . . . and so it is always the structure of metaphor that is projected onto the sequence of metonymy, not the other way around, which is why allegory is always a hierarchizing mode, indicative of timeless order."[64] In its very narrative economy—its institution of timelessness—allegory would seem to work as an ideal instrument of governance, especially what J.G.A. Pocock calls "imperialist" governance, whose "legitimation and organizing categories [are] alike timeless."[65] For our purposes, we might think of the "timeless order" of allegory in two related uses: in the social governance of antebellum America, and in the textual governance of Melville's narratives. The two are parallel and related, I believe, for both the social polity and its literary counterpart require the category of "destiny." Both produce that timeless category through allegory, and, in doing so, both enact what Fineman calls a "hierarchizing" logic, which subordinates those who are "destined" to those whose freedom it is to assign destinies. In short, in its very logic of form, allegory would seem to embody a logic of freedom and dominion, a logic crucial, as we have seen, to the sovereignty both of an imperial nation and of literary authorship.[66]

From this perpective, it is worth remembering that allegory, as a genre, emerged during the same "period from which the Christian empire emerged," as C. S. Lewis reminds us.[67] The very history of allegory is the history of a conjunction between literary representation and political governance, and, in his particular conjunction of the two, Melville would seem to do no more than affirm a historical tradition. His authorial exercise is especially illuminating, however, in bodying forth a logic of governance, for it is altogether exemplary in its legitimating strategies, in the notions of agency and destiny it institutes. From the docile multitudes in *Mardi*, to the doomed Ahab, and back, once again, to the pathetic assembly in *The Confidence-Man*, each of Melville's novels stands as a testimony to the absolute sovereignty of the author. Each is a testimony as well to the double character of that sovereignty, its conjunction of freedom and dominion. In fact, it is the doubleness that makes for the usual relation between author and characters in Melville's writings: a relation of complementarity rather than of equality, a relation that not only operates through an asymmetrical distribution of power, but makes that asymmetry the constitutive grounds of its form.

In this context, Walter Benjamin's remark about the asymmetry between allegorist and allegorical subject—between the power of the former and the powerlessness of the latter—is especially pertinent:

> If the object becomes allegorical under the gaze of melancholy, if melancholy causes life to flow out of it and it remains behind dead, but eternally secure, then it is exposed to the allegorist, it is unconditionally in his power. That is to say it is now quite incapable of emanating any meaning or significance of its own; such significance as it has, it acquires from the allegorist. He places it within it, and stands behind it; not in a psychological but in an ontological sense.[68]

If allegory records "symbolic power struggles," as Angus Fletcher says,[69] Benjamin makes it clear that the struggle is marked above all by its generic imbalance, by the absolute power on the part of the allegorist and the complementary lack of it on the part of his characters. Even more crucially, Benjamin's insight dramatizes the extent to which power inheres in meaning—or rather, in the ability to impose a stable regime of meaning. The allegorist is "unconditionally" powerful because he is free not just to assign meaning but also to fix that meaning, to invest it (as Benjamin goes on to say) in a reified vehicle, "a fixed image and a fixing sign."[70] To put this another way, we might say that the allegorist's power resides in his ability to personify, to create human forms out of immutable meanings. This is why those human forms are at once "dead" and "eternally secure," why meaning here assumes the inevitability of the "ontological," and why allegory confronts us (to recall Benjamin's previous term) with a "petrified" countenance.

In short, what makes the allegorical character powerless is precisely his fixedness, his materialization within a form that never changes. To be personified at all, from this perspective, is already to submit to the dictates of the timeless, the dictates of destiny. This point becomes especially clear when we consider the nature of "agency" in allegory. Here, Angus Fletcher's observation about the emblematic character of the allegorical agent usefully complements Benjamin's sense of that figure's fixedness. In personification, the agent is always "frozen into an eternally fixed form," Fletcher says; such "a fixed agent is tantamount to an image," for "even in narration they are so often sheerly emblematic."[71] In other words, if allegory leaves no doubt about the character of its agency, that emblematic clarity is possible only because its "agent" is always represented as "image," a bounded figure in space. Personification is really a kind of reification then: it reifies the category of "agency," investing it and confining it within a material form—in this case, a human form, a "person." Agency thus personified is necessarily self-contained, for the trajectory of such an agent is already inscribed, staked out and provided for, and embodied always within himself. Indeed, narrative action for him is no more than an autotelic function, no more than the reflexive unfolding of what is already an ontological provision. At once self-propelled and self-governing, autonomous and free, he enacts an edifying career of destined progress.

Put in those terms, the personified agent of allegory is perhaps better known by another name. He is the centerpiece of Jacksonian culture, the "individual," a figure no less autonomous, and no less self-propelled.[72] The laborer Lincoln cited—that remarkable figure who started out a hired hand, made himself self-employed the following year, and further transformed himself into an employer the year after—was just such an instance of agency personified. Individualism, then, might quite properly be called a system of personification, for it too invests and confines agency within a material form, a human form. To say this is not to dispute either the force of individualism, or its reality in the world. Rather, it is to study it as a form of social representation, a form at once congruent with and related to its literary counterpart. Those two meet, in fact, and to their fateful meeting we must add yet another party. For personification, as it turns out, accommodates not just literary texts, and not just the narrative of Jacksonian individualism, but, less obviously though no less crucially, the narrative of Manifest Destiny as well. Like the others, Manifest Destiny too needs a representational form for its agency, and it too discovers that form within the charmed circle of allegory. In the rest of the chapter, then, I will examine these representational forms—these forms of personified agency—in two related uses: on an individual level, the personification of Property, the making of a human agent out of a proprietary relation; and on a national level, the personification of America, the making of a corporeal self out of a geographical expanse.

Americans spoke of their nation as "a body progressing" in time, Tocqueville reported.[73] Numerous antebellum orators bore out his remark. Personified America seemed to have come into being "like Minerva from the head of Jove, sprung at once into full maturity and symmetry, and armed in sovereign panoply."[74] Such a goddesslike apparition was not without a human frame, however. Its bodily parts occupied a prominent place in expansionist rhetoric. John Quincy Adams, for instance, envisioned "the finger of nature" in the Pacific Northwest; President Monroe thought of Cuba as "the mouth of the Mississippi"; the New Orleans *Gazette* presented Florida as the nation's "natural appendage"; C. J. Ingersoll discerned in the Great Lakes America's "national ligaments" and spoke reverently of "the spinal Ohio and Mississippi, with vertebral vitality, uphold[ing] the whole North American body politic."[75] Such was the composition of the nation's allegorical body. Of course, in every instance, that body also happened to be larger than life: not yet fully developed, America would have to grow into it. Thus, personification involved something like developmental biology. America's "natural growth" was at stake here, Secretary of State Edward Everett announced.[76] And while its citizens must "be careful not to impose upon ourselves a regimen so strict as to prevent its healthful development,"[77] there was, at the same time, little doubt about what "growth" would entail, or what sort of body would result. In fact, nothing would be able to stop the corporeal destiny of this personified nation, as Parke Godwin explained:

> Nor would the incorporation of these foreign ingredients into our body . . . swell us out to an unmanageable and plethoric size. . . . [Rather] this tendency to the assimilation of foreign ingredients, or to the putting forth of new members, is an inevitable incident of our growth. . . . Cuba will be ours, and Canada and Mexico too—if we want them—in due season, and without the wicked impertinence of a war.[78]

As a growing body, America could simply grow into Cuba and Canada and Mexico—and it would do so naturally, effortlessly, without any "wicked[ness]." The imperial logic of personification is rather transparent here, but transparency is not always the condition of allegory. It is against this transparent example, therefore, that I would like to examine another instance of America personified, one that would not ordinarily strike us as being in the least imperial: Lincoln's evocation of the "great body of the Republic," first in his inaugural address and, even more extensively, in his second annual message to Congress (1862). Pointing to the dictates of that allegorical body, Lincoln reasoned, "Physically speaking we cannot separate. We cannot remove our respective sections from each other nor build an impassable wall between them. A husband and wife may be divorced and go out of the presence and beyond the reach of each other, but the different parts of our country cannot do this." Indeed, if the integrity of that allegorical personhood were to be violated, if the unthinkable physical separation were indeed to take place, America's body would so assert itself as "ere long [to] force reunion, however much of blood and treasure the separation might have cost."[79]

The "body" of personified America was firmly on the side of the Union and absolutely opposed to "dismemberment"—or secession, which came to the same thing. To personify the nation, on this occasion, was to invoke an organic spatial order, in which conflict could only seem a monstrous violation. What Lincoln dismissed was not only the Southern claim to sovereignty, but any version of history that refused to recognize the primacy of harmony.[80] For his ahistorical "body of the Republic" was nonetheless an attempt to define the character of historical agency. His narrative, in effect, constituted personified America as an agent, an agent eternally committed, in this case, to its own corporeal integrity. But if America was an agent—if agency resided above all in the nation's corporeal self—any other notion of agency must be considered subordinate. Lincoln's allegory worked, then, by a "hierarchizing" logic, as Joel Fineman suggests. What was primary here was a system of order, emblematized by the nation's harmonious "body"; human conflict, insofar as it was allowed to figure at all, could only be secondary and aberrant. In short, Lincoln's plea for harmony operated, paradoxically enough, by an act of subordination: most immediately, by subordinating Southern claims and, more generally, by subordinating the validity of conflict. America was personified strictly for the benefit of the North. With its organic governance, its sovereign dictates, the "body of the Republic" permitted the South no identity except as part of a whole, a whole of which it would always have to remain a part.

The allegory of the body enabled Lincoln ultimately to repress not only the historical provenance of national boundaries—the fact that the "body of the Republic" was itself a product of historical conflict, secured by warfare and annexation—but also the extent to which geography itself was permeated and indeed preempted by the politics of slavery. By the 1840s, to discuss any territorial question, such as California's admission to statehood or the disposition of other territories won by the Mexican War, was to engage in the debate over the justice and limits of slavery. Under those circumstances, Lincoln's appeal to the absolute jurisdiction of the nation's corporeal self, as if it were some sort of freestanding agency, seemed not only perverse but chillingly prophetic of the way that selfhood was to be maintained. The Civil War was a war fought to preserve the Union, the North had always insisted; its primary object was not to end slavery and certainly not to encourage any changes in race relations. Lincoln's hierarchy of historical agencies therefore exactly prefigured the hierarchy of negotiated settlements in postbellum America. In both cases, blacks could not be anything but subordinate, and indeed, their strategic marginalization was altogether necessary for the mending of the nation's body. Not surprisingly, the same speech that celebrated the nation's corporeal personhood also ended with a fervent plea on behalf of the Colonization Society, an organization devoted to the removal of black slaves, one which Harriet Martineau had earlier denounced as a "bald fiction" drummed up to "[alienate] the attention and will of the people . . . from the principle of the abolition of slavery."[81] But Lincoln was altogether consistent in his twin advocacy, for the "fiction" of colonization was merely trying to implement as policy what his corporeal allegory was already representing as reality. Both were attempts at harmonious dominion; both decreed order through the subordination of conflict.

If allegory is, as Fredric Jameson says, a "cultural and historical symptom,"[82] Lincoln's personified America suggests that the "symptom" might equally be the cure. In other words, if the need for personification registers social disorder, the act of personification is already a step toward the resumption of control. Lincoln's exercise summarizes, in this regard, both the motive and the function of allegory in antebellum America. What it summarizes as well is the double logic inherent in that representational form. To personify agency, whether in "America" or in anything else, would seem never to be a neutral exercise, and never to be without a complementary logic. For what inscribes sovereignty must also, in the same gesture, enforce subordination. As a self-governing body, the seat of agency, the "body of the Republic" is hardly an isolated invention in nineteenth-century America. It has everything in common with other instances of personified agency: the free market, with its Invisible Hand, for instance, or the free individual, self-made and self-governed. In fact, the interest of Lincoln's vignette ultimately lies less in its immediate context than in the world of kinship it shadows forth: a world of personifications, a world of free agents putative and compulsory.

And, eloquent as it was, Lincoln's allegory turned out to be readily modifiable when the proper occasion arose. Land speculation was one such occasion. To accommodate that activity, the body of the Republic could quite willingly undergo what it was otherwise reputed not to tolerate—that is, it could be divided, carved up and parceled out, sold and resold. Land in America, the British visitor D. W. Mitchell reported, "might and did pass through a dozen hands within sixty days, rising in price at each transfer."[83] There was an obvious and problematic discrepancy between land as indivisible body and land as highly divisible commodity, between land as a changeless order of organic permanence and land as an ever-fluctuating exchange value on the market. In the rhetoric of commerce, however, that discrepancy was harmonized in yet another reconstituted entity, an even more powerful use of personification. This new entity came about through the characteristic strategy of splitting and reincorporation: by reducing to a part what might otherwise have been seen as an integral whole and, in doing so, at once subordinating and reassimilating that part into a more encompassing order. The nation's corporeal self was thus only part of a larger system of personhood. It had to be united with a human component to make up another integral unit, whose operative logic was not so much the associative logic of contiguous parts as the circulatory logic of the owner and the owned. What resulted was the proprietary self, a figure that assimilated what it owned into a kind of personified economy. Such a construct would allow land to be traded as commodity, its passage "through a dozen hands" being no more than a circulatory function.

This proprietary self is obviously a Lockean self. "Every man has a property in his own person," Locke has written.[84] To be human at all, in Locke's terms, is by definition to be a property owner. Proprietorship is not so much an option as a given, not so much an extrinsic venture as a constitutive relation within the self—the relation between its organic components and its corporate identity. If this makes ownership an ontological provision, it also, by the same token, makes ownership the governing term in the constitution of personhood. Human identity emanates from it, revolves around it, and ceaselessly reaffirms it. Within the terms of our discussion, we might think of this proprietary self as yet another instance of personification—the personification of a proprietary relation.

Such personification was crucial in antebellum America, or at least in the North, for it was the constitution of a proprietary self—the inscription of a contractual relation within the structure of personhood—that underwrote the labor relations of industrial capitalism. In order for "labour-power [to] appear upon the market as a commodity," Marx writes, the laborer "must have it at his disposal, must be the untrammelled owner of his capacity for labour, i.e., of his person."[85] The Lockean self, who "has a property in his own person," is therefore something of a necessary construct in an economy of "free labor." Owning himself, and freely selling what he owns, the laborer enters the market as yet another personification, as Property invested in human shape. In that capacity he figures not only as a party in exchange but, even more crucially, as a *site* of exchange, the site where the property that is oneself is both owned and sold. Embodying both those functions, both the owning and the selling, he ends up personifying the market itself, his human form being no more than an animated habitat for a circulatory economy.

If individualism is indeed a system of personification, as I have tried to suggest, its chief function is no doubt to impersonate Property, to invest market relations in human forms. The most eloquent tribute to its representational power came in fact not from a capitalist, but from the leader of the New York Working Men's party, Thomas Skidmore, author of a book appropriately called *The Rights of Man to Property!* (1829). More than anyone else, Skidmore clarifies the relation between two terms, "Man" and "Property," by showing the extent to which the former is constituted by the latter:

> Title to property exists for all; and for all alike . . . not because of purchase, of conquest, of preoccupancy, or what not; but BE-CAUSE THEY ARE: BECAUSE THEY EXIST. I AM; THERE-FORE IS PROPERTY MINE; as much so as any man's, and that without asking any man's permission; without paying any man price; without knowing or caring farther than as my equal rights extends, whether any other human being exists, or not.[86]

Personhood and proprietorship are one and the same, Skidmore contended. To be an "I" is by definition also to own property; indeed, the "I" cannot be conceived except as the locus of ownership. Nothing better attests to the strength of the established order in antebellum America, to the efficacy of its social personifications. Those concerned about the struggle of "Capital against Labor" need not have worried after all. Such a passionate defense of property, coming from a leader of the labor movement, ought to banish any doubts about "harmony of interests" either as projected ideal or indeed as accomplished fact. Skidmore, of course, imagined himself to be speaking in all militancy. His style certainly seemed more combative than conciliatory. Yet, even as he asserted the right of labor to property, even as he articulated his sovereign demands, what he dramatized instead was the remarkable consonance between adversarial positions, between the voice of Labor and the voice of Capital.

Indeed, Skidmore's militancy is not only compatible with the established order but in some sense generated by it, for his militancy is above all the militancy of an imperial self, one that operates "without caring farther than as my equal right extends, whether any other human being exists, or not." Skidmore here is directly echoing Blackstone, who (we might recall) has characterized "the right to property" as "that sole and despotic dominion which one man claims and exercises over the external things of the world, to the total exclusion of the right of any other individual in the universe." And so, Skidmore too ends up celebrating a "sole and despotic dominion," a personified empire ever jealous of its sovereign rights, and ever indifferent to the rights of "any other human being." It is ironic, of course, that the leader of a labor movement, the spokesman for collective action, should end up glorifying an empire of one. But the full irony of the self's "despotic dominion" becomes clear only when it showed up in a group even more marginal than the New York Working Men's party, only when it pushed its double logic to its vertiginous limit, by building an "empire" out of Indian "liberty."

Indian title had always been a vexed issue in antebellum America. As late as 1821, for instance, the attorney general of the United States had maintained that, "So long as a tribe exists and remains in possession of its land, its title and possession are sovereign and exclusive." In his much-publicized *Johnson v. M'Intosh* ruling of 1823, Chief Justice John Marshall upheld the Indians' "right of occupancy," but insisted, at the same time, on the "preemptive" rights of the United States government.[87] The main task for expansionists, then, was to challenge the former right by appealing to the latter. That turned out to be not very difficult, and nothing was more handy, in this context, than the Lockean notion of property. Land could be legitimately owned, the expansionist argument went, only as labor's property. But because labor was itself a form of private property—the property, that is, of the laboring individual—land ownership, by the same logic, could only mean individual ownership. Any sort of landholding not based on private property, which did not posit at its center the individuated subject, would be correspondingly null and void. Communal landholding, the only form of "ownership" the Indians practiced, therefore had no legal meaning. As John Quincy Adams explained, "separate property is [a] natural and indisputable right," and a "community of goods without community of toil" is not only "oppressive and unjust," but "counteracts the laws of nature" itself. Indians, practicing just such a "community of goods," were obviously disobeying "nature," and their very "right of possession" must stand "upon a questionable foundation." The "Pilgrims of Plymouth," on the other hand, being upholders of private property, "obtained their right of possession to the territory on which they settled by titles as fair and unequivocal as any human property can be held."[88] James Hall put the case even more decisively. The Indians' "insecurity of property, or rather the entire absence of all ideas of property, is the chief cause of their barbarism," he said, and logically concluded that "it is the duty of our government to take the Indians directly under its own control as subjects."[89]

Indian dispossession marked the juncture where representation became action, where the narrative of personified Property actually produced results. To conjoin personhood and proprietorship—to make the former the embodiment of the latter—was already to suggest a way of making nonpersons out of nonproprietors. What doomed the Indians was the very representational form of the self. The thematics of that representation, the specific charges brought against them, were altogether immaterial. And so it happened that the Indians were accused of two contradictory things: they were benighted collectivities, on the one hand, too barbaric to appreciate the blessings of Property, and they were enlightened individuals, on the other hand, civilized enough to desire the same. If the former invalidated their title to land, the latter made their welfare an object of solicitude. It was the second construct that William Ellery Channing had in mind, for instance, when he spoke of the unfortunate Indian, who had been forced to remain a savage because his tribal government, in "withholding protection from property," had "shackle[d] the arm of industry, and forbid[den] exertion for the melioration of his lot."[90] The villain in this scenario was the tribe, needless to say, the barbaric force that, in refusing to honor private property, had "shackled" the enterprising individual. This was also the villain Jackson denounced when he objected to tribal assumption of individual Indian debts as an affront undertaken "without [the] consent" of the subject in question. Pitting himself against that villain, Jackson could accordingly present himself as the champion and defender of the "poor Indian," long enslaved by the "created tyranny" of his tribe, now free at last, through the office of the white man, to enjoy his personal liberty.[91] Beginning with the Creeks in 1814, Indian treaties consistently granted individual ownership to tribal land, giving every Indian the right to property.

Of course, the freedom to own, in this context, really meant the freedom to sell, and to grant every Indian the right to property was not only to break down communal resistance but also to legitimate expropriation as commercial transaction, as the neutral transfer of real estate. Individual allotments, Michael Rogin observes, "subjected [atomized owners] to market mechanisms," and represented "the principal method of dispossessing the Indians."[92] The subjection of the Indian exactly coincided with the constitution of the Indian as personified Property. The attendant narrative not only rewrote land titles, it also represented conflict as progress, Indian dispossession as Indian liberation. This sort of narrative inspired Jackson, in his second annual message to Congress (1830), to speak of the "happy consummation" of his "benevolent policy." The United States government had treated the Indian as a pampered charge, Jackson said, in its policy "to purchase his lands, to give him a new and extensive territory, to pay the expense of his removal, and support him a year in his new abode." Curiously enough, against this cheerful account Jackson also juxtaposed a more somber picture:

> Humanity has often wept over the fate of the aborigines of this country, and Philanthropy has been long busily employed in devising means to avert it, but its progress has never for a moment been arrested, and one by one have many powerful tribes disappeared from the earth. To follow to the tomb the last of his race and to tread on the graves of extinct nations excite melancholy reflections. But true philanthropy reconciles the mind to these vicissitudes as it does to the extinction of one generation to make room for another.[93]

This might not seem much like the "happy consummation" of a "benevolent" policy, but there was actually no contradiction between the "happ[iness]" and the "melancholy" Jackson alternately professed, for those conflicting sentiments were functionally harmonized. Intentional or not, the placement of singulars and plurals in Jackson's speech effectively suggested a differential distribution of fortune, one that consistently distinguished between the "happy" fate of the individual and the "melancholy" demise of the communal. What was to be exterminated were Indians as a tribal plurality, Indians as "aborigines" and "nations"; what was to be preserved was the hallowed individual, that enviable "him" on whom the government had lavished all attentions. To help the latter one must destroy the former. And so the Jacksonian Indian policy, far from being an injustice, seemed positively liberating. Enterprising Indian individuals had every reason to be grateful.

The dispossession of the Indians showed (with a brashness that would have been comic had it not been so brutal) the extent to which the "individual" was a construct—a property relation personified into personhood—and the extent to which that construct was politically and economically motivated. Deployed on the margins of society and on a group indelibly stamped with racial difference, the logic of individualism worked with a clarity of purpose rarely seen elsewhere. It produced, as always, an "imperial" self, but one whose "despotic dominion" was such as to make its bearer a subject. The "rights of man to property," Thomas Skidmore's imperial demand, was all too imperially fulfilled among the Indians: the measure of freedom for one became the measure of subjection for the other. It would be wrong, however, to think of the Indians merely as an ironic commentary on Skidmore, or a warning to him, for what is at stake, in the narrative of Indian "liberation," is not so much the illusion of freedom and the reality of subjection as the complementary logic between the two. That logic would seem, furthermore, to be the constitutive logic of individualism itself, for the "individual" it produces is produced always as a double entity: both sovereign and subject, both the locus of freedom and the locus of dominion. Here too, self and nation seem to mirror each other. In its constitutive doubleness, its representation of freedom and dominion both, the self too might pass for an "empire for liberty."

Melville, as we shall see, knows something about this constitutive doubleness as well. But it was Orestes Brownson who made that doubleness most explicit, and most unforgettable, as he detailed what he called the "law of liberty":

> Liberty, rightly understood, is the true end of man. . . . But there can be no liberty without order. Order is not the end, but the means. Where is not the most perfect order, where each is not in his place, there is no free movement; there is confusion, a clashing and crossing of interests, and the rubbing of one against another, the thwarting of one by another. And order can be maintained only by means of government which reduces all to their places, each to his proper sphere, and maintains him in it.[94]

In an age of "clashing and crossing of interests," the reign of liberty demanded a "government" that would "[reduce] all to their places." Brownson did not elaborate on the nature of this government, but others had already done so. Timothy Dwight, praising his native state of Connecticut, had singled out a particular mode of government as its crowning glory. "There is not a spot on the globe where so little is done to govern the inhabitants," he said, "nor a spot where the inhabitants are so well governed."[95] The government in question could only be a kind of self-government, then: not government of the inhabitants, but government by the inhabitants of their own individual selves.

The method was unsurpassable, but Connecticut could hardly claim to have invented it. Indeed, this form of "government" seemed to be the rule in America. Michel Chevalier, the French visitor to America in the 1830s, was especially struck by it. "The Americans, therefore, can dispense with Caesar," he wrote. "Yet it is not to be inferred," he went on to say, "that they can and will long dispense with authority, or that they are even now free from its control." For in America, as it turned out, everyone was "ready to act the part of constables. This is real self-government; these are the obligations and responsibilities, that every citizen takes upon himself when he disarms authority." Robert Rantoul, Jr., agreed. In America, he said, "where the sovereignty is in the whole people," citizens "must fit themselves to be wiser and better sovereigns than any race of kings." What that meant, as it turned out, was that everyone must learn "conscientiously to discharge his private duty of self-government."[96] In short, the American method of government, as Chevalier and Rantoul saw it, was a highly internalized method, operating from within "every citizen." This form of government, self-government, was also what Jefferson had in mind when he celebrated his nation's unique combination of freedom and dominion. America, Jefferson said, was to be "such an empire for liberty as the world has never surveyed since the creation; and I am persuaded no constitution was ever before so well calculated as ours for extensive empire and self-government."[97]

The best government for an "empire," according to Jefferson, was "self-government": the government of the self by the self. Only such a form of government could set America apart, make it an empire that "the world has never surveyed since the creation." By the same logic, only such a form of government could exempt it from the proverbial fate of empires and guarantee it unexampled longevity. Individualism was central to America's defense. As Lyman Beecher explained, proper government "must act in the government of mind . . . with reference to the formation and continuance of character, and free agency, and accountability." To defend itself, a civil society must insert an "all-pervading and efficient control" within each individual, for "ours must be a self-government or despotism." Theodore Parker put the point even more emphatically. A society might "defend itself" against external threat, he said, "by means of armies, forts, fleets, and all the artillery of war," but when the threat came from "within itself," from "domestic harm," it must build its defenses on "the mind and conscience of the individual," by instilling in everyone certain "personal statutes." Thus, "to preserve itself, . . . society is to preserve the individuality of the individual."[98]

Located in each and every individual, self-government had the advantage of being everywhere and nowhere, at once ubiq-

uitous and invisible—an important defensive advantage, as
Beecher and Parker both recognized. The production of individuality was thus crucial to an Empire for Liberty, both to the
making of it and to the maintenance of it. The making and
the maintenance were altogether analogous, in fact, for both
revolved around a common representational form of the self—
the self as personified Property. That venerable personification
turned out to be as much at home in America's civil society as
it was on the frontier. Unlike its pioneering kindred, however
(whose property was after all tangible, and therefore mun-
dane), the proprietary self, in its metropolitan sophistication,
would body forth a more interesting kind of property. What
that involved might be glimpsed from the following, a curious
account of the self's "possess[ion]," in William Ellery Channing's *Self-Culture* (1838):

> It is worthy of observation, that we are able to discern not only
> what we already are, but what we may become, to see in ourselves
> germs and promises of a growth to which no bounds can be set.
> . . . This is indeed a noble prerogative of our nature. Possessing
> this, it matters little what or where we are now; for we can con-
> quer a better lot.[99]

Here, the proprietary individual lay claim not to a tract of
land, but to a "better lot": a sort of temporal real estate, the
self's property in time. This was even better than the American West, for unlike the geographical expanse, the temporal
province had "no bounds." Such a domain took shape, of
course, only because personification, in its projective enclosure of time, had effectively spatialized the future, incorporated it into itself, as "a better lot" to which it had title. The
self's proprietary jurisdiction, then, was nothing short of a jurisdiction over time: as an 1842 *Manual of Self-Education* explained, the "destiny of each individual is, to a large extent,
in his own possession."[100]
What the proprietary self owned was not just his "person,"
as Locke stipulated, but also the "destiny" of that person. But
if so, in order to own this property—this destiny one was supposed to possess—one must also continually purchase it. One

must continually trade merit for reward, personal worth for personal advancement. This made the self not just a personified marketplace, but, even more crucially, a marketplace across time, the site of temporal exchange, where one's "better lot" might be bought and owned. Of course, such an exchange also happened to be something of a tautological enterprise, for if one's destiny was already in one's possession, what one "bought" could only be something one already had. Tautology seemed, indeed, to be the ultimate (and logical) form of the proprietary self. Owning in order to sell and selling in order to buy, he ended up embodying a circular marketplace, an orbit of reflexive exchange. Buying his own future, he always got what he bargained for.

The "possession of one's destiny" registered, in this sense, not just the freedom of opportunity but also its obverse, something like an orbit of fate. But this too is only to be expected, for the proprietary self, here as everywhere, must underwrite a complementary logic. If the possession of his destiny enabled this self to expand his domain of freedom, what such a "possession" also incurred was a sphere of obligation, where the proprietary self, always getting what he bargained for, had only himself to blame for a bad bargain. His very province of selfhood would seem, from this perspective, to be a double-edged construct, at once empire and prison. Aggrandized to the point where he became a sovereign agent, he became, at that very point, a sovereign subject, someone whose destiny was internally accountable—someone who could always be accounted for. Here was the "self-governing" individual Beecher and Parker looked to for America's civil defense. What gave this individual his defensive value, indeed, was his very tautological character, for what he embodied, in his expanded province of selfhood, was ultimately a field of strategic attribution, where everything could be read into and accounted for.[101] Self-governing and self-accounting, sovereign within himself and subject unto himself, such an individual not only became a free agent on his own, he also enabled his nation to become an "empire for liberty."

The production of such strategic individuality was the implicit burden of social governance in antebellum America. More explicitly, it was the burden of antebellum reform, with its emphasis on self-government and individual accountability.[102] In education we might expect to find its most vocal exponents. "To whom are mankind indebted for the noiseless but resistless progress of good principles, whereby greater changes are effected in the condition of the whole human family, than have grown out of the efforts of the mightiest conquerors, or than have followed the most renowned revolutions of empire?" Robert Rantoul, Jr., asked, and the answer, predictably, was, "To those whose moral education has fixed in their hearts permanent and actuating principles of conduct."[103] This faith, in the benefit of making the individual "fixed" and "permanent," was echoed by Horace Mann, the best known champion of school reform. Education, he said, "is a thousand times more lucrative than fraud, and adds a thousand-fold more to a nation's resources than the most successful conquests,"[104] for the asset it produced was nothing other than the "individual," an asset infinitely more valuable, and infinitely more lasting, than anything either fraud or conquest could boast:

> Indeed, so pervading and enduring is the effect of education upon the youthful soul, that it may well be compared to a certain species of writing-ink, whose color, at first, is scarcely perceptible, but which penetrates deeper and grows blacker by age, until, if you consume the scroll over a coal-fire, the character will still be legible in the cinders.[105]

The youthful soul, penetrated by the "writing-ink" of education to acquire a timelessly "legible" "character," seems to me the most fitting image for the making of individuals in antebellum America. It also seems a fitting image for the making of characters in Melville's writings. The relation between the two—between the enterprise of social personification and the enterprise of literary personification—is the subject of the following chapters.

2 ◆ *Author as Monarch*

In *Mardi* Melville saw himself doing something infinitely superior to anything he had done before. He did not consider his earlier books, *Typee* and *Omoo*, worthy productions: not worthy, because they had not come freely into being, because he had felt "irked, cramped & fettered" writing them. Disliking that mode of authorship, Melville was now ready for something different: he "long[ed] to plume [his] pinions for a flight," he told John Murray. *Mardi*, the embodiment of that "flight," was therefore to be "no *Typee* or *Omoo*, but different stuff altogether." Here, finally, was a book after his own heart, a book where he could exercise "that play of freedom and invention accorded only to the Romancer & Poet."[1] Because *Mardi* was in a wholly separate category from its predecessors, Melville was almost ashamed to acknowledge the other two. "Unless you should deem it *very* desirable," he told Murray again, "do not put me down on the title page as 'the author of *Typee* and *Omoo*.' I wish to separate *Mardi* as much as possible from those books."[2]

Melville's account of his first three books is hardly a model of impartial judgment, but in its very partiality—in its marked likes and dislikes—it does say something about his premises, about his aspiration and predilection as an author. *Typee* and *Omoo* are not strictly factual, of course, a circumstance Melville knows perfectly well; all the same, he will not credit them with the "freedom" and "invention" that most certainly contributed to their making. Those two are honored epithets, he seems to think, and they belong to *Mardi* alone. Melville is not simply being supercilious here, for by "freedom" and "invention" he seems to have meant something rather definite, something *Typee* and *Omoo* have only in short supply. What is it, then, that makes these two books not free, and not inventive, according to his estimate?

Because Melville himself is somewhat vague on this point, we can only speculate, perhaps, that *Typee* and *Omoo* have not been "free" and "inventive" in the way he wants, in the way he values. They have been altogether too plausible, too seemingly real. Even though they were not actually all "facts," they could easily have been. Only in a local sense are the two books free and inventive; globally considered, they are quite unfree, and uninventive, for their purported authenticity turns out to constitute a limit—a limit as to what might be invented without giving away the invention. Whatever liberties Melville takes, they will have to be within the bounds of probability. This kind of "invention," at once circumspect and circumscribed, is, for Melville, really no invention at all: it bears only the mark of submission, not the mark of freedom. This is why he has felt "irked, cramped & fettered" writing his first two books. It is an ignoble constraint. The newly liberated author of *Mardi* would have none of it.

What that newly liberated author wants, to say it in a different way, is not just the freedom to invent occasionally and plausibly, but an absolute freedom to invent what he pleases, a freedom that makes him the sole arbiter in his fictive domain. This notion of "freedom"—freedom as exclusive jurisdiction—lies at the heart of Melville's new conception of authorship, and it accounts not only for his dislike of *Typee* and *Omoo* but also, more generally, for his aversion to "narratives of facts."[3] Those narratives, in their allegiance to "facts" (and not to the person who writes them), can only offend an author who wants his sovereignty to be absolute. Such narratives owe their existence to something other than the author's imagination: they are not created by him, and they might not even properly be called his. To avoid that problem, Melville now chooses to write what he calls a "*real* romance," something that is "no *Typee* or *Omoo*, & is made of different stuff altogether."[4] This "different stuff" is obviously not "facts," but emanations, it seems, from a creative genius, from him and from nowhere else. *Mardi* is an attempt at "creating the creative," Richard Brodhead suggests.[5] It is also an attempt to elevate the author from a mere writer to a sovereign creator, someone whose jurisdiction is exclusive and undisputed, someone who, thanks to his "freedom and invention," is able to reign, "like many a monarch,"[6] in his fictive domain: reign supreme, and reign alone.

Melville's belief in the sovereignty of the "creative"—by now, a more or less commonplace assumption—might not seem especially noteworthy to us. And yet such an assumption has not always been commonplace, as Raymond Williams points out. Among Elizabethan writers, for instance, "creation" often carried a pejorative meaning. Not until the eighteenth century was the word "creative" coined, and its positive association with art became conventional only in the mid-nineteenth century.[7] In short, the figure of the "creative artist" is not without its own history, and it might be useful to study the emergence of that figure and the attendant elevation of his calling—to study it not just as an episode in literary history, but as a phenomenon concurrent with and perhaps connected to other historical events. It is possible, for instance, to think of the artist's "calling" in the context of Max Weber's argument about the Protestant idea of "calling" and its relation to what he calls the "spirit of capitalism."[8] It is possible, that is, to think of the "creative" not as a natural or timeless concept, but as an idea historically conditioned and historically inscribed, an idea taking shape among a particular set of social practices. Melville, it seems to me, offers an especially suggestive example here, for his idea of creative freedom—his implicit sense of it as a kind of exclusive sovereignty—carries within it echoes of other definitions of freedom, echoes that, at first sight, might seem rather remote from the artistic realm.

Blackstone, for example, had used a phrase Melville would have understood, "sole and despotic dominion," to describe the right to property, a right invested, we might recall, in a man's freedom to establish his claims "to the total exclusion of the right of any other individual in the universe."[9] Blackstone is speaking within a well-defined liberal tradition, that not only associates "liberty" with "property" but interprets the former as a subset of the latter.[10] Because "property" is the more encompassing of the two terms, because "liberty" is classified as a species of "property" (which is how Madison presents it, for instance, in his essay "Property and Liberty"[11]), "liberty" must exist not just as something one enjoys but, more crucially, as something one possesses. But if so, if liberty is indeed a kind of property, it must also operate as property operates, which is to say, it must be exclusive in its entitlement.

"Exclusion of others," C. B. Macpherson observes in his well-known study, turns out to be central to the liberal definition of freedom,[12] for where liberty is imagined as a possessory right, its proper possession must require a corresponding security of title, and a corresponding exclusion of rival claims. Melville's thinking about freedom certainly seems to have proceeded along those lines: in chapter 161 of *Mardi*, for example, we find "a Voice from the Gods" telling us that the "real felicity" of freedom "is not to be shared," since it is "of a man's own individual getting and holding" (528–29). This is by no means a random thought, and it seems to have worked its way not just into such occasional remarks, but also into a general pattern of authorial practice. Melville's very idea of authorship—his desire to have exclusive jurisdiction over his fictive domain, his need to exclude the rival claims of the world's "dull common places"—might be considered an authorial variant within a much broader tradition, one that conjoins "liberty" and "property," what Macpherson has called the tradition of "possessive individualism."

If Melville's idea of authorship is indeed informed by a tradition of property rights, *Mardi* would seem to offer an instance of proprietary jurisdiction. Here, much like a proprietor, the author presides over his creation, establishes clear and undisputed title, excludes the claims of "facts." Melville's success in these matters no doubt explains his peculiar fondness for *Mardi*, his sense that he is finally practicing the highest form of authorship, the "freedom and invention accorded only to the Romancer & Poet." Of course, how that authorial freedom actually comports itself—the kind of textual correlatives it engenders—remains an open question. We might want to ask, for example, about the status of the fictive characters it produces, the structure of agency and destiny it institutes, the legitimating strategies it deploys. *Mardi* is exemplary here as well, for Melville's commitment to liberty and property turns out, ultimately, to be not just a belief, but also a poetics, a principle of textual governance that structures the form of the book. His reference to himself as a "monarch" is especially suggestive, for in this word (and its often literal application), we get a hint of the poetics Melville will embrace—the principle of textual sovereignty commensurate with a principle of proprietary sovereignty.

"Monarchy" (or some comparable version of it) is of course a metaphor traditionally associated with liberty and property. James Otis, noting that "one of the most essential branches of English liberty is the freedom of one's house," has observed, for instance, that a "man's home is his castle, and whilst he is quiet is as well guarded as a prince in his castle."[13] Otis's princely estate, being real estate, is not something every authorial "monarch" can boast. Melville, however, is not without a "castle" of his own, a linguistic edifice, something created exclusively by his mind and therefore also belonging exclusively to that mind. Every "Romancer & Poet" can lay claim to this kind of property, for their entitlement is inscribed in their very creativity, in their sole and exclusive authorship. Such literary assets are no doubt gratifying, though they are hardly unproblematic. For if the author's fictive creation does indeed count as his property, it must also count as his "sole and despotic dominion," as Blackstone suggests. It must count, that is to say, as a field of sovereignty, over which he presides, in supreme command, like a "monarch."

The emergence of the imperial under the auspices of the creative is not altogether accidental here, nor is it altogether idiosyncratic. To see it in context, we need only look at the following exposition by Timothy Walker, from his "Defence of Mechanical Philosophy," a much-publicized defense of technology that also confers on its creative spirit an imperial armature:

> Now it was, that mind began to develop its energies, and assert its empire over all other things. . . . We look with unmixed delight at the triumphant march of Mechanism. So far from enslaving, it has emancipated the mind, in the most glorious sense. From a ministering servant to matter, mind has become the powerful lord of matter . . . it rests, like the Omnipotent Mind, of which it is the image, from its work of creation, and pronounces it good.[14]

The "creation" Walker celebrates here is technological rather than literary, but his sense of what such a "creation" means is almost exactly analogous to Melville's. Where Melville speaks of the "freedom" his "invention" affords, Walker discerns in the "march of Mechanism "an "emancipat[ory]" power. And where Melville imagines himself a "monarch," Walker portrays a "powerful lord" ensconced in an "empire" of his own "creation." For both of them, "creation" entails not only the freedom of ownership but also the freedom of dominion. One's creation is not only one's to possess, it is also one's to "lord" over.

Within the terms of our discussion, we might think of both Walker and Melville as "imperial" selves, selves whose individualism is imperially articulated. The making of such a self, I have tried to suggest, is not only instrumental to the making of the nation but in many ways expressive of it, reproducing in the province of selfhood an internalized version of the national polity. In the case of Melville and Walker, the mutuality between self and nation appears, more specifically, as the inscription of the imperial in the proprietary, as the reproduction of the nation's terms of sovereignty within the self's terms of ownership. In other words, where self and nation coincide, the proprietary individual would seem, quite literally, to be a representation of empire. The representation is embedded in his very form of selfhood: being "imperial," he is fashioned like an empire and acts like one. Melville and Walker have every reason, by this logic, to call themselves "lord" and "monarch"; and they are in good company. The same logic would lead the U.S. Commissioner of Patents, Thomas Ewbank, to discuss proprietary inventors in imperial terms. Speaking of future inventors of motors, for example, he summed up their keen competition by noting: "We are ignorant who will receive the crown."[15]

In *Mardi*, the conjunction of the proprietary and the imperial raises especially interesting questions about the representational form of the book. Here, in this prized possession of an imperial self, we should not be surprised to find a textual polity that is likewise "imperial," one that takes as its controlling form the polity of an expansionist nation. *Mardi* thus dramatizes a juncture between a politics and a poetics, between a mode of social governance and a mode of authorial governance. Putting it more bluntly, we might think of it as the juncture where literary property represents imperial polity, where the brutal efficiencies of nation building replay themselves in what Richard Poirier calls the "brutal efficiencies of literary form."[16]

Using this as a working hypothesis, I will now examine a curious instance of authorial governance in *Mardi*, the astonishing proliferation of names. Even the most random sampling easily produces over a dozen names at once meaningless and unfamiliar to most readers, names such as Tongatona, Blandoo, Voyo, Raymonda Zonoree, Titonti, Ogro, Tripoo, Indrimavoki, Tarzillo, Vivivi Jojijorora, Jorkraki, Mujo, and Oloo. Indeed, hardly a chapter is free from the name of some legendary hero, king, sage, or fool, whose name is mentioned just once and no more. These names invoke no human face and no personality, and unlike historical names (such as John Jacob Astor in "Bartleby"), they carry no recognizable social content, and seem to signify nothing.

Why does Melville invent names in such abundance? A few of them are useful in an obvious and limited way. To vindicate a theory, for instance, Melville has only to invent a name and use that as documentary evidence. When he reports that "among these people of Odo, the matter of eating and drinking is held a matter of life and death," Melville need only point to one Tyty: " 'Drag away my queen from my arms,' said old Tyty when overcome of Adommo, 'but leave me my cook' "

(175). And when he tries to persuade us that "the most solemn oath of a native of Valapee is that sworn by his tooth," he gives us this reference: " 'by this tooth,' said Bondo to Noojoomo, 'by this tooth I swear to be avenged upon thee, oh Noojoomo!' " (207).

Names such as these are at least easy to account for. They are clearly made to order, to suit the author's convenience. But such cases are relatively rare. More characteristically, names are as gratuitous as they are abundant. Such useless multitudes might seem hard to justify, and indeed they cannot be justified, at least not in terms of the book's narrative economy. They acquire meaning and validity only in relation to some other supervening principle. We might call it the principle of authorial pleasure, for the names, useless as they are to the book, are nevertheless quite useful from Melville's standpoint, that of a deliberately "creative" author. The act of naming is, after all, the simplest and clearest sign of creativity—a "mode of self-expansion" (to use Gérard Genette's term[17]) especially congenial to a sovereign author. Repeated over and over again, it affirms in Melville the magical powers of a wizard of words, conjuring up a world of sounds and just sounds, a world with no reality outside their dependency on their creator. Such names dramatize the author's power in the most absolute sense. By merely putting letters together Melville creates an entity, and because the permutation of letters is practically inexhaustible, he can do so endlessly. Only from the perspective of the narrative are the names useless; from Melville's perspective their uses are infinite and infinitely gratifying.

What we are witnessing in Melville's nominating frenzy, is a rift between author and text, a conflict between authorial pleasure and textual economy. Of course, the match is unequal: there is never any doubt who will prevail. Like a true "monarch," Melville must lord over what he creates—he must deploy his creativity as a means of dominion. This explains why names in *Mardi* are so short-lived, why they tend to be faceless and unresisting. Names that crop up at every turn can be dispatched equally precipitously. "Their production is their

obliteration," we might say. [18] Only their continual erasure can
give their author a chance to make up more names, to prove
his creativity yet again. Melville has, in short, embraced the
privilege of naming but spurned the responsibility that conventionally attends that power—the responsibility of bringing
life to a phonic concoction, of matching substance and sound.
If names in *Mardi* are, in the words of a contemporary reviewer, "legion,"[19] that is only because they are disposable,
replaceable, always at the mercy of their author. Authorial
freedom in *Mardi*, then, requires not only the freedom to "invent" but also the freedom to destroy, the latter being not so
much the antithesis to the former as its obverse and correlative.

The rapid appearance and disappearance of names in *Mardi*
attest to an essentially complementary relation between author and characters, an asymmetrical distribution of privilege
and obligation. The "freedom and invention" of the former
can manifest itself in the latter only as fated obsolescence.
Such a complementary relation, as I have tried to suggest, is
ultimately not just a literary phenomenon. It has wider uses as
a social instrumentality, underwriting a logic of freedom and
dominion that an imperial nation, an "empire for liberty," can
hardly do without. It is ironic, then, that even as Melville
proclaims his authorial sovereignty, even as he celebrates his
sole and exclusive ownership, his text, at that very moment,
traces its kinship to something that, far from being sole and
exclusive, extends beyond the domain of *Mardi*, beyond even
the domain of the literary.

The complementary logic of freedom and dominion dictates, in any case, not only the ephemerality of names, but also
the ephemerality of *Mardi*'s supposedly human characters. Unlike the characters in *Typee* and *Omoo*, who command an impressive capacity for survival (even the hated Captain Guy
manages not to die), characters in *Mardi* seem docilely reconciled to annihilation. Among the characters we can name and
remember, Annatoo is the first to be dispatched, meeting her
death in a storm. Aleema follows, Samoa and Jarl come next,
and at the end Yillah presumably also dies. If we add those

minor characters whose deaths are either reported or indirectly described, the death toll swells to an alarming degree. These peripheral deaths include the captain of the *Parki* and his crew (71–72), the diver whose fractured skull Samoa tries to replace (295), most of the sons of Aleema (306), the willful boy who does not accept Pani for a guide (347), and the merry bowsman fallen from the boat (618). Not even the good old *Acturion* is spared, perishing in the deep with all its crew. In fact, by the end of *Mardi*, all the characters from the first fifty chapters, with the exception of the narrator, die or disappear in one way or another.

Quite apart from the sheer numbers, what seems especially odd about these deaths is their utter pointlessness. Most occur for no apparent reason: the plot has no need for them, and they make not the slightest difference, emotional or otherwise. The one exception to this rather distressing rule is the death of Aleema, and the difference between this and the other deaths is instructive. For all the stilted language in which it is conveyed, Aleema's death is an event and we remember it, partly because his vengeful sons regularly show up to remind us, but, more fundamentally, because it is an integral part of the story, an incident whose significance extends beyond the immediate moment of its occurrence. Death does not eliminate Aleema from the story. If only as a curse he lives on, casting a tenacious shadow on the narrator's career. Aleema has not died in vain, but the other characters are not so fortunate. For most of them, death amounts to absolute erasure. Once they die, the story moves on as if they had never existed.

Annatoo, to take one example, dies in just this fashion. She is a vivid personality while still alive, and it seems only fitting that her death should create some turbulence in the narrative. But she simply disappears by falling overboard during a storm (presumably at the point when Melville has finally exhausted his store of acid comments about marriage for which she has provided the occasion). Her unceremonious dispatch, however, turns out to be more generic than personal—an indication of things to come rather than a sign of Melville's misogyny—for Annatoo's enemy, Jarl, hardly fares any better. More than any other character, Jarl deserves to die a special death, a death commensurate with his role as the narrator's faithful friend and constant companion. What he actually gets is this:

> Dismal tidings!—My faithful follower's death.
>
> Absent over night, that morning early, he had been discovered lifeless in the woods, three arrows in his heart. And the three pale strangers were nowhere to be found. But a fleet canoe was missing from the beach.
>
> Slain for me! my soul sobbed out. Nor yet appeased Aleema's manes; nor yet seemed sated the avengers' malice; who doubtless, were on my track. (364)

This passage, the full account of Jarl's demise, is hasty, threadbare, perfunctory. "My soul sobbed out," the narrator claims, but his performance is hardly convincing. Indeed, the only discernible sentiment in this eminently undistressed passage turns out to be Melville's own impatience to say what needs to be said and move on. Even before the end of the paragraph his attention has shifted to newer and more exciting dangers awaiting his narrator.

To make things worse, Jarl seems to have been killed not only casually, but for no reason related to himself. Our usual explanation—that he has to die because of guilt by association—is precisely one Melville refuses to offer (among the countless topics discussed by the philosophical characters, guilt by association never comes up). Explanation will have to come elsewhere, I think, for *Mardi* simply does not honor those modes of causation that render the text thematically intelligible. What it does honor is the author's freedom—in this case, to dispose of his characters in whichever way he pleases. Jarl dies not because he deserves it, not because his death in any way illuminates his life, but because—as the author's instrument and possession—he must die when Melville wants him to, he must submit to death and function in death. Jarl's death makes sense only within a textual field in which authorial dictates are always primary and characters are always subordinate. In a weird alienation of act from agent, Jarl and the death of Jarl stand as two unrelated facts, cut off from each other by the intervening figure of the author, who engineers acts of killing to suit his needs.[20]

And indeed, Jarl's death is meaningless only from the character's point of view. From Melville's perspective, his death is full of meaning, for nothing better demonstrates the extent of the narrator's guilt. Taji's guilt has to be demonstrated vicariously, because even though he himself tries to feel guilty, and even though an entire chapter is set aside for that effort (chapter 42, "Remorse"), his performance is quite unsatisfactory:

> As I gazed at this sight, what iron mace fell on my soul; what curse rang sharp in my ear! It was I, who was the author of the deed that caused the shrill wails that I heard. By this hand, the dead man had died. Remorse smote me hard; and like lightning I asked myself, whether the death-deed I had done was sprung of a virtuous motive, the rescuing a captive from thrall, or whether beneath that pretense, I had engaged in this fatal affray for some other, and selfish purpose; the companionship of a beautiful maid. But throttling the thought, I swore to be gay. Am I not rescuing the maiden? Let them go down who withstand me. (135)

The narrator "swore to be gay," and he succeeds in doing just that—it does not take much work. This pathetic attempt to feel remorse explains why Jarl has to be killed. For what animates the passage is certainly not guilt but Melville's failure to convey it. He must convey it by some other means then: not as an experiential fact, but by substitution, displacement, and transference—in short, by the "meaningful" death of a surrogate. Jarl dies primarily as a cipher, a signifying vehicle: his death produces the meaning that the narrator himself fails to. When the latter exclaims upon hearing Jarl's death, "Slain for me!" he is speaking more truth than he imagines.

But to say that Jarl's death "signifies" Taji's guilt is also to say that his life is not quite his: it has been alienated from him, appropriated by a signifying economy in which his life and death matter only in reference to someone else. He is a bearer of Taji's meaning, or rather, of Melville's. And as a bearer of meaning he is really nothing more than a personified attribute.

His "person" functions only as an allegorical sign—a sign of somebody else's guilt. His status as sign, in fact, gives him his identity—he is at once meaningful and docile—and in that peculiar character he exactly illustrates Walter Benjamin's point about the docile meaningfulness of allegorical figures. The subject of allegory, Benjamin writes, is "incapable of emanating any meaning or significance of its own; such significance as it has, it acquires from the allegorist." Such characters "are assembled according to their significance; indifference to their existence allowed them to be dispersed again."[21] This more or less sums up the fate of Jarl, and of most of the other characters as well. Aside from its obvious political allegory, what makes *Mardi* more subtly allegorical is a process of signifying appropriation—a process that enables the author continually to produce his characters as signs, harness them to his scheme of reference, make them carry his meaning. In this manner, he constitutes the entire textual field as a field of authorial "significance."

As we can see, Melville's freedom as an author has something to do with his freedom as an allegorist.[22] It has something to do as well—and the conjunction here is suggestive—with his freedom as a proprietor. He gets to become a proprietor, in fact, in the process of becoming an allegorist, for it is the act of personification that allows him to own his characters as signifying property, human ciphers created by him, belonging to him, and bearing a meaning he assigns. Allegory is logically a proprietary mode, it seems, and as such it gives Melville every right to make free with Jarl's life. This freedom might strike us as brutal, but in the tradition of property rights (as in the tradition of allegory), such freedom is altogether legitimate. "Liberty of estate," after all, is understood to reside "properly in the propriety of their goods, and a disposing power of their possessions."[23] This freedom to "dispose of" one's property is what Locke chooses to emphasize in his *Second Treatise of Government*, where he describes the freedom of individuals as the "perfect freedom to order their actions and dispose of their possessions and persons as they think fit."[24] In one sense, then, Melville is only doing what he is entitled to do, disposing of Jarl as he thinks fit. Of course, this particular form of "disposal" is not one Locke would have endorsed, although, given his latitude of definition, it is hardly one he can reject out of hand.[25]

From Jarl's standpoint, Melville's freedom of signification can appear only as an arbitrary imposition of meaning. If this rehearses, on the one hand, the familiar double logic of freedom and dominion, it also suggests, on the other, a necessarily ambiguous boundary between the two. For what Melville insists on, and what he ends up exercising, is finally not just the right to signify but the right to signify as he pleases, not just the freedom of authorship but its arbitrary sovereignty. He is proceeding as much from the latter as from the former when he disposes of Jarl, for to some extent he is simply getting rid of a character he finds increasingly tiresome. The doughty Viking has not kept pace with his author's changing interests. Between chapter 52, when the narrator and his company arrive in Mardi, and chapter 118, when Jarl's death is reported, Melville has transformed *Mardi* from a narrative of action to a narrative of discourse, for which he has also created a new set of characters—Media, Babbalanja, Mohi, and Yoomy—making the original cast altogether redundant. Uncouth and inarticulate, Jarl has no place in the world of abstruse discourse that Melville now fancies. He belongs to an earlier, earthier part of the story, and when that comes to an end he too must go.

Getting rid of Jarl would not have been difficult, because a peaceful exit is already in sight, in the form of the "wondrous kindness between Jarl and Borabolla" (292). The latter has "repeatedly besought Taji to allow his henchman to remain on the island" (292), and nothing would have been more natural than to take advantage of that offer. Melville seems initially tempted by that peaceful solution—Jarl is indeed left behind in Mondoldo—but in the end he cannot bring himself to acquiesce in Jarl's harmless release. Harmless release would have undermined the author's signifying freedom; it would have diminished his sovereign proprietorship. Characters cannot be truly "possessed" by the allegorist, Walter Benjamin has ob-

served, unless they become "dead, but eternally secure." Only
"as corpses" can they "enter into the homeland of allegory."[26]
For that reason, Melville must insist on seeing the end of Jarl,
whose death embodies his authorial sovereignty as both the
right to signify and the right to signify arbitrarily, the right to
freedom and the right to dominion.

In this double logic, a logic at work throughout *Mardi*, we
see a principle of social governance—an "empire for liberty,"
as it were—enacted in textual terms. But if the workings of
society have something to tell us about the workings of literature, the latter, in its unhampered performance, in turn has
something to say about the former. For what we see, in *Mardi*'s
reign of significance, is how unoxymoronic the phrase "empire
for liberty" is, and how seamlessly it works as a functional complementarity. This paradox begins to emerge in the death of
Jarl. With the death of Samoa the paradox becomes unmistakable.

Samoa has grown "impatient of the voyage," we learn in
chapter 102, and has asked to be allowed to return to Odo.
What ensues is remarkable:

> [Samoa] besought permission to return to Odo, there to await
> my return; and a canoe of Mondoldo being about to proceed in
> that direction, permission was granted; and departing for the
> other side of the island, from thence he embarked.
>
> Long after, dark tidings came, that at early dawn he had been
> found dead in the canoe: three arrows in his side.
>
> Yoomy was at a loss to account for the departure of Samoa;
> who, while ashore, had expressed much desire to roam.
>
> Media, however, declared that he must be returning to some
> inamorata.
>
> But Babbalanja averred, that the Upoluan was not the first
> man, who had turned back, after beginning a voyage like our
> own.
>
> To this, after musing, Yoomy assented. (311–12)

What seems especially odd here is the narrative sequence.
Melville begins by telling us about Samoa's departure, reveals
his death along the way, and as soon as that is done, moves on

once again to discuss, through the new characters, the reasons and proprieties of turning back from a voyage, little caring that the subject discussed has just been reported to be dead. One thing is clear: Melville has lost all interest in Samoa, and acts to get rid of him. What is also clear, however, is that he is by no means willing simply to let Samoa go. Here too, authorial freedom, to dispose of an unwanted character, seems inseparable from authorial dominion. And so Samoa has to die. Interjected as an aside, his death is not important enough to warrant full treatment but not trivial enough to be overlooked. In a literal and rather gruesome sense, Melville means to have the last word on Samoa, who, being a human cipher in life, must also die as one, much as Jarl does.

In the deaths of Jarl and Samoa we see the governing terms of Melville's authorship, a persistent and rather frightening compound, at once proprietary and imperial, enforcing a logic of dominion no less than a logic of freedom. Jarl and Samoa are casualties of this logic, and yet these two are finally no more than local instances of a much more central phenomenon, for *Mardi*'s chief casualty is (as we might expect) the narrator himself. This character has always annoyed and puzzled critics.[27] Unlike his more reasonable forerunners in *Typee* and *Omoo*, the narrator in *Mardi* is someone who undergoes a transformation before the book is half over, a protagonist who turns into a minor character and remains one, silent and invisible, until his resurrection in the last fifty pages. These are familiar facts, but they are worth going over, partly because the details have remained intriguing, and partly because, in his checkered career—in his initial privilege and his subsequent fall from grace—the narrator gives us the most graphic summary of the operating terms of Melville's authorship.

On the face of it, Taji's downfall is even harder to explain than that of his companions. Their boorishness and ignorance put them at a disadvantage; he labors under no such handicap. Unlike Jarl and Samoa, the narrator is witty, articulate, even learned, and has a decidedly conversational bent (he used to complain about the lack of a companion on the *Acturion* who could talk "sentiment and philosophy," "someone who could page me a quotation from Burton on Blue Devils" [5]). All in all he seems a natural candidate for the lofty metaphysical discourse that takes up the rest of the book. Melville's decision to brush him aside is, for that reason, all the more strange.

The strangeness increases if we further remember the close alliance between author and narrator in the early part of *Mardi*. In the first fifty chapters the narrator is not so much a character as a voice, and as a voice—a fluid linguistic presence—he seems to inhabit the same narrative space as the author. His language, lively, hyperbolical, bombastic, reigns almost as a naturalized fact: there is no indication that Melville is presenting him deliberately, through his speech. Even more crucially, author and narrator work in unison as they jointly preside over a number of narrative functions. One of the authorial privileges in *Mardi*, we have seen, is the privilege of naming, but that privilege is by no means exclusively Melville's. For the narrator, too, has a genius for naming, and supplies everyone with fanciful geographical and literary titles. Jarl, for instance, is "the Viking" and "the Skyeman"; Samoa is the "the Islander," "the Upoluan," as well as "Belisarius" (98); Annatoo is "the Calmuc" (110). In chapter 32, after running through the different nomenclature of the swordfish ("Indian sword fish," "Bill fish," "Xiphius Platypterus"), the narrator decides to "substitute a much better one of my own, namely, the Chevalier" (104)—and "Chevalier" the fish remains for the rest of the chapter.

In granting his narrator a knack for naming, Melville is not trying to represent a quirky habit; he is, once again, simply allowing the narrator to do what he himself delights in doing. Because the two are essentially engaged in the same activity, Melville never notices his narrator's odd habit. The blurred boundary and interchangeable function between author and narrator make it unclear at many points just who the "author" is. Perhaps Melville alone is responsible for those utterly nonsensical names (such as Jojijorara) presented to us as absolute givens in the story. But is it Melville or the narrator who christens the whaleboat "the chamois," the sperm whale "the cachalot," Annatoo "the Calmuc," and Jarl "the Skyeman"?

The overlapping province of author and narrator gives rise to a composite linguistic presence in *Mardi*. It "authorizes" the narrator, making him not only a figure of authority but an author within the text. In that capacity he gives us a striking demonstration of authorship as Melville conceives of it and, to a large extent, as he himself practices it. Like Melville, the narrator acquires property when he turns author. He nominates, and he owns what he names, for as always in *Mardi*, names are deeds of entitlement: they belong to the namer, not the named.[28] When the narrator calls Jarl a "Viking" and rhapsodizes over the title, his rhapsody amounts to a declaration of ownership:

> My life for it, Jarl, thy ancestors were Vikings, who many a time sailed over the salt German Sea and the Baltic; who wedded their Brynhildas in Jutland; and are now quaffing mead in the halls of Valhalla, and beating time with their cans to the hymns of the Scalds. Ah! how the old Sagas run through me! (12)

Jarl is the ostensible subject of the passage, but his part in it is at best incidental. Such fanciful words and ideas about his ancestry have nothing to do with him; they belong to the narrator. As the final sentence makes clear, the true hero of the passage is the speaker: the old Sagas run through "me" and not Jarl.[29] The supposed tribute to the "Viking" is really a smug display of the narrator's own wit. Hardly the portrait of a friend, it seems more a deed of ownership. What the narrator actually owns is words: but even as he flaunts his verbal property, he also collects, in the same gesture, his human property, underwritten here quite literally with words.

Linguistic ownership, then, would seem to be the supreme form of ownership in *Mardi*. And because ownership is exclusive, linguistic usage in this book is no less so. Only one person can be the proprietor here, and only one person can talk. This accounts for the volubility of the narrator and the voicelessness of his companions. Jarl is "exceedingly taciturn, and but seldom will speak for himself" (13), Melville makes a point of telling us, and the same is apparently true of Samoa and Annatoo. It is no coincidence, perhaps, that the narrator's com-

panions comprise two South Sea Islanders and a "Viking"—
savages all, with no claim to the English language and perhaps
for that reason unworthy of speech. In the first fifty chapters
of *Mardi* there is no Toby, no Doctor Long Ghost, to banter
words with the narrator.

Indirect discourse, rather than dialogue, is what befits such
savages. Indirect discourse is abruptly introduced, for instance, when Samoa gives an account of what happened to the
Parki. "Now, this story of his was related in the mixed phrase-
ology of a Polynesian sailor," the narrator tells us (67), and,
having no patience with such gibberish, he proceeds to tell the
story himself, using his own words and his own point of view.
His treatment of Annatoo repeats the same pattern. A fearful
shrew she may be, but when it comes to things verbal she turns
out to be quite inept. She may lie about her pilferings, and she
may "[shower] a whole torrent of objurgations into both ears
of Samoa," but not a single word actually passes her lips. The
same muteness seems to afflict Jarl as well. On a few occasions
he actually comes up with such pronouncements as "Ay, ay
sir, pulling as hard as ever we can, sir" (28), but even those
moments are rare. Jarl does not, as a rule, speak for himself.
What he has to say is usually said for him:

> At last he [Jarl] very bluntly declared that the scheme was a crazy
> one; he had never known of such a thing but thrice before; and
> in every case the runaways had never afterwards been heard of.
> He entreated me to renounce my determination, not be a boy,
> pause and reflect, stick to the ship, and go home in her like a
> man. Verily, my Viking talked to me like my uncle. (17)

Jarl's unfastidious advice must be made over before it can be
admitted into a text as fastidious as *Mardi*. But "making over"
here must work in a double sense: in the sense of being im-
proved upon, reformed into a consciously literary diction; but
also in a proprietary sense, of being turned over to the narrator's possession. What is at stake here is not who the speaker
is (that much is undisputed), but who owns the words Jarl is
supposed to be speaking and, even more seriously, who owns
Jarl. If one could speak of a politics of discursive modes, what

blazons forth from this passage is surely the politics of the "imperial" self—whose very utterance is appropriative, whose expansive selfhood resembles nothing better than an imperial polity. Armed, on this occasion, with its linguistic projectile—with its strategic use of indirect discourse—this imperial voice not only secures the propriety of Jarl's speech but also secures Jarl as property. It is no accident, then, that at the end of the passage the narrator should refer to Jarl as "my Viking." Nor is this the only instance when he refers to his friends in the possessive form. Jarl is quite routinely "my Viking" (and, on special occasions, "my royal old Viking" [100]), just as Samoa is variously "my Islander," "my Upoluan," "my Belisarius." Such a practice is only to be expected, for the logic of authorial sovereignty, as Melville sees fit to confer it on his favored surrogate, is ultimately a logic of appropriation no less than a logic of ownership, a logic of dominion no less than a logic of freedom.

Melville would have been horrified, of course, by the suggestion of kinship between literary property and imperial polity. Still, some half-complacent, half-uneasy sense of his book's imperial logic must have prompted him to thematize that logic into some heavy-handed seignorial trappings for his narrator. Beginning with *Mardi* (and repeated, perhaps for a different effect, in *White-Jacket* and *Redburn*), Melville makes his narrator a gentleman, a cut above ordinary seamen, mingling with them only for mysterious reasons. "Abroad of all ships in which I have sailed," the narrator tells us, "I have invariably been known by a sort of drawing-room title." And this comes about "because of something in me that could not be hidden; stealing out in an occasional polysyllable; an otherwise incomprehensible deliberation in dining; remote, unguarded allusions to Belles-Lettres affairs; and other trifles superfluous to mention" (14). Not satisfied with such advantages, the narrator reports an even more fantastic rumor about his social elevation, circulated, he tells us, by the adoring Jarl: "He must have taken me for one of the House of Hanover in disguise, or, haply, for bonneted Charles Edward the

Pretender, who, like the Wandering Jew, may yet be a vagrant" (14).

The narrator seems to have forgotten Jarl's supposed ignorance when he attributes to his friend such a learned hunch. Jarl's fond fancy, one suspects, is really the narrator's own: it is he who would like, if not seriously to claim kinship with royalty, at least to depict others fantasizing about it. Not satisfied with being a mere gentleman, the narrator wishfully puts himself among the monarchs of feudal Europe. Theirs is the sort of power he would like to claim for himself, and, to some degree, theirs is the sort of power he exercises in the first part of *Mardi*. Jarl is clearly his obedient servant, and even though he ordinarily looks upon the old sailor with "humorous complacency" (34), when the need arises he can easily "assume the decided air of a master" (90). His lordship over Samoa is equally unmistakable. From the very first, using the "mild, firm tone of a superior," the narrator establishes his own "unquestioned supremacy" (96). Indeed, the only intractable soul on board the *Parki* is Annatoo, who "through Samoa would then have the sway" (96). But the narrator guards against this eventuality by securing "my Viking" and by keeping Samoa "docile" (96). So before long "the command of the vessel [is] tacitly yielded up to myself" (97).

Imperial narrator and docile companions make up a configuration of characters strikingly different, as Edwin Eigner points out, from anything we have seen in Melville's two previous books.[30] But the narrator's supremacy rests ultimately not on his social origins, imagined or otherwise, but on the fact that he is a different kind of character from the others. He does the speaking, they are spoken of. His existence is coextensive with the narrative; theirs is cursory, incidental. The narrator, in his very mode of being, is already a breed apart. Along with the author, he inhabits a privileged sphere, an exclusive linguistic realm to which all other characters are denied access. Sovereignty and subordination would seem to be inscribed, then, in the very linguistic structure of the book. This hierarchical arrangement, in turn, is naturalized by a rhetoric of species difference. The narrator cannot help but dominate, the book suggests, because what he is dominating is really not men but brute animals:

> I like him [Samoa]; it was as you fancy a fiery steed with mane disheveled, as young Alexander fancied Bucephalus; which wild horse, when he patted, he preferred holding by the bridle. (97)

Here, graphically rendered, is the narrator's sovereignty in word and deed. That sovereignty, we can also see, is primarily a relational category: it can exist only in relation to something else, something produced, by a complementary logic, as a pole of subjection. Such sovereignty inevitably recalls the form Melville himself practices: an authorial sovereignty that also dictates, as its operating condition, an attendant field of dominion. Indeed, what we are witnessing seems once again to be a reflexive bond between author and narrator, where the former's relation *to* the narrative translates, by a sort of osmotic correspondence, into the latter's relation *within* the narrative.

The intimate bond between author and narrator in the first fifty chapters makes the latter's ultimate downfall all the more remarkable. Because Melville is understandably silent on the subject, his reasons for demoting Taji can only be speculated upon. Accompanying circumstances suggest a web of intriguing connections. The timing of Taji's demotion—its odd concurrence with the deaths of Jarl and Samoa—seems especially significant. In fact, the three companions are mysteriously bound up in a common fate, dictated not by who they are or what they do, but by their genetic chronology in relation to the author. The three are of the same vintage, compositionally speaking, and Melville apparently thinks of them as a single unit. All three are active in the first fifty chapters, but upon their arrival in Mardi and during their visits to Odo, Valapee, Juam, Mondoldo, and Maramma (chapters 53 to 117), they steadily lose ground until, by chapter 120, they are completely usurped by the new Mardian characters. Characters in *Mardi* seem to divide into two generations: Jarl, Samoa, Yillah, and the narrator compose the first; Media, Babbalanja, Yoomi, and Mohi make up the second. Thus divided, it becomes clear that characters from the first generation die (or otherwise fade into insignificance) more or less at the same time. Their synchronized exits bear witness to an intervening hand, the author's hand. The passing away of one generation, and the ascendancy of the other, have almost nothing to do with the logic of the narrative, and everything to do with the logic of the author's pleasure.

Thus, the narrator's fate cannot be understood apart from that of his companions. Like them, he too is a human cipher, a bearer of authorial significance. What happens to him is more interesting from our point of view, for in his downfall, in the rupture between him and the author, we are finally able to see the latter, undisguised and unassisted, in a rare but not altogether unexpected appearance. The first sign of that rupture takes place, in fact, as early as chapter 53. On that fateful occasion, the narrator, to take advantage of the natives' mistaken belief that he is Taji, decides to be "received under that title" (164). That might seem harmless enough, until we remember what naming means in *Mardi*. The narrator, the customary donor of names, now finds himself in the unprecedented position of a recipient. Saddled with a "title," he becomes alienable property, which is to say, he becomes just like everybody else. No longer the imperial "I" of the first-person narrative, no longer the proprietor in the text, he is now reduced to the same state to which he has previously reduced others.

To be named, then, amounts to an ontological transformation for the narrator. It shifts him from one side of *Mardi*'s complementarity to the other—from the pole of freedom to the pole of dominion—and makes him everything that he was not. No other event better emblematizes the rupture between author and narrator. Unlike the other instances of naming, where it is sometimes hard to tell the narrator from Melville in their joint authorship, and their joint entitlement, this occasion admits of no ambiguity. The naming is done solely and exclusively by Melville, and the name comes solely and exclusively from him. Taji plays no part in it except as the receptacle of a "title," something for the author to claim. Far from being a unifying ritual between the two, this act of naming ushers in a hierarchical separation between author and narrator, turning them into creator and object, owner and owned.

As the author's newly minted property, Taji must await his turn to be disposed of, and that happens, appropriately, right after the demise of his two companions. Three important chapters chronicle that occurrence: chapter 118 ("Taji receives Tidings and Omens"), chapter 119 ("Dreams"), and chapter 120 ("Media and Babbalanja Discourse"). These chapters represent the turning point in *Mardi*, and in their sequence of appearance they offer an excellent summary of Melville's logic and logistics, of the participating parties and the rise and fall of their respective fortunes. To start things off, Taji receives the news of Jarl's death in chapter 118. That event seems to signal a collective end for the first generation of characters, and clears the stage for their successors in chapter 120 ("Media and Babbalanja Discourse"). But the stage is not limited to just these fictive beings. The author, too, has a part to play, and in the intervening chapter (chapter 119), Melville reveals and dramatizes himself, as if to take credit for the changes in his narrative. After three pages of extravagant recitations, the chapter concludes with the following:

> My cheek blanches white while I write; I start at the scratch of my pen; my own mad brood of eagles devours me; fain would I unsay this audacity; but an iron-mailed hand clenches mine in a vice, and prints down every letter in my spite. Fain would I hurl off this Dionysius that rides me; my thoughts crush me down till I groan; in far fields I hear the song of the reaper, while I slave and faint in this cell. The fever runs through me like lava; my hot brain burns like a coal; and like many a monarch, I am less to be envied, than the veriest hind in the land. (368)

Here, once again, is the first-person singular, more than restored to its former eminence. This frenzied, feverish "I," though, is no longer the familiar one of the early chapters. The speaker is not Taji at all, but the author himself, speaking without mediation from the "cell" where he "slave[s] and "faint[s]" in the act of writing. The speaker claims to be toiling

under an intolerable yoke, driven to distraction by the ardor
of his labor. Yet, amidst his extravagant complaint one senses
an even more extravagant pride, evident in his very manner
of complaint. For the speaker clearly enjoys talking about his
woes and burdens: he is ecstatic about them. If authorship is,
as he says, a compulsive ordeal, it is charged all the same with
a demonic grandeur, wildly intoxicating and wildly empower-
ing. In any case it is no ordinary affair, but something that
requires superhuman effort and superhuman endurance—a
task fit only for a "monarch."

Melville's fantastic language assiduously draws attention to
that task of authorship, and in doing so he brushes aside the
narrator to stamp his insignia directly on the text. Such a self-
dramatizing author clearly needs no fictive surrogate. The con-
fused boundary between author and narrator is redefined, in a
way that makes the narrator obsolete. Henceforth he is no
longer a part of the author, and shares neither his freedom nor
his power. He is just another thing the author owns. If the
dissociation between author and narrator begins when the narrator receives a name, it culminates in the dramatic appearance of the author as author. At this crucial juncture, between
the passing away of the old dispensation and the installment
of the new, Melville steps forward to reveal himself as the un-
mediated, unmistakable creator of his text.

The narrator's downfall thus establishes the author's clear
and undisputed title. Property relations, one suspects, ultimately dictate the fate of the narrator: he has become too
prominent, too privileged, too domineering—in short, too authorial for Melville's jealous comfort. In his downfall we see
the logic of literary possession at its clearest and most uncom-
promising. Earlier, Melville has refused to tolerate the rival
claims of the world's "dull common places." Now he refuses to
tolerate even his own narrator, his deputy and surrogate. The
author's proprietary jurisdiction, like Blackstone's, and like
Thomas Skidmore's, can only be an empire of one. It is truly
a "sole and despotic dominion," as Blackstone says, and as
such it must insist on "the total exclusion of the right of any
other individual in the universe." It is altogether fitting that

Melville should desire now to be the sole monarch, a point he makes emphatically clear when he publicizes the following bit of information:

> As we glided away, King Media issued a sociable decree. He declared it his royal pleasure, that throughout the voyage, all stiffness and state etiquette should be suspended: nothing must occur to mar the freedom of the party. To further this charming plan, he doffed his symbols of royalty, put off his crown, laid aside his scepter, and assured us that he would not wear them again, except when we landed; and not invariably, then. (208)

Media's self-elected abdication from kingship would have been gratuitous except, of course, in the context of his author's proprietorship. Such an author will ultimately tolerate no principle of sovereignty comparable with his own. Media cannot be the commanding figure the narrator once was (and no other character in the second part of *Mardi* can either), because that office is meant never to be filled again. From this point on the narrative will be rendered, appropriately, in the first-person plural, the royal "we." It will be answerable only to the author.

The conspicuous authorial presence in *Mardi* has struck a number of critics. Richard Brodhead reads the book as a kind of allegory of the creative artist, an allegory whose true subject is not the characters but the author himself. In the act of writing, Brodhead suggests, Melville "comes to see that [*Mardi*'s] true action is not his characters' adventures but his own creative process; that its real voyage is the imaginative one he has undertaken in conceiving *Mardi*, that the real object of its quest is nothing his characters seek but the mental world he himself discloses through the act of creating his book."[31] Edwin Eigner, struck by the same preeminent centrality of the author, has harsher things to say. Pointing to Pierre as an example of the Melville-like author, he goes on to outline an authorial practice that almost exactly describes Melville's own practice in *Mardi*:

> Pierre alters the style, the meaning, the very nature of his book while he is writing it, but there is never any suggestion that the

changes are inspired by anything that happens within his manuscript. Rather Pierre's novel changes because Pierre changes. The alterations in his book are brought about by his own development, of which the developing manuscript is an effect and an index, never a cause.[32]

What becomes clear, from the accounts of both critics, is that Melville has replaced his characters not only as the center of interest in their fictive domain, but as the very locus of signification. *Mardi* refers only to him: it acquires meaning only in relation to his development as a writer, only when it becomes an allegory of authorship. Within the terms of our discussion, nothing better illustrates the process of "signifying appropriation," a process where the allegorical underwrites the proprietary in a reign of authorial meaning. *Mardi* belongs to Melville in every sense of the word. The book is his, his private allegory—emblematic of his creative process but also subsumed by it, by his continual production of the fictive universe as his authorial universe. The "authorial" turns out to be the all-encompassing category here, but if so, its boundless jurisdiction must rest on a radical aggrandizement of the self, and a corresponding subjection of the Other.

The phenomenon here is akin to what Terry Castle calls the "spectralization of the Other." She sees it as intrinsic to individualism, whose ultimate fantasy is to reduce all principles of otherness into projections from one's own self.[33] Such spectralizations, I further argue, are proprietary ventures as well, for the Other is not just spectralized, it is also internalized in the process, incorporated and possessed. Here as elsewhere, the proprietary self, to operate as such, must operate like an imperial polity: to render absolute its own jurisdiction, it needs to make over the Other in its own image.[34] This need is especially true in *Mardi*, where the inscription of the appropriative in the proprietary is so central that the author must end up literally being an "imperial" self, a veritable "dominion." In that capacity, he reproduces, in his literary endeavor, what we might call the textual corollaries of empire building.

One of those corollaries seems to be a unilingual regime. As we have noted, speech in *Mardi* is primarily something the author owns, and—ownership being exclusive—speech here also tends to be monotonous. Instead of a rich array of tones and accents, styles and vocabularies (as we might expect from a novel the bulk of which is conversation), *Mardi* presents us with an uncanny uniformity of speech. Even though the speakers are supposedly very different people, and even though they do espouse different ideas, their conversational style is remarkably unvaried in its fanciful archaism, its convoluted syntax, its stiff and stilted diction. Far from being an orchestration of voices, *Mardi* presents an orchestration of ideas articulated, oddly enough, in only one voice.[35]

Mardi's monotony is the logical consequence, I think, of its commitment to proprietorship. To the extent that speech is the author's asset, and to the extent that the characters too are the author's property, one voice is all Melville needs, and one voice is all he will countenance, for monotony is, in some sense, his constitutive proof of ownership.[36] Speech in *Mardi* is therefore rarely a distinguishing trait for different characters. It is hard to tell who is speaking from what is being said, and to ensure identification Melville almost always has to include the name of the speaker along with his speech. Consider, for instance, the following example:

> "In safety, afar off, you may batter down a fortress; but at your peril you essay to carry a single turret by escalade. And if doubts distract you, in vain will you seek sympathy from your fellow men. For upon this one theme, not a few of your free-minded mortals, even the otherwise honest and intelligent, are the least frank and friendly. . . . Do you show a tropical calm without? then, be sure a thousand contrary currents whirl and eddy within. The free, airy robe of your philosophy is but a dream, which seems true while it lasts; but waking again into the orthodox world, straightway you resume the old habit. And though in your dreams you may hie to the uttermost Orient, yet all the while you abide where you are." (369–70)

Whose voice is it? Obviously it is Melville's voice, but if we were to pick among the characters, most of us would probably pick Babbalanja (just because he is given to long speeches). Babbalanja might, in fact, have spoken those words, but on this occasion the speaker happens to be Media. As we can see, speech in *Mardi* has nothing to do with the speakers: it is without emotion, without density, and without nuance—without any trace of human difference. It is there not to represent the characters but to signal authorial ownership, not to enliven but to foreclose. Here, then, is the language of the imperial self, cast in its imperial extreme: a uniform (and uniformed) language, a language stamped not only with its author's insignia but with his appropriative passion.[37] That passion, indeed, seems to extend beyond the province of language to cover *Mardi*'s entire assembly of narrative effects. For even as the fictive universe becomes the author's signifying universe—and even as fictive causality gives away to authorial intervention— the text too coalesces along certain lines, in such a way as to permit what we might call an incorporation of the reader's sphere.

The fate of Yillah is a case in point. A vanishing lady, in any form of narrative, usually carries a great deal of suspense, but in *Mardi* the suspense is altogether minimal. Yillah's disappearance will not upset most readers, because we all know it is just a handy way for Melville to set his characters off on their wanderings. We do not worry too much about Yillah, partly because we see through the cause of her disappearance, but, most of all, because Melville himself does not worry. His indifference, the very transparency of it, makes it impossible for the reader to feel otherwise. Melville's authorial sentiment is never a strictly bilateral affair between him and his characters, for a vectorial motion is already inscribed in it, a sentiment directed at the reader as both subject and target. Just like everything else, the reader's sphere in *Mardi* is subject to appropriation, and Melville stakes his claims on that promising terrain by populating it with an ideal occupant, an imaginary reader created much as his characters are created and, being his creation, owned much as his characters are owned.

The only problem is that Melville happened to be dealing with real readers. Ownership of real people might not be as easy as ownership of fictive characters—an obvious enough detail, and yet it seemed not to have been the case for Melville. The fact that it was not obvious to him, that he expected *Mardi* to be beloved by its readers, seems to me one of the most telling clues to the book. Here, too, something like the "spectralization of the Other" seems to be at work—in this case, the spectralization of the actual reader into an ideal one. Only such an operation can lead Melville to think that readers will welcome his book. The reader as Melville imagines him (or fails to imagine him) has something to tell us about *Mardi*'s principles of authorship. By the same token, the responses of the actual readers, and Melville's responses to them, have something to tell us about *Mardi* as well, for against those historical transactions we might be able to see what is peculiar, and perhaps what is amiss, in Melville's fictitious dealings with his readers.

In the "Preface" to *Mardi* Melville writes, "Not long ago, having published two narratives of voyages in the Pacific, which, in many quarters, were received with incredulity, the thought occurred to me, of indeed writing a romance of Polynesian adventure, and publishing it as such; to see whether, the fiction might not, possibly, be received for a verity" (xvii). Critics were quick to respond:

> In his preface, Mr. Melville intimates, that having previously written truly which was believed to be fiction, he has now attempted a romance "to see whether it might not possibly be received as a verity." We think he need be under no apprehension that the present volumes will be received as gospel—they certainly lack all show of truth or naturalness.

> As Mr. Melville's facts have been mistaken for fictions, he wishes to see if his fictions will be mistaken for facts. On this point he may set his mind entirely at rest. Although it is by no means a good way to make people receive the false for the true, by forewarning them of your design, there can be no reader so intensely verdant, as not to discern the grossness and utter improbabilities of the fabrications in *Mardi*.[38]

Interestingly, what both critics objected to was not so much the fictiveness of *Mardi* as the transparency of the fiction (the book not only "lack[s] all show of truth and naturalness," but Melville has even gone so far as to "forewarn" his readers of his "design"). Likewise, both resented Melville's snide hope that his fiction would "be received as a verity," indignantly pointing out that "there can be no reader so intensely verdant" as to be guilty of that error. In short, what most infuriated them was Melville's attitude toward his readers: his utter presumption and utter disregard.

Other critics responded in much the same way. Annoyance, protest, some measure of self-vindication and even self-identification were the standard reactions to *Mardi*. At least four reviewers were moved to discuss their professional duties as critics, as if they felt compelled to speak out, to give themselves title and substance against the author's spectralizing impulse.[39] Among the four, Henry Cood Watson of the New York *Saroni's Musical Times* went to the greatest length and turned his review of *Mardi* into a championship of the critic:

> True, it is the province of the hapless critic to peruse all kinds of books—the good and the bad, or worse yet, the indifferent—the serious and the grave. But, in his distribution of his task, it is his consoling privilege to appropriate a different season for each class of work, reserving dull trash and all manner of figurative strictures for his hours of penance. . . . Mr. Melville is hard upon the critics. We somewhat question the good taste of his remarks on the topic. The only difference between critics and other readers is that the former *print* their opinion. Oral and published criticisms generally agree, except when injudicious friends abuse the privilege of criticism to write up a book, or when malicious enemies attempt the reverse.[40]

For Watson, a full account of his duties as a critic served as a critique of *Mardi*. With a degree of discernment for which we rarely give them credit, nineteenth-century reviewers seem to have seized upon and responded to what is surely one of the most striking facts about the book: its spectralization of the Other, its production of the reader as an ideal person, which is also to say, a species of nonperson. Watson was, if anything, gentler than most critics, whose scathing reviews left Melville with no doubts about what actual readers thought of his book.

The recorded responses to *Mardi* make Melville's faith in its popular success all the more curious. We might dismiss his hope that *Mardi* might be "received as a verity" as a rhetorical hope, but there was nothing rhetorical, or disingenuous, in his other hopes for the book. Melville expected *Mardi* to do well, and in all the letters to his publishers, he expressed a strong conviction that his book would bring in large profits and public acclaim. Melville's enthusiastic recommendation of the book cannot be put down as the calculated move of an author. True, he needed the money and bargained eagerly for it, but he also thought the book was going to sell, and expected his publishers to come around to the same opinion. To John Murray, Melville insisted that "you may not form as high an idea of the book *now*, as you may, when you see it."[41] And three months later, he again wrote, "But I can give you no adequate idea of it. You must see it for yourself."[42] In fact, Melville's confidence in the book seemed to grow the more he thought about it. When he wrote to John Murray on 25 March 1848, he initially asked for an advance of £150. By 28 January 1849, he was demanding no "less than 200 guineas."[43] Even when Murray rejected the book, on the ground that it was fiction, Melville's confidence remained unshaken, and when he negotiated with his new publisher, Richard Bentley, his terms remained unchanged. Melville eventually received 200 guineas from Bentley, and *Mardi* was published in the "handsome style" that he wanted, as a three-decker novel at 31s.6d. for the set. All the accompanying circumstances of negotiation and publication indicate that Melville intended *Mardi* to be what he called a "hit."[44] From our perspective, these expectations seem insane. But the more interesting question is, What enabled Melville to have such insane expectations?

Once he recovered from the shock of the book's popular failure (though never from his bitterness), Melville was quite able to explain why *Mardi* was a flop:

And I can not but think that its having been brought out in England in the ordinary novel form must have led to the disappoint-
ment of many readers, who would have been better pleased with
it, perhaps, had they taken it up in the first place for what it really
is. Besides, the peculiar thoughts and fancies of a Yankee upon
politics and other matters could hardly be presumed to delight
that class of gentlemen who conduct your leading journals; while
the metaphysical ingredients (for want of a better term) of this
book, must of course repel some of those who read simply for
amusement.[45]

Melville's attempt to explain the failure of his book amounts
to an attempt to evoke various kinds of readers and to imagine,
from their points of view, why they might have disliked Mardi.
He comes up with quite a few specimens: mindless readers,
who are disappointed when the book is not what the adver-
tisement says it is; snobbish (English) readers, who frown upon
the presumptuous Yankee; and frivolous readers, "who read
simply for amusement." The portraits are hardly flattering, and
Melville is anything but penitent as he elaborates upon them.
Still, the exercise amounts to an attempt to imagine the reader
as something other than what he wants, something other than
what suits his convenience. To make sense of the poor reception of Mardi necessitates an effort to imagine an alien Other,
an Other outside the jurisdiction of one's selfhood, something
one cannot own.

Even to the last, Melville persisted in believing that Mardi
would find an audience "for whom it is intended." Who might
such readers be? It is interesting to speculate for a moment on
Melville's ideal reader—"ideal" both in the sense that he is
desired and in the sense that he has no material reality. Actual
readers objected to the "prosiness," "puerility," and "down-
right nonsense" in Mardi, found the book "vapid," and wondered at the "audacity of the writer which could attempt such
an experiment with the long suffering of his readers."[46] The
ideal reader, presumably, has no such objections. He has no
objections, one suspects, because he is tame and submissive, a
willing soul, a meek reflection of the authorial ego. If this fig-

ure seems somewhat familiar, that is because we have met him before among the characters. He resembles those unfortunate creatures in every respect: he too is created and possessed by the author, and being so created, and so possessed, he too can be disposed of, as his owner thinks fit.

The reader "for whom [Mardi] is intended" is a fiction then, as perhaps all imagined readers are.[47] This fictive reader, though, is a fiction created by an imperial self, a self that annihilates what it refuses to imagine and appropriates what it projects as its own. Melville does not actually kill his readers (as he kills his characters), but he does turn them into specters and incorporates them as well into his proprietary domain. Only a spectral reader will put up with the effrontery he feels entirely at liberty to perpetrate. To write as he does in *Mardi*, he needs such docile specters. The absence of a recalcitrant Other among his characters enables Melville to reign as a "monarch"; the absence of a recalcitrant Other in the reader's sphere persuades him that *Mardi* is going to be a "hit."

Of course, such fictive victories are never without their cost. *Mardi*, a work of unsurpassed freedom for Melville, is a story of fated demise for his characters. The text that establishes its author's clear and undisputed title subjects its characters to a continual drama of appropriation. In this double logic of freedom and dominion, we see the constitutive doubleness of Melville's authorial sovereignty. Such a doubleness also happens to be the doubleness of an imperial self or, within the terms of our discussion, the doubleness of an "empire for liberty." Far from being a flight from the world of "dull common places," *Mardi* internalizes that world. What Melville says about the Koztanza is indirectly and ironically pertinent here, for just as Lombardo has "abandoned all monitors from without," honoring only the "autocrat within—his crowned and sceptered instinct" (597), so Melville, in his very aspirations to be a "monarch," ends up yielding his book to the "autocrat within."

3. ◆ *Author as Subject*

"No REPUTATION that is gratifying to me, can possibly be achieved by either of these books," Melville confided to his father-in-law about *Redburn* and *White-Jacket*. "They are two *jobs*, which I have done for money—being forced to it, as other men are to sawing wood."¹ A year later, writing to Richard Henry Dana, Jr., Melville complained again, using almost the same words: "these books of mine [were written] almost entirely for 'lucre'—by the job, as a woodsawyer saws wood."² Authorial peevishness hardly makes Melville a good judge of his own books, but it does say something about the yoke of obligation under which he fancies himself to be laboring. And while writing for money might not necessarily strike everyone as a sign of servility, to the author of *Mardi* it could mean nothing else. If *Mardi* represents Melville's accession to sovereign authorship, *Redburn* and *White-Jacket* mark an ignominious retreat, a hateful surrender to the reader. From that surrender only one thing can result: "When a poor devil writes with duns all round him, & looking over the back of his chair—& perching on his pen & diving in his inkstand . . . what can you expect of that poor devil?—What but a beggarly *Redburn*!"³

Melville's authorial psychology is of some interest here, given the vehemence and persistence of his contempt for his readers and—no less vehement and no less persistent—his sense of being in their power, of being supervised by them and indeed tyrannized by them. My emphasis in this chapter, how-

A different version of this chapter originally appeared in *Nineteenth-Century Fiction* 36, no. 3 (December 1981): 296–317. Copyright © 1982 by the Regents of the University of California. Used with permission.

ever, is not on authorial psychology as such, but on its representational form. If Melville is indeed writing under duress in *Redburn* and *White-Jacket*, if he indeed fancies himself the slave of "duns," what kind of narrative—what features of plot, metaphor, rhetorical address—is he likely to adopt? What fictive universe answers to his complaint? My approach focuses, in short, not on how Melville feels, but on the textual correlatives to those feelings. If we could speak of a poetics of authorial sovereignty in *Mardi*, its counterpart in *Redburn* and *White-Jacket* must surely be called a poetics of authorial subjection. It is the poetics of a newly chastened—bitterly chastened—author, one that will allow him to represent and to give meaning to his imagined powerlessness.

By any standard, authorial powerlessness makes up only the most incidental part of any power structure, but for Melville his plight has a sharp and urgent reality—so much so, that certain forms of public injury seem no more than a metaphor for his personal grievance. "No Indian, red as a deer, could have startled the simple people more," Redburn says at one point, referring to his intrusive presence among the rural population in an English church.[4] Melville, at his most aggrieved, might have added, "No Indian, red as a deer, could have been more persecuted." *Redburn* and *White-Jacket* are attempts to figure forth the "persecuted" artist. They are attempts, more specifically, to identify that artistic powerlessness with other forms of powerlessness, to credit it with the same meaning and the same weight.

There is something preposterous about such a project, of course. Melville had nothing in common, after all, with the historically powerless—with Indians, for instance, in the mid-nineteenth century—and his self-abasement is perhaps no more than another measure of his aggrandized selfhood. He was a "failed patrician," to be sure, and as such his plight was both historically demonstrable and intensely felt, as Walter Herbert and Michael Rogin have reminded us.[5] Still, such plight notwithstanding, it takes an imperial self to clothe his personal woes in the mantle of public injuries. Among twentieth-century writers, of course, this is an altogether familiar occurrence—Sylvia Plath's appropriation of the Holocaust as subjective metaphor comes immediately to mind.[6] Something of the same impulse is already at work in Melville, I suggest, for *Redburn* and *White-Jacket* too are subjective appropriations of sorts. They too try to harness the public in order to signify the private, and they do so, moreover, not only by way of metaphor (as with Plath), but also by way of narrative. In fact, their very textual coordinates might be seen as a subjective figuration, a transposition from the public domain, where powerlessness has a shape and a logic that Melville now claims as his own.

On this count, *Redburn* and *White-Jacket* would seem to have retained more than a little of the "possessive individualism" *Mardi* so abundantly displays. And yet, it is just this appropriative spirit, this extravagant claim made on one's own behalf, that enables Melville to speak on behalf of others, to give voice to what is habitually voiceless. Melville might not be as powerless as he thinks, but he certainly shows us what it feels like to be powerless. For even though both his books are really about himself, about his plight as an author, they nonetheless echo the plight of others. Those others inhabit his books as spectral presences—as attributes, as positions, as styles of conduct and figures of thought. They are the absentee tenants within a fictive edifice. "A book never arrives unaccompanied," Pierre Macherey writes, "it is a figure against a background of other formations, depending on them rather than contrasting with them."[7] *Redburn* and *White-Jacket* are "figures" in just this sense. More than accompanied, they are haunted, metaphors of powerlessness that they are, by the specters of those for whom powerlessness is anything but metaphor.

As "figures," *Redburn* and *White-Jacket* might also be called allegories of authorship, allegories of Melville's writerly affliction. This is not how they are usually regarded, and indeed there is nothing conventionally allegorical about the textual surface of either book.[8] They are allegorical, however, in the way that *Mardi* is, in practicing what I have tried to call a form of "signifying appropriation." Here, as in *Mardi*, the fictive universe is continually produced as the author's signifying universe: a universe in which every sign bears a meaning, and in which every meaning belongs subjectively to the author. "Manifest subjectivity" is the condition of allegory, Walter Benjamin has observed.[9] C. S. Lewis, speaking in a different context, echoes that point. "Allegory," he says, "is the subjectivism of an objective age."[10] *Redburn* and *White-Jacket* seem to bear out both those remarks, for their signifying universe— their universe of authorial meaning—is indeed one of manifest subjectivity: manifest, not only because the "authorial" is constitutively present, but also because it is constitutively appropriative. Indeed, in making the world meaningful only in reference to itself, in making its imperial selfhood the locus of signification, this "manifest subjectivity" might even be said to have a Manifest Destiny of its own. *Redburn* and *White-Jacket* are deeds of possession, then, in the same measure that they are allegories of authorship. For only allegory gives Melville the freedom to invest his story in the story of others, to appropriate their ordeal for his subjective figuration.

Melville, needless to say, has a very different idea about who is doing the appropriating, and what is being appropriated. The very narrative medium of *Redburn* and *White-Jacket* attests, in fact, to his sense of being exploited, tyrannized, dispossessed. On this relatively abstract level of narrative coordinates, we will see the articulated forms of his sentiment. For, to the extent that the two books are allegories of authorship, the allegory is to be found, I believe, not in substantives but in relations, not in any particular feature of the plot but in its textual configuration, its economy of time and space. Of Melville's first five books, only *Redburn* and *White-Jacket* dwell on the return voyage, something the author in his previous writings has neglected (or refused) to consider. Where *Mardi* is all voyage out, *White-Jacket* is all voyage homeward. The altered status of authorship apparently demands a corresponding remapping of the narrative terrain.

Even more important than the redistribution of quantifiable narrative space, however, is the altered meaning of the very idea of "space" as an experiential category. Unlike space in

Mardi, felt always in its expanse, space in *Redburn* and *White-Jacket* is experienced always as confinement. This striking reversal comes about in part through the ascendancy of the ship as an ever-present and ever-noticeable site, so encompassing as to seem like an entire universe. Where voyage in *Mardi* signifies boundless mobility, voyage in *Redburn* and *White-Jacket* is never anything other than a constricted sojourn within the unvarying "world" of an encircling vehicle. The *Highlander* and the *Neversink* contain, limit, and overshadow their respective narratives. Perpetually voyaging and yet perpetually changeless, they make a mockery of any movement for which they are the supposed agencies. The ordeal on shipboard is not so much the ordeal of being stationary (a sad enough affliction in itself) as the even crueler ordeal of being transfixed in navigation, of voyaging under an inescapable sameness. This sense of imprisonment is rooted in the familiar conceit of the ship as an image of the world, a conceit Melville evokes often in *White-Jacket*: "In truth, a man-of-war is a city afloat, with long avenues set out with guns instead of trees, and numerous shady lanes, courts, and by-ways. . . . Or rather, a man-of-war is a lofty, walled, and garrisoned town, like Quebec."[11]

There is no escape from the ship, just as there is no escape from a "walled and garrisoned town." The prisonlike atmosphere on board stems less from the ship's physical bulk than from its figurative compass, from its status as a symbol of confinement. There is no escape from it, not only because it is always present as a physical site, but because it marks a metaphoric enclosure. As "a city afloat," an image both of what it leaves behind and what it journeys toward, the ship operates as a traveling synecdoche, a moving part of an encircling whole. Its own unvarying environment is only part of a universe that is just as unvarying: a universe of such relentless sameness that origins and destinations always meet (as Redburn says) in an "unexpected resemblance" (127).[12] Such a ship as the *Highlander* goes only from one place to another exactly like it, only from New York to Liverpool, its mirror image, a point Melville underscores: "Liverpool, away from the docks, was very much such a place as New York. There were the same sort of streets pretty much; the same rows of houses with stone steps; the same kind of sidewalks and curbs; and the same elbowing, heartless-looking crowd as ever" (202). Indeed, the overwhelming "sameness" between England and America is such that it bursts upon Redburn as a "humiliating fact," a source of "continual mortification" (202).

Redburn's curiously strong reaction (perhaps overly strong) no doubt has something to do with the pointlessness of his voyage: if Liverpool is indeed just like New York, he might as well have stayed home. But it would seem to have something to do as well with how his author feels. For the narrator's "mortification" is surely Melville's own as he finds himself back where he started, performing the "same" job he thought he has outgrown, catering to the "same" readers he thought he has transcended—as if *Mardi*'s "voyage thither" had never been. The juncture seems to me an exemplary instance of the allegorical in *Redburn*: a narrative register of authorial sentiment. That sentiment, though, is ultimately less interesting than the logic that underwrites its representation. In other words, if Melville is indeed beset by a sense of futility as he turns from *Mardi* to *Redburn* and *White-Jacket*, what predisposes him to spatialize that futility, to represent it as a geographical universe of pervasive "sameness"? The broader question concerns the coincidence between an experiential category and a spatial economy or, to put it even more broadly, between a representation of space and a representation of agency. The interest of such a question is not strictly literary. As I have tried to suggest, it is central to the logic of both selfhood and nationhood—both "manifest subjectivity" and Manifest Destiny. What emerges from *Redburn*, indeed, is something like an experiential account of those two phenomena, from the standpoint of someone who imagines himself a docile subject.

The world in which Redburn voyages, a world of "sameness," also happens to be a world in which one voyages in vain, in which "all this talk about travel [is] a humbug" (203). The conjunction of the two facts is hardly fortuitous, for what makes travel a futile exercise (a mere "humbug") is precisely the ubiquity of "sameness": sameness between Liverpool and

New York and, even more fatally, between the prisonlike *Highlander* and the world it mirrors. In such a world, where one runs into the same thing no matter what one does or where one goes, action itself becomes pointless. For temporal endeavor here is by definition doomed to repeat what has always been there and will always be there. A world of absolute "sameness" permits no one to make a difference. Within the terms of our discussion, we might speak of such a world as the world of a spatialized narrative, where time is always subordinated to space, the former's possibility being contained always by the latter's circuit of identity. For Melville, no other economy of time and space better represents his sense of authorial futility. Yet subjective as this representation is to him, it also happens, as we have seen, to be something of a collective representation. In Manifest Destiny, in the providential design that sets forth America's future greatness, we find the same spatialized narrative, the same subordination of time, the same inscription of temporal unfolding within a spatial figure.

Redburn, in this light, would seem to have appropriated nothing less than the narrative of Manifest Destiny itself. Given Melville's mood, however, it has appropriated not the winning side but the losing side, enacting not its drama of freedom but its drama of dominion. Here, the subordination of time to space brings no guarantee of one's future greatness; it only underscores the futility of one's present existence. In short, what *Redburn* articulates is something like the underside of Manifest Destiny: not the narrative of the ascendant, but the narrative of the dispossessed. That thankless narrative Melville has now reserved for his own use—quite logically, we might add, for to represent his own powerlessness he needs no better metaphor than the fate of the imperial casualty. *Redburn* might be seen, in fact, as a textual correlative to that fate: an economy of time and space that is also an economy of powerlessness. That economy shows forth in the very first chapter of *Redburn*, in Melville's account of a glass ship named *La Reine*, a ship made evidently of imperial timber:

> I will only make mention of the people on board of her. They, too, were all of glass, as beautiful little glass sailors as any body

ever saw, with hats and shoes on, just like living men, and curious
blue jackets with a sort of ruffle round the bottom. Four or five of
these sailors were very nimble little chaps, and were mounting up
the rigging with very long strides; but for all that, they never
gained a single inch in the year, as I can take my oath. . . .

The name of this curious ship was *La Reine*, or The Queen,
which was painted on her stern where any one might read it,
among a crowd of glass dolphins and sea-horses carved there in a
sort of semicircle.

And this Queen rode undisputed mistress of a green glassy sea,
some of whose waves were breaking over her bow in a wild way, I
can tell you, and I used to be giving her up for lost and foundered
every moment, till I grew older, and perceived that she was not
in the slightest danger in the world. (8–9)

Clearly an instance of what Edwin Honig calls the "threshold symbol"—an emblematic exegesis and prefiguration of a
subsequent development—the glass ship at once anticipates
and clarifies what it means to inhabit the world of *Redburn* (or
to author the text of *Redburn*).[13] True to its name, *La Reine* is
a symbol of dominion. It is also the site where a politics of time
and space begins to emerge. The fossilized vessel, a sort of mar-
itime Grecian urn, is an extreme case of timelessness, and it
shows, with proportionate clarity, just what timelessness can
mean. Melville's point is not unlike Keats's, for here too,
timeless permanence must rest on a kind of paralysis, a kind of
living death. In spite of the sailors' "very long strides," they
"never gained a single inch in the year." To be on board *La
Reine* is to be utterly futile, utterly inconsequential. It is to
labor in vain. Melville, who understands the vanity of labor as
well as anyone—who has described his own authorial labor as
two "jobs" in which nothing "gratifying" "can possibly be
achieved"—must have recognized on the glass ship a rather
familiar kind of horror.

In this context, we learn that *La Reine* is the sea's "undisputed mistress," that she is "not in the slightest danger" even
in a rough sea, for the ocean too has been spatialized into a
mere appendage to her queenly presence. Her sovereignty is so
absolute and so self-evident that her very title is "painted on

her stern where any one might read it." That being so, she reigns "undisputed" over a world of docile subjects: a world of "glass sailors," "green glassy sea," and "glass dolphins." For Melville, this tyrannical vessel is obviously a signifying vessel—a symbol of the tyranny that has overtaken him—and the glass ship ominously marks his passage from *Mardi* to *Redburn*, from the reign of the sovereign author to his inglorious subjection. The "monarch" of the earlier book is monarch no more; *La Reine* has taken his place.[14]

La Reine is clearly another instance of the allegorical, another instance where the author "manifests" himself through a significant—perhaps overly significant—narrative detail. As an index to Melville's psychology, the glass ship is interesting enough. It is even more interesting, however, as an index to social governance. For what we witness, in this imperial emblem, is an imperial representation of time and space, whose dominion inheres in its very representation. The rest of *Redburn* extends that emblematic figure into a sustained narrative. And so, *La Reine* and her glass sailors never truly recede from the book. One of those sailors, or at least one remarkably like them, happens to have ventured forth from that "threshold symbol," to make his way through the rest of *Redburn*. His story makes up "the Sailor-boy Confessions and Reminiscences of the Son-of-a-Gentleman, in the Merchant Service." Like other racially and culturally inferior "children of nature," this sailor has to be a "boy" and "son," for in *Redburn* (as in antebellum America), powerlessness coincides with a certain temporal economy. Infancy is the attributed age of the dominated, and, as we will see, infancy here is not only inscribed, it is actively induced—a fact that explains one of the most curious and most discussed phenomena in *Redburn*, the narrator's "inconsistent" characterization.[15]

To rehearse a few well-known facts, Redburn appears in the early chapters of the book as a precocious young man, upon whose "soul the mildew has fallen" (11). Well schooled by poverty, he is angry, cynical, misanthropic almost by necessity—a youth made "to think much and bitterly before [his] time" (10). He is quite wrong, however, to suppose that "never again can such blights be made good; they strike in too deep, and leave such a scar that the air of Paradise might not erase it" (11). The "scar," contrary to what he says, turns out to be altogether erasable, and it takes considerably less than the air of Paradise to do the work. The transformation takes place the moment Redburn sets foot on the *Highlander*. From that point on, the once cynical youth stalks around, a paragon of gullibility. Redburn's inconsistency annoyed quite a few nineteenth-century reviewers. *Blackwood's* observed that "Redburn, a sharp enough lad on shore, and who, it has been seen, is altogether precocious in experience of the world's disappointments, seems converted, by the first sniff of salt water, into as arrant a simpleton as ever made mirth in a cockpit." That sentiment was echoed by the *Southern Quarterly Review*, which complained that Redburn, "as a character, is not symmetrically drawn. He forgets his part at times; and the wild, very knowing and bold boy ashore, becomes a sneak, and a numbskull aboard ship."[16]

Odd as it might seem, Redburn's "inconsistency" actually makes sense if we think of it as a particular way of computing time—or, rather, a way of *not* computing time, of treating it as a constant deductible. *Redburn* is, in this regard, the exact opposite of a *Bildungsroman*: where the *Bildungsroman* registers time as accretion, *Redburn* registers it as deficit.[17] In short, Redburn's apparent regression has less to do, I think, with the development of the self than with the politics of time, less to do with organic characterization than with temporal accounting. Redburn is "inconsistent" as a character because he fails to achieve a cumulative identity over time, but that failure is altogether consistent with the book's timeless environment. It is also consistent, more generally, with the "zero of human society" certain races are said to inhabit.

That astonishing phrase is Lewis Henry Morgan's. "The hunter state is the zero of human society," the famous ethnologist had written, "and while the red man was bound by its spell, there was no hope of his elevation."[18] Morgan here spoke of Indians as being "bound," apparently of their own volition, to the zero of human society. In practice, however, that zero point was rather deliberately conferred. Something like a temporal "subtracting machine"[19] seemed to have been at work in antebellum representation of Indians, under whose ministrations the savages would always remain "children"—a device put to good use, as we have seen, by Andrew Jackson, Francis Parkman, Horace Greeley, and others.[20] Indeed, so formidable was that subtracting machine that the Indians sometimes seemed not only affixed in time but actually regressing in time, bound not just to the "zero" of human society but to some negative number. Henry Rowe Schoolcraft, in his magisterial *History of the Indian Tribes of the United States* (1857), invoked just this sort of temporal arithmetic to measure the Indians' regression. Since "man was created, not a savage . . . but a horticulturist," according to him, and since "the civil and social state was the original type of society for man," the Indian, having no horticulture, and no civil society, must be understood to be "liv[ing] in a state of very great declension from his original state."[21] The same "declension," not surprisingly, seems to afflict Melville's protagonist as well, for in his eagerness to make Redburn a "boy" and "son," Melville is simply resorting to the same temporal arithmetic Schoolcraft found so useful. He too has brought in a subtracting machine and, in his overzealous application, he too has gone beyond the zero point. Caught in a subtracting frenzy, failing to stop where he ought to, he comes up eventually with an infantilized Redburn, an "inconsistent" character born out of time's deficit accounting.

Accounting—both as a way of reckoning time and, more generally, as a problem of economics—has everything to do, of course, with Melville's professed motive in writing *Redburn* (and *White-Jacket*). Given his sardonic mood, it seems altogether fitting that a book "written for lucre" should have as its protagonist a "loser," someone who accumulates not capital but deficits, and who does so not just by temporal accounting, but by accounting of a more regular sort. Redburn's labor, unlike his author's, turns out to bring in no "lucre" at all. In fact, it actually puts him in debt, an outcome Melville anticipates when he shows the narrator, much earlier in the book, vainly trying to read *The Wealth of Nations*. The book does nothing for Redburn, and he soon gives up, "without getting any profits myself for my pains in perusing it" (87). Adam Smith's topics—"the productive power of labor" and the "Wages and profits of labor"—have no meaning for Redburn, for his labor turns out to be altogether unproductive and unprofitable, as we find out at the end of the book. Upon discharge from the *Highlander*, he is set "adrift without a copper" (307). Not only has he earned nothing "after slaving abroad for more than four mortal months," he ends up—thanks to Captain Riga's peculiar mode of accounting—actually owing seven dollars and seventy-five cents.[22]

At stake here is not just money but (anticipating *The Confidence-Man*) what money figures and configures. On an obliquely ironic level, Redburn's profitless venture no doubt mirrors Melville's own, for from a certain standpoint (say, that of *Mardi's*), *Redburn* might indeed be called a profitless enterprise, because "no reputation that is gratifying" can possibly be gained by such a book. Money in Melville is perhaps above all a representational form, "endlessly tropic and infinitely hermeneutic," as Marc Shell would say.[23] Operating here as a retroactive threshold text, Redburn's negative accumulation of capital at once literalizes and reallegorizes a more central mode of negative accumulation in the book—the negative accumulation of time in the person of the infantilized narrator.

Of course, infantilization is itself a metaphor, as we have said, for Melville's sense of authorial powerlessness. To him, the socially infantilized seems a fit emblem for the artist infantilized by "duns." If this seems a wildly subjective claim, it nevertheless attests, in its very subjectivity, to a reality that is anything but subjective. For the logic of infantilization is ultimately not peculiar to *Redburn*, and not peculiar to Melville. It owes its meaning and its currency to a historical situation, to the social economy of time in nineteenth-century America, where "infancy" served not only as a figure for powerlessness, but also as its calculus. In a curious way, *Redburn* is most historical where it is most metaphoric. To the extent that the book is a "figure" against a "background," as Macherey says—

and to the extent that this "figure" is a matter of subjective appropriation—*Redburn*'s background might be imagined only by resisting Melville, only by restoring a context to what he has subjectively decontextualized. Not to resist Melville, of course, is to trace a wholly different background (and indeed a wholly different genealogy) for the infantilized narrator.

Chapter 62, the chapter in which Redburn and Harry go their separate ways, is especially useful in suggesting another background—an authorial background—for the narrator's infantilization:

> "I have no doubt, Goodwell will take care of you, Harry," said I, "he's a fine, good-hearted fellow; and will do his best for you, I know."
>
> "No doubt of it," said Harry, looking hopeless.
>
> "But I need not tell you, Harry, how sorry I am to leave you so soon."
>
> "And I am sorry enough myself," said Harry, looking very sincere.
>
> "But I will be soon back again, I doubt not," said I.
>
> "Perhaps so," said Harry, shaking his head. "How far is it off?"
>
> "Only a hundred and eighty miles," said I.
>
> "A hundred and eighty miles!" said Harry, drawing the words out like an endless ribbon. "Why, I couldn't walk that in a month."
>
> "Now, my dear friend," said I, "Take my advice, and while I am gone, keep up a stout heart; never despair, and all will be well." (310)

One can hardly think of a more excruciating moment in the book—excruciating not from the surfeit of emotions but from their utter asymmetry. Melville does not explain why Redburn has to leave in such a great hurry (all we know is that some letters "compelled [his] departure homeward" [304]). Nor does he explain why Redburn fails to bring Harry home with him, a conceivable and even logical gesture under the circumstances. All we are presented with, at the end of the book, is Redburn's act of desertion, unrelieved by any mitigating circumstances, and the spectacle of Harry desolate and penniless in a strange land.

Bruce Franklin and James Duban are certainly right to upbraid Redburn for being so heartless and so phony.[24] And yet those are hardly his habitual traits; their sudden appearance at the end of the book seems more puzzling than revelatory. The oddness of the episode is an oblique sign, I think, of an alien presence, one "looking over the back of [the author's] chair—& perching on his pen & diving in his inkstand." It is the sign, in short, of an imagined overseer, the "duns" who read Melville's books and who supervise his writing in anticipation. Questionable attachments, which certainly include the attachment between Redburn and Harry, must be rendered unquestionable to please that supervisory body.[25] Nor is Melville simply being paranoiac here. *Blackwood's*, for instance, was already referring to Harry as the "male brunette" and counseling Melville that "plain, vigorous, unaffected writing of [shipboard scenes] is a far superior style of thing to rhapsodies about Italian boys and hurdy-gurdies."[26] The intimacy between the two friends has not been exactly discreet (Redburn calls Harry "my zebra"), and so objectionable a thing must eventually be contained, deflated, sanitized—all of which Redburn does with disciplined aplomb. His cheerful indifference revokes and demotes his intimacy with Harry, turning it into something it ought to have been all along.

In executing his duty, Redburn acts like a monster in one sense, but in another sense his monstrosity is altogether in keeping with the book mode of accounting, one that enforces negative accumulation. Product of that bizarre arithmetic, Redburn must come away from the book, not just with a temporal deficit, and not just with an actual deficit of seven dollars and seventy-five cents, but with an experiential deficit as well.[27] The final episode cancels out any "growth" he might have undergone in Liverpool: if his affective faculties have shown some development then, they are now restored to their properly infantilized state. Child that he is, Redburn can have only one desire. He must carry out what Tommo only promises to do in *Typee*: he must dutifully hurry back to "home" and "mother." As the subtitle of the book already indicates, Redburn is equipped only to be a "son," and nothing proves it better than his desertion of Harry.

Still, the act of desertion, unperturbed as it would like to appear, is not altogether unnoticeable. It is surely not just a matter of self-betraying projection (or even a matter of narrative irony) that Redburn should choose, at the moment when he himself is most phony, to make an issue of Harry's "sincerity," and inevitably to draw attention to his own lack of it. Redburn's insincerity is dramatized, I think, because that is what Melville wants: it is meant as a demonstration, a flaunting performance of duty, rather than a mute compliance with the requisite. Melville is not just placating the reader; he is also representing the act of placating, a double operation by which the reader's authority is at once complied with and reexhibited as coercive agency. Insofar as the infantilized narrator is a figure of submission, within the figure is inscribed both the submissive author and, by implication, a critical portrait of the reader to whom the author must submit, for submission would not have been necessary—would not even have been contemplated—if the supervisory body had not been posited as tyrannical.

Only the presence of such a tyrannical reader can account for that curious phenomenon in *Redburn*—what we might call its orchestrated literary offenses, a pattern of publicized misdemeanors and effusive apologies. Over and over again, the narrative voice indulges in what it freely admits to be improper conduct—digressions, suggestions of idleness, choice of unsuitable topics—all of which calls forth Redburn's self-admonitory fervor. After an account of the sailors' depravity, for instance, comes this apology: "Now you must not think, that because all these things were passing through my mind, that I had nothing to do but sit still and think; no, no, I was hard at work" (34). Soon afterward, after bringing up "an uncle of mine," a member of Captain Langsdorff's Arctic Expedition, Redburn again checks himself with, "But I meant to speak about the fort" (35), and puts an end to what he implies to be an inappropriate digression. But sticking to the point is just what Redburn cannot do, for another digression follows almost immediately—this time a fond recollection of a bygone past when "the sky overhead was blue as my mother's eye, and I was so glad and happy then" (36). Once again the narrative voice scolds itself ("But I must not think of those delightful days" [36]), only to suffer a relapse in the next breath, resulting in yet another recollection of the idyllic past, followed by even more self-scolding ("But it would not do" [36]). And so the list goes on. Yet the misdemeanors would have gone completely undetected if Redburn had not called attention to them. They are summoned into being by the very gestures offered to correct them. Impropriety and self-reprimand are animated by an oddly inverted causal relation: Redburn does not chide himself because he has made a mistake, he makes a mistake because he needs to chide himself. The point of this compulsive exercise, it seems, is not to eliminate such blunders, but to make self-censorship and apology a more or less permanent feature of the narrative, in a perverse inclusion of the reprehensible within the field of deliberate rhetorical strategy.

The system of orchestrated literary offenses confirms as stylistics what we already know from the book's narrative action: Redburn is not only infantile but pathetically so. Even more important, what the self-correcting style demonstrates is the genealogy of this pathetic creature. For the infantilized Redburn does have parents: he is the offspring of "duns," readers who make him what he is, readers whose pleasure attends his genesis. About the character of those readers there can also be little doubt. For Redburn, we can now see, is not simply infantile, but painfully and unmistakably infantilized. His touching anxiety and submissiveness, the audible tremor in his voice, the very diction of his speech—all proclaim him to be a product of harsh antecedents, a child chastened into what he is by virtue of what he has been through. He is a child with a history. But if so, that history is perhaps less Redburn's than Melville's. It is the history of an author "forced" to produce books "from my pocket, & not from my heart"—an author forced to produce what he calls a "nursery tale."[28] It is no accident that this nursery tale should end up being a double-edged tribute to the readers Melville honors and ahbors, and no accident, either, that those readers should be inscribed, dutifully and maliciously, as a legislating, supervising, infantilizing figure. In *White-Jacket* that figure of tyranny will come even more dramatically to the foreground.

Turning from *Redburn* to *White-Jacket*, we turn from a "nursery tale" to one that (even Melville admits) is rather "man-ofwarish in style."[29] The two books would seem to have little in common either thematically or stylistically, and yet in contrary fashion they complement, contextualize, and elucidate each other. Both are allegories of authorship, I suggest: allegories of the subjugated author and his tyrannical reader. *White-Jacket*, of course, gives no initial sign of either writerly subjection or readerly tyranny. Indeed, the narrative voice seems to have moved to the other extreme of the rhetorical spectrum: White-Jacket, apparently, has no fear of the reader, and from the outset a gruff chumminess prevails. The opening sentence signals just that: "It was not a *very* white jacket, but white enough, in all conscience, as the sequel will show."[30] In its very lack of ceremony, in launching forth impulsively, without bothering about preliminary details, the opening sentence greets the reader with open arms. Such an impetuous remark is itself the proof of intimacy; it invokes the confiding and the confided, the trusting author and his trusted readers.

The abrupt opening of *White-Jacket*, and the minimal "Note" to the American edition (a product of Melville's successive revisions), differ quite markedly from the extensive introductions that characterize the genre.[31] Most sea authors find it advisable to dilate on their history, their motives for going to sea, and their reasons for writing a book.[32] Among the identified sources for *White-Jacket*, Samuel Leech's *Thirty Years From Home* contains no less than a preface, a laudatory letter from Richard Dana, Jr., testimonials from several ministers, and finally, an entire first chapter devoted to the author's early life.[33] Implicit in such elaborate preliminaries is the assumption that the reader is as yet unacquainted, untrusting, that he needs to be informed, persuaded, won over. *White-Jacket*, on the other hand, dispenses with all such proof of character—presumably because readers need none of it, because they already "have confidence" (as we might say) in the narrator.

What emerges from *White-Jacket*'s rhetorical apparatus is, once again, a double portrait. It invokes the image not only of trusted readers, but also of a narrator presumably as trusted by them as they are by him. White-Jacket is a known quantum, the text suggests, and in that character he betrays an interesting kinship with his infantile predecessor in Melville's "nursery tale." Redburn too is a known quantum: he is advertised, from the very first, as a "boy" and "son," and he proves to be just that. White-Jacket, on the other hand, is not so much a knowable personality as a legible generality. He can be easily known, easily "read," because the social meanings of his identity can hardly be mistaken. White-Jacket is a gentleman, a fact evident from the very first chapter of the book, where he displays an erudition altogether unseamanlike. On the initial conversion of shirt into jacket, he observes that this is a "metamorphosis . . . transcending any related by Ovid" (3). When the jacket is further metamorphosized through stuffing and quilting, it stands, "stiff and padded, as King James's cotton-stuffed and dagger-proof doublet; and no buckram or steel hauberk stood up more stoutly" (4). The last sentence of that chapter informs us that the jacket is "gleaming white, as the White Lady of Avenel" (5).

Literary allusions in *White-Jacket* are of course never merely literary; nineteenth-century reviewers certainly did not respond to them as such. English reviewers, noting the book's learned diction, habitually expressed doubts about the author's class affiliation and indeed his identity. American reviewers, on the other hand, were generally impressed. The *Literary World* applauded Melville for his "union of culture and experience," and noted that "the sharp breeze of the forecastle alternating with the mellow stillness of the library . . . distinguish the narratives of the author of *Typee* from all other productions of their class." The *Southern Literary Messenger*, in a similar vein, suggested that "this practical experience from the 'fo'k'sle' uniting with a love of elegant learning and with an educated taste . . . has distinguished Melville from all other writers of his class. . . . It is not often that the stains of the tar-bucket and the inkstand are seen upon the same fingers."[34]

Literary allusions promote social legibility. So too do allusions to such acquaintances as "Hawthorne of Salem" (283) and "my friend Dana" (99), and to such future events as a "ball given by the Russian Minister, the Baron de Bodisco" (290), where White-Jacket renews his acquaintance with the commodore of the *Neversink*.[35] Information of this sort makes any external recommendations unnecessary. As the bearer of a set of legible credentials, White-Jacket stands as an open book, winningly filled out, ever readable. And readability, in this context, is inseparable from respectability: the union of the two commends White-Jacket to his readers as a friend and intimate.

Social legibility has obvious benefits, as the favorable reviews of *White-Jacket* demonstrate, and as Melville's own experience in the past ought perhaps to have taught him. Unguarded empathy with the common sailor in *Typee*, William Charvat points out, had only lent fuel to hostile critics, who readily accused Melville of all the vices he described in other seamen.[36] After *Typee* Melville became more judicious in such matters, and in this respect he might have taken his cue from Dana himself. *Two Years Before the Mast* (1840), a resounding popular success, begins with the author discarding the "tight dress coat, silk cap and kid gloves of an undergraduate at Cambridge" and going to sea "for the sake of health."[37] Dana's respectability is, if anything, even more pronounced than White-Jacket's, and more firmly established from the outset. Melville's narrator is in good company when he makes similar disclosures about his social elevation. Such disclosures are finally less a matter of snobbery than a matter of necessity: to be read, one is duty-bound to be legible.

The continuity between *Redburn* and *White-Jacket* resides, I suggest, on just this point. Its chummy style notwithstanding, *White-Jacket* turns out, like its predecessor, to be something of a dutiful performance. Like *Redburn*, it shadows forth, in its very expressive form, an implicit hierarchy between reader and author: between the one who dictates and the one who complies, between the inspecting and the inspected. White-Jacket's very legibility, from this perspective, attests to Melville's sense of obligation, for if the narrator's credentials embody an enviable privilege on the one hand, they also suggest, on the other hand, an unenviable duty to be what readers expect one to be.[38] Such legibility elevates its subject, but it also freezes him at that altitude, turning him into a social type, a fixed profile, an emblem of respectability. In this, *White-Jacket* would seem to have something in common with its predecessor as well, for to be legible in *Redburn*, as we have seen, is likewise to be ossified, frozen, becalmed. *La Reine's* name, significantly, is "painted on her stern where any one might read it" (9). The permanence of her queenly title goes hand in hand with her legible sovereignty. The same legibility, and the same chilling permanence, characterizes not just the glass ship and the glassy world of which she is the "undisputed mistress" (9) but also, more generally, the unchanging landscape of *Redburn*. Jackson, one of the more memorable figures in that landscape, illustrates just this point:

> His nose had broken down in the middle, and he squinted with one eye, and did not look very straight out of the other. . . . one glance of his squinting eye was as good as a knock-down, for it was the most deep, subtle, infernal looking eye, that I ever saw lodged in a human head. I believe, that by good rights it must have belonged to a wolf, or starved tiger; at any rate, I would defy any oculist, to turn out a glass eye, half so cold, and snaky, and deadly. (56–57)

With a face like this, Jackson obviously cannot be anything other than a villain. His whole life—the full story of his villainy, half comic and half sinister—can be read in this introductory portrait, so much so that all subsequent action seems no more than a repetition of this initial tableau.[39] Perpetually imprisoned and perpetually revealed in his own portrait, Jackson would have made a fit inhabitant on *La Reine*, for like the glass sailors, he too is affixed in space, a figure exhibited as physical parts. He too is legible and, in his legibility, reduced to ossified form.

White-Jacket's legibility seems merely to remap Jackson's onto a new signifying field: he is socially legible where Jackson is physiognomically so. White-Jacket can be easily read, partly because his credentials are unmistakable but, more crucially, because his entire temporal career is laid out in spatial display, emblazoned in the cloak of respectability that makes up his identity. That he should be named after his attire is only too fitting, for that is indeed what he is: not a person but a jacket, an outer garment, all surface and all visibility.[40] (The jacket, we might add, is no ordinary jacket, but a curious affair, once supplied with an abundance of pockets, subsequently "masoned up" to guard against the ship's "pickpockets" [37]—surely not an insignificant detail.) Naming the book after the jacket is fitting as well, for that too is what it is: not a book but the jacket of a book, perhaps the only thing that a wood-sawing author is capable of producing.[41]

Writing a jacket is not, however, necessarily easier than writing a book, for the jacket, as it turns out, manages not only to clothe but also to constrain, a propensity that makes it something of a straitjacket as well. Only such a conceit can account for the sense of liberation that accompanies the demolition of the jacket—and the end of the book. Chapter 92, "The Last of the Jacket," reports this happy event. The narrator has just plunged into the ocean from the topmast (having mistaken his jacket for the sail), but luckily resurfacing, he

> essayed to swim toward the ship; but instantly I was conscious of a feeling like being pinioned in a feather-bed, and, moving my hands, felt my jacket puffed out above my tight girdle with water. I strove to tear it off; but it was looped together here and there, and the strings were not then to be sundered by hand. I whipped out my knife, that was tucked at my belt, and ripped my jacket straight up and down, as if I were ripping open myself. With a violent struggle I then burst out of it, and was free. Heavily soaked, it slowly sank before my eyes.

Sink! sink! oh shroud! thought I; sink forever! accursed jacket that thou art!

"See that white shark!" cried a horrified voice from the taffrail; "he'll have that man down his hatchway! Quick! the *grains*! the *grains*!"

The next instant that barbed bunch of harpoons pierced through and through the unfortunate jacket, and swiftly sped down with it out of sight. (394)

As Howard Vincent points out, Melville has revised his sources considerably here, making the jacket much more of a straitjacket.[42] In *Life on Board a Man-of-War* (Melville's primary source for this episode), the jacket had merely "incommoded" the narrator; White-Jacket, on the other hand, is "conscious of a feeling like being pinioned in a feather-bed." In the original source the jacket was preserved, in Melville it is not only discarded but "ripped open." The white jacket must be "ripped open"—must be sunk "out of sight"—before *Moby-Dick* can come into being. Indeed, in this unabashedly allegorical moment, we already see the displacement of one book by the other: the "barbed bunch of harpoons" that "pierced through and through" the jacket belong more properly to a whaler than to a man-of-war. The destruction of the jacket occasions no grief, presumably because it has always been something that "pinioned." The final, joyous moment of liberation, yet another retroactive threshold text, recasts the entire narrative as its antecedent—as what must have been in order for the ending to be what it is. The story of *White-Jacket* might be read, then, as a story of how its jacket "pinions." Chapter 67, "White-Jacket arraigned at the Mast," especially invites that reading.

Chapter 67 is partly derived from John Sherburne Sleeper's *Tales of the Ocean*, Howard Vincent tells us.[43] Sleeper's story is an eyewitness account of what happens to someone else: another sailor, unjustly flogged, kills both the captain and himself, while the narrator comments from a distance. When Melville incorporates that episode into *White-Jacket*, he significantly changes it into a first-person story, making the

main action White-Jacket's. In doing so, of course, he forfeits
Sleeper's safeguard and exposes his narrator to the danger of
being flogged, something quite outside the bounds of respectability. (Samuel Leech, a respectable narrator, includes in
Thirty Years From Home no fewer than three incidents of "hair-
breadth escape from the lash," each time coming close to that
ordeal but always escaping untouched.[44]) The problem for
Melville then is the problem of rescuing his narrator from what
is actually a self-imposed danger. The plot that he comes up
with is very odd indeed—deliberately so, one is tempted to
think, for on the verge of martyrdom, White-Jacket is
snatched away, just in the nick of time, and by a totally unexpected agent:

> "Captain Claret," said a voice advancing from the crowd. I
> turned to see who this might be, that audaciously interposed at a
> juncture like this. It was the same remarkably handsome and
> gentlemanly corporal of marines, Colbrook, who has been previ-
> ously alluded to, in the chapter describing killing time in a man-
> of-war.
> "I know that man," said Colbrook, touching his cap, and
> speaking in a mild, firm, but extremely deferential manner; "and
> I know that he would not be found absent from his station, if he
> knew where it was." (280–81).

The intervention is not only unprecedented, it is altogether
unearned. Nothing in *White-Jacket* has prepared us for this astonishing development. Corporal Colbrook is not a memorable character, having appeared only once before in a minor
portrait—as a vain, dandyish, sentimental creature, a "complete lady's man," hardly a candidate for the heroic role that
seems suddenly to have devolved upon him. But even that discrepancy worries Melville less than the possibility that Colbrook might not be remembered at all, which is why he stops
(his nervousness having apparently gotten the better of him)
to remind the reader that Colbrook is indeed an authentic
character and a legitimate choice, since he "has been previously alluded to, in the chapter describing killing time in a
man-of-war."

It is a most unusual bit of information to emerge from a narrative climax. Even though this is not the first time that Melville has felt the need to refresh his reader's memory by supplying reminders, one is struck, all the same, by the gracelessness of this particular specimen.[45] In the thick of an explosive crisis the story comes abruptly to a halt, and the author steps forward to reiterate certain facts about his composition. The recitation brings the reader conspicuously into the text; it is his presence, his incredulity, that Melville is addressing. But if the reader is in the text, he is decidedly not of it: Melville's reminder, in its nervousness no less than in its deference, shows plainly the degree to which the reader is alien, intrusive, feared. This is an odd way of acknowledging the reader, but the oddity is perhaps the point. From its deliberate inception to its ungainly end, White-Jacket's impasse seems to me a perfect instance of the engineered impasse. The logic here is exactly analogous to that of the orchestrated offenses in *Redburn*. The point, once again, is not to slip imperceptibly out of a jam, but to go about it as obtrusively as possible and, in doing so, to render equally obtrusive that which dictates the jam in the first place. Less a concession to respectability than a *representation* of that concession, chapter 37 stands as an oblique and unflattering portrait of the reader. This figure has obviously little in common with that model of cordiality implied by the book's rhetorical address. No longer the indulgent friend of the socially legible narrator, he has grown narrow-minded, dully censorial. Clearly unwelcome, he is nevertheless not unfamiliar. We have seen him before in *Redburn*, in the parting scene between Redburn and Harry. In *White-Jacket*, his straitlaced propriety helps to make the book the straitjacket that its author eventually and delightedly "pierce[s] through and through."

Chapter 37 shows the straitjacket in good order. Constraint is only half the story, however. Proper narrative conduct ultimately entails not only renouncing the improper but also pronouncing the obligatory. And, to please the reader, nothing is more obligatory than a rhetoric of naval reform, more specifically, a critique of flogging. Not much was controversial about such a critique. By the spring of 1850, when *White-Jacket* first appeared, the abolition of flogging was by and large a settled matter; "so far from Melville's *White-Jacket* bringing about the movement that resulted in the abolition of flogging in the navy," Charles Anderson observes, "it was the very currency of this agitation that brought forth his attack."[46] Nineteenth-century readers agreed. George Ripley remarked that Melville's opinions "coincide[d] with the prevailing tendencies of the public mind."[47] Other critics, mostly naval officers, had less charitable things to say. According to them, *White-Jacket* was simply a bit of hack propaganda, written with an eye to sales and profits. Commodore Charles Henry Davis, for instance, identified Melville with a new "class who pursue philanthropy as a means of livelihood, and expose the evils of society in order that they may eat," and predicted that this attack on the navy would be recognized by most people as an effort to "make the work racy and saleable."[48]

Melville, self-acknowledged author of two "jobs" "done for money," might not have disagreed with the commodore. But the crucial issue here, it seems to me, is not motive or even belief (Melville was no doubt speaking the truth when he told Evert Duyckinck that he was "offering up devout jubilations for the abolition of the flogging law"[49]), but the popular appeal of reform rhetoric and its usefulness—as Melville's naval critics charged—in securing "a means of livelihood." *White-Jacket*'s humanitarian fervor, according to these cynical souls, was really just a marketing device, something drummed up to make the book "racy and saleable." The naval officers obviously had their own reasons to think this about Melville, but their view of reform is suggestive all the same. If reform was indeed a profitable thing to advocate, what was it that constituted its market appeal?

Part of the answer is to be found, I think, in the appealing dimensions of *White-Jacket*'s reform rhetoric, which (like much else in the book) also has a straitjacket of its own. As we might expect, such a straitjacket is most useful as a quarantining device. Judiciously administered, it enables its users—writer and readers alike—at once to isolate and localize an objectionable phenomenon, at once to identify and consign it to a manageable site. What this means, more specifically, is a reform rhetoric that is consistently differential, one that steadfastly separates out two realms: a realm of abnormality, which sorely needs treatment, and a realm of normality, which administers the cure. According to this reasoning, naval reform is necessary only because such reform is unnecessary anywhere else, only because abuses in the navy are peculiar to the navy. Flogging, in this view, is an "unparalleled anomaly," a "monstrous grafting of tyranny upon freedom" (297), a hideous blot on the otherwise unblemished national landscape. Flogging spoils the blessings of America, blessings enjoyed, apparently, by every citizen, with the sad exception of the seamen, for whom "our Revolution was in vain; [for whom] our Declaration of Independence is a lie" (144).

Reform rhetoric of this sort turns out also to be exercises in patriotic piety. By singling out and dwelling on naval abuses, as if America were faced with nothing worse, such rhetoric tacitly marginalizes other problems besetting the nation: a nation torn by internal strife and sectional conflict, unsure about its future, perched on the edge of the Civil War. The book's fiery language is, for that reason, oddly soothing. It is comforting to know exactly where the evil is, and to be able to fence it off, as an isolated problem within a body politic that is otherwise free of abuse.

Differential incrimination, however, is not the sole appeal of reform rhetoric. For even as it divides the world into separate spheres, and even as it isolates blame within one particular site, it also enters into an unspoken alliance, oddly enough, with another kind of rhetoric, one that is anything but isolationist. Taken together, in fact, this composite rhetoric assumes a strikingly expansionist hue. If its professed aim, on the one hand, is to isolate the navy as a seat of malaise—a site of "tyranny" grafted upon American "freedom"—its implicit charge, on the other hand, is to broaden the domain of the otherwise exemplary nation. In short, the compartmentalization of naval anomaly directly sanctifies the expansion of the American norm:

Seventy years ago we escaped from thrall; and, besides our first
birth-right—embracing one continent of earth—God has given
to us, for a future inheritance, the broad domains of the political
pagans, that shall yet come and lie down under the shade of our
ark, without bloody hands being lifted. God has predestinated,
mankind expects, great things from our race; and great things we
feel in our souls. The rest of the nations must soon be in our rear.
We are the pioneers of the world; the advance-guard, sent on
through the wilderness of untried things, to break a new path in
the New World that is ours. . . . And let us always remember that
with ourselves, almost for the first time in the history of earth,
national selfishness is unbounded philanthropy; for we can not do
a good to America but we give alms to the world. (151)

The "New World that is ours" is supposedly temporal (it is the
New World of the future, the "wilderness of untried things"),
but it seems to have a geographical component as well, for as
Melville tells us, it is to include "the broad domains of the
political pagans," designated here as America's "future inheritance." If the emergence of this jingoistic voice at the end of
a chapter called "Flogging Not Necessary" seems incomprehensible from one point of view, from another it is no more
than a tribute to the historical conjunction of Manifest Destiny and Jacksonian reform. Those two make good allies, for
the compartmentalizing impulse of the latter ultimately complements the expansionist impulse of the former. Both operate
through what we might call an institution of the discrete: both
posit as their normative site a discrete site whose mission is to
convert other sites correspondingly defined as less than normative, less than acceptable. Needless to say, both endorse
the incorporation of the anomalous into the orbit of the norm.

In this curious conjunction, the conjunction of an imperial
enterprise and a humanitarian enterprise, we see both the
terms and the implications of the spatial economy we have
been witnessing in *Redburn* and *White-Jacket*. That spatial
economy, we can now see, is at once hierarchical and expansionist: hierarchical, because its discrete compartments are
never equal compartments, and expansionist, because unequal

compartments always impel takeover attempts. Such a spatial economy represents the world as a map of discrete sites and unequal attributes—of "freedom" and "tyranny"—a map whose very representation is already the ground for reform, and the ground for expansion. The privileged site on this map belongs, needless to say, to the advocate of those activities. It belongs to his readers as well. All *they* are required to do is to benefit from the American Revolution and the Declaration of Independence, and help extend those benefits to the less fortunate. It is a position Melville's readers relished.

Melville seems to relish it less. Indeed, to the extent that the language of Manifest Destiny is the language of the straitjacket—to the extent that it represents the politic and the obligatory—its status within *White-Jacket* seems altogether uncertain. For example, we can read such passages as linguistic specimens, as samples of the requisite embedded and exhibited in the text—analogous, in their status as *represented* discourse, to other represented acts of concession to the reader.[50] And if the final goal of the narrative is to "rip open" its straitjacket, we should not be surprised to see trial efforts along the way. Some such gesture seems to be at work even here, in that astonishing, improbable aphorism at the end of the paragraph: "National selfishness is unbounded Philanthropy." No advocate of Manifest Destiny would put it quite that way, of course, and the deadpan incisiveness at once summarizes and cuts through everything that has gone on before.[51] *White-Jacket* abounds with such local puncturing efforts, efforts aimed not so much at "ripping open" the textual fabric as at showing its strain. Those moments almost always come with some violence, and, as if in reaction against the discrete spatiality operating in the expansionist rhetoric, they almost always embody an alternative form of spatial representation.

If compartmentalization governs *White-Jacket*'s official rhetoric, a mingling of the incongruous would seem the logical countermovement, as in fact happens in many of the less decorous moments in the book. When Jack Chase is first introduced, for instance, we are told, "No one could be better company in forecastle or saloon; no man told such stories, sang such songs, or with greater alacrity sprang to his duty. Indeed, there was only one thing wanting about him; and that was, a finger of his left hand" (13). The shock effect here comes not only from the detail of the missing finger, altogether out of place in this sentimental portrait but, most of all, from the phrase "only one thing wanting," which, in refusing to be the senseless cliché it usually is, gathers material meaning by conjoining two realms of signification: one in which the "thing" wanting matters not a bit, and the other, in which that "thing" turns out to be all too literal, all too tangible. The violence here is the violence of conflation and superimposition, and its effect is to collapse the reign of segregated sites, the reign of discrete spatiality. An even more striking instance of such violence comes when the narrator recounts his polishing duties:

> Upon one occasion, even, when woolen rags were scarce, and no burned-brick was to be had from the ship's yeoman, I sacrificed the corners of my woolen shirt, and used some dentrifice I had, as substitutes for the rags and burned-brick. The dentrifice operated delightfully, and made the threading of my carronade screw shine and grin again, like a set of false teeth in an eager heiress-hunter's mouth. (171)

The metaphor here might be unbecoming, but it is certainly not undeliberate (we get not just false teeth, but specifically those in an eager heiress-hunter's mouth). The giddy incompatibility, between the "delightful" performance of shipboard duties and the less than delightful business of fortune-hunting, makes the metaphor finally less an exercise in analogy than an exercise in incongruity, and once again it enacts a spatial violence, yoking together what is usually understood to be separate and discontinuous. Metaphors turn out to be Melville's primary instrument of spatial desegregation,[52] and nothing demonstrates this better than the metaphors in *White-Jacket*'s rather graphic battle scenes.

The very presence of those battle scenes is something of an incongruity, because the *Neversink* never engages in any actual combat, and properly speaking has no war stories of its own.

Battle scenes have to be imported as "told stories," recollections by war veterans, or simply fantasies, and in that contrived fashion they propagate various chatty metaphors of war. Wads for gun carriages, for example, are "big as Dutch cheeses" (68); a canister shot is packed in a tin case "like a tea-caddy" (68); grapeshot "precisely resemble bunches of the fruit" though they "would be but a sorry dessert" (68). There are also a "long nine-pounder rammed home with wads of French silks, cartridges stuffed with the finest gunpowder tea, cannister-shot full of West India sweetmeats" (317); guns smoke "like rows of Dutch pipe-bowls" (318); sailors scrambling up the ladder to their respective guns are "like eating-house waiters hurrying along with hot cakes for breakfast" (68), and the surgeon's steward presiding over the amputation table is "like an over-conscientious butler fidgeting over a dinner-table just before the convivialists enter" (256). Gastronomic metaphors such as these turn war into a regular feast for ordinary readers.[53] Against the logic of compartmentalization they weld together, even more spectacularly, two incongruous realms, the man-of-war's and the reader's, and in each case the effect is at once to domesticate war and to militarize civilian America, to assert the continuity and indeed the identity between these supposedly disparate spheres. Because war is talked about with so little astonishment, and in such homey language, it becomes a pedestrian affair, a routine diet. But if so, the pedestrian and the routine are likewise transformed by the same gesture into something unrecognizable. Home becomes warlike even as war decks itself out in domestic colors.

And yet these metaphors ultimately do no more than reproduce, in dramatic miniature, what *White-Jacket* is already doing as a whole, and what sea stories tend to do as a genre. For the logic that domesticates war is the same logic that dictates the inclusion of lurid war stories in high-minded reform literature. Samuel Leech, every bit as ardent as Melville on the subject of naval reform, is even more graphic in his depiction of the bloodshed on the *Macedonian*.[54] But *White-Jacket*'s war stories are ultimately less lurid than lyric, as we can see in

the following example, related by none other than the noble
Jack Chase:

> "A third shot killed my powder-monkey without touching
> him."
> "How, Jack?"
> "It *whizzed* the poor babe dead. He was seated on a *cheese of
> wads* at the time, and after the dust of the powdered bulwarks had
> blown away, I noticed he yet sat still, his eyes wide open. 'My
> *little hero!*' cried I, and I clapped him on the back, but he fell on
> his face at my feet. I touched his heart, and found he was dead.
> There was not a little finger mark on him." (319)

The tone of the passage is hard to characterize, but if one sentiment is conspicuously lacking, it is moral outrage. In the telling of the story there is a sense of jubilation, a mixture of wonder, staged suspense, and above all, an ill-concealed and
impious delight in the magical power of the enemy's cannon
fire, which accomplishes a death without even leaving behind
"a little finger mark."

White-Jacket's war stories celebrate the spectacle of atrocity.
They also celebrate (and this is indeed the right word) the
spectacle of the atrocious reader. Such stories could have been
written only for an audience of connoisseurs, connoisseurs of
bloodshed, and with a submission so deliberate as to seem a
kind of offense, the narrative at once gratifies and travesties
their appetite. This is the imperial underside of the vigilant
reformer, and in the conjunction of the two, in the harmony
between war stories and moral sermon, Melville projects his
most damning portrait of the reader. What he ends up project-
ing is something much larger: something that enveloped and
constituted the reader in his historical moment, something
that produced the reader as jingoist and reformer both. And
so what emerges, in Melville's oblique portrait of the reader, is
yet another portrait, still more oblique but hardly less pertinent. This portrait features what George Ripley called America's "prevailing tendencies"—Manifest Destiny and Jacksonian reform, the two collapsed now into a single image, their
boundaries blurred both by their historical filiations and by

Melville's incongruous rhetoric. Those historical phenomena, and their attendant injuries, are now private metaphors for Melville, since he too fancies himself an injured party, injured by the "imperial" reader. To him, his own fate, the fate of the afflicted artist, is altogether analogous to the fate of the dispossessed, the infantilized, the reformed.

Of course, the distance between him and the others—between someone who laments his fate in metaphors and others who suffer it in person—calls into question Melville's claim of powerlessness. Nothing more tellingly qualifies that claim than the figure of dominion he rhetorically subjects himself to, the figure of the reader. We have seen that figure in a number of guises, variously censorious and despicable, but responsible, in every guise, for what Melville perceives to be his own tribulations. But to imagine the reader in this fashion is to do some compartmentalizing of one's own. Melville, too, localizes blame within a site he designates. Conveniently objectionable, the tyrannical reader allows the artist to feel sublimely persecuted.[55] Harry Bolton in *Redburn*, Melville's ultimate figure of the persecuted artist, shows how this works. An "Orpheus" among "leopards and tigers" (278), Harry's ordeal is to "sing his songs to this ruffian crew, whom he hated, even in his dreams, till the foam flew from his mouth while he slept" (278). The following passage usefully glosses the relation between the persecuted artist and his persecuting audience:

> And indeed, in his striped Guernsey frock, dark glossy skin and hair, Harry Bolton, mingling with the *Highlander*'s crew, looked not unlike the soft, silken quadruped-creole, that, pursued by wild Bushmen, bounds through Caffrarian woods.
>
> How they hunted you, Harry, my zebra! those ocean barbarians, those unimpressible, uncivilized sailors of ours! How they pursued you from bowsprit to mainmast, and started you out of your every retreat! (253)

At once "uncivilized" and "unimpressible," aggressive and obtuse, the "wild Bushmen" stand as the definitive trope for the philistine readers, readers Harry Bolton and Herman Melville apparently share. Barbarism of this sort is obviously more dangerous than the exotic strain in *Typee*. Closer to home and vaster in numbers, barbaric readers threaten to bring down the very fabric of civilization, as casualties like *Mardi* already attest. Such is their power, and so infested is the *Highlander* by their savage presence, that being on board is "like going into a barbarous country, where they speak a strange dialect, and dress in strange clothes, and live in strange houses" (65). Horace Mann might have said the same of the urban ghettos, whose inhabitants, he thought, were rapidly "plung[ing]" into the "weakness and helplessness of barbarism."[56] Mann's barbaric working class congregated in the very heart of the metropolis; Melville's barbaric readers dominate those regions where he has once "chartless voyaged."[57] In both cases, barbarism signifies at once inferiority and menace, and requires at once accommodation and defense. The surprising kinship here, between Melville's rhetoric of authorial affliction and Horace Mann's rhetoric of social cataclysm, suggests that Melville might not be where he would like to position himself within the topography of power. What it also suggests is the essentially inverse relation between the rhetoric of professed vulnerability and the structure of enforced dominion. The category of "threat," like the category of "defense," emanates (in the nineteenth century no less than in the twentieth) from the powerful rather than the powerless. Melville's allegories of authorship, in their assumed figure of subjection, exemplify just that logic. Uncanny ventriloquisms for the powerless, they remain imperial ventriloquisms.

4. ◆ *Blaming the Victim*

"IN MY PROUD, humble way—a shepherd-king,—I was lord of a little vale in the solitary Crimea; but you have now given me the crown of India."[1] With characteristic effusion Melville writes Hawthorne to thank him for his "joy-giving and exultation-breeding" letter about *Moby-Dick*. The effusion is characteristic, not only in sentiment but also in expression, for as we have seen, it is something of a habit for Melville to convey his authorial aspirations in the idiom of empire. Earlier, in *Mardi*, he has fancied himself a "monarch."[2] That fancy has apparently survived—*Redburn* and *White-Jacket* notwithstanding—and Melville now returns to it, to give it yet another airing. *Moby-Dick*, he says, is to be an "imperial folio," one designed to capture the "revolving panoramas of empire on earth."[3] The same conceit, and perhaps an attendant sense of kinship, seem also to have prompted his curious tribute to Nicholas the Czar, whose "ringed crown of geographical empire encircles an imperial brain," in whose shadow "the plebeian herds crouch abased" (129).

Whatever hopes Melville might entertain about an "imperial brain," a "geographical empire" is clearly not his to have. Not an actual one, at any rate. Yet writing an "imperial folio" is in some ways almost as gratifying as ruling an empire, as his own experience in *Mardi* suggests. *Moby-Dick* will not, all the same, be as imperial, or as free, as *Mardi*, for unlike the sovereign author of the earlier book, Melville has no illusions now about his absolute dominion. The reception of *Mardi*, and the

An earlier version of this chapter appeared in *Raritan: A Quarterly Review*, 7, no. 2 (Fall 1987), 93-112. Copyright © 1987 by *Raritan*, 165 College Avenue, New Brunswick, NJ 08903. Used with permission.

writing of *Redburn* and *White-Jacket*, have taught him at least a hostile regard for the reader. *Moby-Dick* is, in that sense, very much a sequel to its predecessors: it takes up old grudges, settles them, and compensates for them, but also derives from them a keener sense of the adversarial and, correspondingly, a subtler and more effective instrument of control. Where *Mardi* casually dismisses the reader, a docile specter, *Moby-Dick* is anything but casual. Having constituted his audience as a category of threat, the author must proceed to erect defenses.

The most powerful defense, for Melville, is the idea of an autonomous literary domain. If readers everywhere are tyrannous and despicable, if these "ocean barbarians" have taken over what he once claimed as his own, authorial freedom might be recovered only by positing a transcendent realm, at once independent of its environment and impervious to it. The spatial goal in *Moby-Dick* is therefore exactly the obverse of that in *Redburn* and *White-Jacket*. If Melville's project there is to designate a seat of malaise, his project in *Moby-Dick* is to locate an island of immunity. In either case, he is committed to what I have tried to call an institution of the discrete, a faith in the self-contained and self-sufficient. This commitment accounts for the recurring images of charmed insularity in *Moby-Dick*. The ambergris is one such example: Melville marvels that the "incorruption of this most fragrant [substance] should be found in the heart of such decay" (343). No less marvelous, the doubloon, "nailed amidst all the rustiness of iron bolts and the verdigris of copper spikes, yet, untouchable and immaculate to any foulness, it still preserved its Quito glow" (359).

Untouchable and immaculate, eternally enclosed and eternally secure, ambergris and doubloon are emblems of the literary masterpiece Melville would like to produce. Like that masterpiece, they too are models of freedom: they are free from their environment, free from contagion and even from kinship. Such then is Melville's ideal image of the book, transposed, we might say, into material forms. Oddly, these material forms, transcendingly free as they are, nevertheless come equipped with an environment, understood to be corrupt and hostile, against which and in defiance of which they can measure their own freedom. For ambergris and doubloon happen to be surrounded by "decay" (343) and "foulness," "ruthless crew" and "ruthless hands" (359). To be the marvels that they are, they must be accompanied by something distinctly unmarvelous. The inviolate needs a corrupt world in order to prove its inviolability. Even in Melville's logic, freedom is always part of a complementary formation, set in a landscape of polarized attributes and discrete repositories. Freedom not only entails an obverse; it is itself constituted by that obverse.

The complementary logic here—the genesis of freedom alongside an obverse—is worth noting, for such a logic, I suggest, is ultimately not peculiar to doubloon and ambergris, and not peculiar to the literary text of which they are the material emblems. It is, more generally, the logic of the "imperial" self, as we have seen, and, even more generally, the logic of an "empire for liberty." In each case, freedom is only the positive pole within a double formation, a constitutive polarity of terms. Within this context, the emblematic polarity in *Moby-Dick*—the polarity between the incorruptible ambergris and the surrounding corruption, between the untarnishable doubloon and its tarnished habitat—must appear as no more than a memorable variation on what is by now a familiar theme. What animates this polarity, what gives it its characteristic structure, is not merely a logic of the literary text, but equally a logic of the self and, beyond the self, a logic of the nation— all three of them being double formations, all three bodying forth, separately and together, a kindred logic of freedom and dominion, sovereignty and subjection.

All of this would seem to align *Moby-Dick* directly with *Mardi*, a book even more enamored of freedom, and even more haunted by freedom's obverse. One important difference, however, sets the two books apart, and makes them contrary testimonies in Melville's poetics. In *Mardi*, freedom is primarily a sovereign right, something that the author claims for himself and that enables him to write as he pleases. In *Moby-Dick*, however, freedom is primarily a disciplinary postulate, something that the author imputes to his characters and that enables him to judge them, as free agents, responsible and punishable for their deeds. Freedom of this sort points to a negative individualism: one that produces individuals as "subjects," figures whose very freedom of action already constitutes the ground for discipline.

The self as "subject" is nothing new in Melville; in *Redburn* and *White-Jacket* he has offered himself, the persecuted artist, as one such example. But here too, *Moby-Dick* seems to have departed from its predecessors and gone beyond their purview, for if Melville has previously invoked the subjected self as a token of the reader's dominion, he is now able to use the same figure, paradoxically, as an instrument of his own sovereignty. The negative individualism in *Moby-Dick*, then, is one that actually empowers its author, allowing him to govern his characters, to dispense justice and assign destiny—and to do so by an internal mechanism, namely, by constituting his characters as agents of that justice and that destiny. Under this new dispensation, Melville's own exercise in freedom will entail a corresponding attribution of freedom; his own authorial sovereignty will reside in the creation of fictive characters as sovereign subjects.

Sovereign subjects abound in *Moby-Dick*, and not just human ones, but specimens from the animal kingdom as well:

> It does seem to me, that herein we see the rare virtue of a strong individual vitality, and the rare virtue of thick walls, and the rare virtue of interior spaciousness. Oh, man! admire and model thyself after the whale! Do thou, too, remain warm among ice. Do thou, too, live in this world without being of it. Be cool at the equator; keep thy blood fluid at the Pole. (261)

If the whale had been human, it would have been applauded as a hero, a hero of Jacksonian individualism. Not being human, it is applauded in *Moby-Dick* as a heroic beast, a model of transcendent freedom, one that "live[s] in this world without being of it." But if the whale is free, its freedom is measured, nonetheless, not in and of itself, but over and against something else. Its "strong individual vitality" inheres, after all, in its ability to defy its environment, to stay cool at the equator and warm among ice. The whale is something of a defensive model, and from that standpoint its "thick walls" and "interior spaciousness" become vital assets.

Still, if this is a defensive model, the defense turns out to be not literal (since whales do get killed regularly in the course of the book), but literary. What the whale defies is the unworthy reader, the "timid untravelled man [who tries] to comprehend" it (378). To that reader, the whale "is an unwritten life" (118); it will always be "that one creature in the world which must remain unpainted to the last" (228). Even Ishmael, neither timid nor untraveled, finds himself utterly at a loss here: "If then, Sir William Jones, who read in thirty languages, could not read the simplest peasant's face . . . how may unlettered Ishmael hope to read the awful Chaldee of the Sperm Whale's brow?" (292–93). Melville has every reason, then, to call his book *Moby-Dick* (rather than *Ahab* or *Ishmael* or *The Fatal Voyage of the "Pequod"*), for as a literary model, especially a defensive one, the whale indeed has no match. It will always resist the reader, it will triumph over him, because its transcendent freedom is also a kind of transcendent illegibility: it cannot be read, because it refers to nothing other than itself. It luxuriates in what John Irwin calls "divine indeterminacy," a condition that prevails when the sign is simply its own representation.[4] The whale is doubly autonomous then, doubly self-contained, not only in its physical compass, but also in its circularity of reference.[5] Its "divine indeterminacy" reconstitutes the "imperial folio" as self-referential text.

Thus far, self-containment would seem nothing but a positive asset, something that protects both the whale, and the book that is named after the whale, from the unworthy and the sacrilegious. Yet, as we all know, protection is only half the story. For the whale also happens to be an engine of destruction. Only a few chapters earlier (chapter 76), its sublimely indeterminate head has appeared as a repository of "battering-ram power" (284), an "impregnable, uninjurable wall" capable of "inconsiderable braining feats" (285), the most spectacular of which is no doubt performed by Moby-Dick's "solid white buttress" (468). Self-containment, at least in the whale, is responsible for the "doom of boats, and ships, and men" (292). The "thick walls" that ensure freedom are also the "dead, blind wall" (284) that kills.

The strange conjunction here, between freedom as idealized privilege and freedom as destructive agency, should not surprise us, for it is just this conjunction, this yoking together of contrarieties, that commends the whale to Melville. In its alternate freedom and dominion, the whale is finally no more than an exceptionally enviable specimen in the gallery of double entities we have thus far examined. The achievement of *Moby-Dick* lies precisely in its ability to normalize this doubleness, by segregating it in such a way that the polarities seem to occupy two entirely different realms. Freedom, by this arrangement, becomes primarily a literary privilege: it belongs to the author, conferring on him a sovereignty he is understood to command absolutely. Dominion, on the other hand, becomes primarily a punitive consequence: it inflicts itself on the fictive individual, conferring on him a fate he is understood himself to have incurred.

In Ahab, we see both principles at work. The punitive logic dictates his end, of course, but the literary logic measures his offense. That offense is grave indeed—altogether unpardonable from a certain standpoint. Ahab is a monstrous reader, as a number of critics have suggested; his monomania threatens to reduce indeterminate text to determinate meaning.[6] His goal is to penetrate "that inscrutable thing" (144), the "impregnable, uninjurable wall" (285) that is both whale and text: "If man will strike, strike through the mask! How can the prisoner reach outside except by thrusting through the wall? To me, the white whale is that wall, shoved near to me" (144). If Ahab were to have his way, the category of the "inviolate" would exist no more, and neither doubloon, nor ambergris, nor even a literary text, could find refuge in it. That would be a blow indeed to Melville. For this, if for no other reason, Ahab is doomed never to have his way. *Moby-Dick*, in that respect, once again allegorizes the author's battle for sovereignty. It also allegorizes his revenge on the reader.

Ahab's sins, as a reader or otherwise, have been abundantly

documented. My focus in this chapter, however, will not be on those sins, but on the punitive logic his author administers. To dispatch Ahab, to disarm him, to make him die not only inevitably but also deservedly, Melville needs an executory instrument, a logic that explains and justifies the fate of this character. That logic is only too easy to come by, for it is already a provision in individualism. What we might expect to find in Ahab is an individualism that afflicts its bearer, one that apprehends and incriminates, one that disciplines the self in its very freedom. And that, in fact, is what we do find.

Being a product of individualism, Ahab is by definition a free agent. But, since his individualism happens to be the negative variety, he is, also by definition, an overdetermined character. He is both doomed and free: free, that is, to choose his doom. This is a strange logic, to say the least, but within the terms of negative individualism, nothing is more reasonable, or more necessary, for such a logic—a logic that inscribes discipline in freedom—is just what makes the autonomous self governable as such. Embracing this logic, *Moby-Dick* will find itself in intimate communion with antebellum America, for both the text and the nation agree about what it means to be "doomed"—about the cause, character, and trajectory of that unfortunate condition.[7]

The narrative of doom in *Moby-Dick* comes into play even before Ahab appears. His ship is introduced with the accompanying information that "*Pequod*, you will no doubt remember, was the name of a celebrated tribe of Massachusetts Indians, now extinct as the ancient Medes" (67). The crucial words here are "now extinct"—and it is crucial, too, that the word should be "extinct," rather than "exterminated." "Extermination" betrays the work of an exterminator; "extinction," on the other hand, suggests a natural process, as if time alone were responsible for this fated course of events. Melville is not alone in favoring the word. As we have noted, Andrew Jackson had used the same word in his Second Annual Message (1830) to defend his Indian policy. "To follow to the tomb the last of his race and to tread on the graves of extinct nations excite melancholy reflections," Jackson admitted, but quickly added that "true philanthropy reconciles the mind . . . to the extinction of one generation to make room for another."[8] The usefulness of the term becomes even clearer in the following observation by Benjamin Lincoln, the Revolutionary general from Massachusetts. Commenting on the imminent demise of the Indians, he predicted:

> If the savages cannot be civilized and quit their present pursuits, they will, in consequence of their stubbornness, dwindle and moulder away, from causes perhaps imperceptible to us, until the whole race shall become extinct.[9]

Dying from "imperceptible" causes, Indians obligingly solved the problem for white settlers. "Extinction" is what happens in an autotelic universe: it naturalizes the category of the "doomed," not only by recuperating it as an evolutionary category but, most crucially, by locating the cause for extinction within the extinct organism itself.[10] If Indians die out it is their own fault. Their extinction is a function of their "stubbornness," their benighted refusal to quit their savage ways. This is the logic of blaming the victim; within the terms of our discussion, we might also call it the logic of negative individualism. The strategy here is to equate phenomenon with locus, to collapse cause and casualty into an identical unit, to make the Indian at once the scene and the agent of his own destruction. No less than the whale, the Indian too is a self-contained figure. He is both necessary and sufficient for his own condition: his impending doom refers to nothing other than his own savage self.

The Indian, as he is described by antebellum ethnographers and politicians, is therefore always the subject of a predestined narrative, in which he is responsible for, guilty of, and committed to a fated course of action, in which he appears not only as both victim and culprit, but also as a legible sign of his own inexorable end. Negative individualism could have found no better exponent. Ahab's kinship with the Indian is, under the circumstances, only to be expected. A single narrative works for both, for like the doomed savage, Ahab too is a product of negative individualism. He too is a victim of his own fault, and an instrument of his own fate. *Moby-Dick*, then, is not just a story of doom, but the story of a particular kind of doom, self-chosen and self-inflicted. As such, it has more than a little in common with another story of doom, Francis Parkman's *The Conspiracy of Pontiac*, a book also published in 1851, one written to record the "final doom" of those "destined to melt and vanish before the advancing waves of Anglo-American power."[11]

The *Pequod* is, for that reason, a "cannibal of a craft" (67), "apparelled like any barbaric Ethiopian emperor" (67), and manned by a "barbaric, heathenish, and motley" crew (109), repulsive in the "barbaric brilliancy of their teeth" (353) and their "uncivilized laughter" (353). Less civilized still are the five "tiger-yellow barbarians" (463) reserved for Ahab's whaleboat. Such barbaric trappings are obviously meant to suggest something about Ahab himself; in "The Try-Works" we are expressly told that "the rushing *Pequod*, freighted with savages, and laden with fire, and burning a corpse, and plunging into that blackness of darkness, seemed the material counterpart of her monomaniac commander's soul" (354). Ahab, indeed, is not without savage airs of his own. He walks on a "barbaric white leg" (110), for instance, and even though we do not ordinarily think of him as being animal-like, he has been shown on occasions to manifest a "sudden, passionate, corporal animosity" (160), and to emit a "terrific, loud, animal sob, like that of a heart-stricken moose" (143).

All the same, Ahab's barbarism has to do less with his "animosity" than with what Melville in *White-Jacket* has referred to as "barbarous feudal aristocracy," a condition associated with Czarist Russia, "immovable China," and to some extent England.[12] Ahab's "dictatorship" (129) is best understood in this context—in the equation between "barbarism" and "feudal aristocracy." Given such a definition, the repeated references to Ahab as "Khan of the plank" (114), "sultan" (130), and "Grand Turk" (130) are nothing if not ominous. More verdict than tribute, such allusions hardly describe Ahab: they merely brand him as a thing of the past. At once regal and barbaric, he takes his place among other candidates for extinction. "Social czarship" (130), "sultan's step" (130), and "Egyptian chest" (160) all conspire to make him a hopeless anomaly (and a sure casualty) in the age of the "Nantucket market" (143). Barbarians are doomed, in *Moby-Dick* as in antebellum America, because they have outlived their allotted time span, because their very nobility marks them as anachronistic. The Indian (John Quincy Adams called him the "lordly savage") perished not in spite of but because of his "stateliness," his "heroic virtues," his "fine figure, commanding voice, noble beauty."[13] Ahab perishes because he inhabits "the nameless regal overbearing dignity of some mighty woe" (111)—because, where feudalism equals barbarism, regality *is* woe.

The constellations of terms that seal Ahab's fate are therefore exactly those that sealed the fate of the Indians. Yet seeing Ahab as an allegory of the Indian would be wrong, for the representational relation here is not so much one between the two as one encompassing both of them. Both are encompassed, that is, by a punitive representation of the self, what I have called negative individualism. Thus filiated in their genesis, Ahab and the Indians logically share a common end. We might speak of this punitive representation as broadly allegorical, for it operates through a set of signifying attributes, out of which it produces both "persons" and "destinies." Indeed, if we are right to detect in *Moby-Dick* a "hideous and intolerable allegory" (177) (whose existence Melville denies), that allegory works, I believe, primarily as an economy of ascription, as the production of narrative through the assignment of attributes. Ahab and the Indians are both bearers of attributes. They happen to inhabit two (apparently) disparate realms, one literary and the other social, but that fact finally matters less than the attributes they share. Those attributes make them analogous characters, produce them as analogous signs, and inflict on them analogous narratives—narratives of extinction.

Ahab's archaic speech (like the eloquence so often ascribed to Indians[14]) is therefore only another signifying attribute, another sign of his doom. At stake here is more than a question of language, for what the language embodies is actually an outmoded syntax of being. At its most memorable, this syntax takes the form of Ahab's famous resolve: to "dismember my dismemberer." This syntax of vengeance makes Ahab the coeval of "sultans" and "Khans," for vengeance is the alleged code of the primitive. "Vengeance, and fortitude . . . are duties which [Indians] consider as sacred," Jedidiah Morse reported in his much-reprinted article on "America" in the American edition (1790) of the *Encyclopaedia*. In agreement, Francis Parkman noted that "revenge" was one of the "ruling passions" among Indians. It was this passion that he dwelled on, at the end of *The Conspiracy of Pontiac*, as he imagined the "savage spirit" of Pontiac revisiting the scene of his murder and exulting in the "vengeance which overwhelmed the abettors of the crime," even as other tribes gathered to "revenge his fate."[15] In a somewhat different vein, René Girard also suggests that "primitive societies have only private vengeance."[16] It is this primitive obsession that sets Ahab apart, and spells his doom. Captain Boomer of the *Samuel Enderby*, a man unburdened by such primitive obsession, appears, in this regard, not only as a contrast to Ahab, but also as a salient example of doom averted:

> "No, thank ye, Bunger," said the English Captain, "he's welcome to the arm he has, since I can't help it, and didn't know him then; but not to another one. No more White Whales for me; I've lowered for him once, and that has satisfied me. There would be great glory in killing him, I know that; and there is a shipload of precious sperm in him, but, hark ye, he's best let alone; don't you think so, Captain?" (368)

Vengeance clearly means nothing to Captain Boomer. Indeed, if he were ever to hunt Moby Dick again, it would not be for revenge, but for glory and profit—glory, in killing what no one has so far managed to kill, and profit, already beckoning in that "shipload of precious sperm." Both in what he values and in what he dismisses, Captain Boomer stands as a rebuke to Ahab. In that capacity he comically echoes Starbuck, for it is Starbuck, that eminently unprimitive character, who objects most strenuously to the idea of vengeance. What he says is this, "I came here to hunt whales, not my commander's vengeance. How many barrels will thy vengeance yield thee even if thou gettest it, Captain Ahab? it will not fetch thee much in our Nantucket market" (143).

Vengeance is wrong because it is unprofitable, Starbuck reasons. This is not simply crass materialism, either, for in spite of the talk about "barrels," about what vengeance will "yield" and "fetch," Starbuck is concerned with profit less as an end in itself than as a signifying economy, by which things can be calibrated, their meanings affixed, and their values ascertained. Only such an economy will permit Starbuck to assess Ahab's vengeance and reject it for its deficient value. And only such an economy will permit violence to end. Starbuck's strategy, in other words, is always to resist vengeance-as-vengeance, always to position it within a system of exchange. Vengeance can be validated, according to him, only if it can be substituted—only if it can be exchanged—for a different set of terms, like its value on the Nantucket market.

Ahab, of course, has no use for substitution and exchange.[17] His universe is one of mimetic repetition: in trying to dismember his dismemberer, he is trying to be like the whale, to do what the whale has done to him.[18] Vengeance affirms the primacy of temporal continuity, of mimesis in time. Starbuck, with no desire to imitate a "dumb brute," rejects not only mimesis but also the very idea of "continuity." Starbuck is an Emerson in the whaling business, we might say, and Emerson's defiant wish to be "an endless seeker with no Past at my back"[19] might have served equally well as his motto. Like Emerson, Starbuck cultivates the art of discontinuity, the art of discrete substitution.[20] Exchanging the whale (or vengeance on the whale) with what it will "fetch," he brings together two separate terms, the whale and its market value, and substitutes one for the other. There is no resemblance, of course, between the two terms, not even a logical connection, but that is precisely the point. Substitution, even as it exchanges one term for another, affirms the primacy of discontinuity.[21]

Discontinuity is also what Melville affirms as he proclaims

himself "lord of [his] little vale." The freedom of the literary domain requires discontinuity, necessarily posits it, for the very possibility of freedom rests on the presumed ability of the literary artifact to set itself apart, to transcend mimesis, to rest within an impervious tissue of words. Melville and Starbuck would seem to be logical allies, at least on epistemological grounds. Starbuck, of course, is less worried about representation than about revenge: mimesis in time rather than mimesis in space is what he objects to. Unlike Melville, who values the discontinuous primarily as a spatial privilege—as the discrete separation of the literary object—Starbuck values the discontinuous primarily as a temporal privilege, as the privilege of not revenging, not repeating a prior event. Whether as spatial construct or as temporal postulate, however, discontinuity is, for both of them, the very condition of freedom: it liberates Starbuck from his antecedents, just as it liberates Melville from his surroundings. A common hope animates both, and if they were to win out, time and space in *Moby-Dick* would both observe the same law, the law of discontinuity.

Starbuck does not win out, although Melville does. Their differential fate points to a certain strain within *Moby-Dick*, to its contrary sense of possibilities and liabilities. And yet Starbuck need not have died. He (and indeed everybody else on the *Pequod*) could have survived without violating the logic of the plot. The fact that he does die, that his author deliberately makes it happen, suggests at once capitulation and control on Melville's part. For *Moby-Dick* manages, of course, to contain the terms of Starbuck's defeat within the terms of Melville's triumph—manages, that is to say, to contain its temporal disaster within a spatial order. Yet even that fact diminishes not at all the particular horror of Starbuck's defeat, a defeat his author scarcely "ha[s] the heart to write" (104). The "immaculate manliness we feel within ourselves" must "[bleed] with keenest anguish" at this tragic event, Melville says, for Starbuck's tragedy is the tragedy of American democracy itself:

> But this august dignity I treat of, is not the dignity of kings and robes, but . . . that democratic dignity which, on all hands, ra-

diates without end from God; Himself! The great God absolute! The centre and circumference of all democracy! His omnipresence, our divine equality!

If, then, to meanest mariners, and renegades and castaways, I shall hereafter ascribe high qualities, though dark; weave round them tragic graces . . . if I shall spread a rainbow over his disastrous set of sun; then against all mortal critics bear me out in it, thou just Spirit of Equality, which hast spread one royal mantle of humanity over all my kind! (104–105)

According to this passage, Starbuck's battle is the battle to enthrone democracy and to unseat the "dignity of kings and robes." It is a battle, we might infer, between the progressive and the primitive, between the "Spirit of Equality" and Ahab's barbaric "czarship." Given such an array of terms, there is no question what the outcome ought to be. Yet it is just this outcome that fails to materialize. In spite of its excited apostrophes, this celebrated passage on democracy actually predicts not victory but disaster. It is about the "dark" qualities, "tragic graces," and "disastrous set of sun" that await the democratic man.

Generalized as the defeat of American democracy, Starbuck's defeat is unbearable to contemplate because it represents a breakdown of what should take place, a reversal in the book's teleological opposition of terms. The tragedy here is the tragedy of failed succession, of deficient "valor" on the part of those slated for ascendancy, of "sultanism" stubbornly refusing to be deposed. It is the tragedy of the progressive failing to supplant the primitive. Instead of proceeding helpfully according to plan, time in *Moby-Dick* actually sides with Ahab's antiquated feudal barbarism. Even worse, that feudal barbarism seems quite capable of implicating the future in its wake. Time, it would seem, is resolutely, relentlessly continuous: there is no question here of substitution, no unexampled beginnings, no freedom even from vengeance. Starbuck's temporal economy—his dream of the discontinuous—fails abysmally.

Anxiety about the wayward workings of time is not peculiar

to *Moby-Dick*. Antebellum expansionists expressed similar worries about the problem of succession, about the shape of America's future. If the Indian is allowed to be "lord paramount of that wide domain," Representative Strother speculated in a 1819 congressional debate on the Seminole War, "the progress of mankind is arrested and you condemn one of the most beautiful and fertile tracts of the earth to perpetual sterility as the hunting ground of a few savages."[22] This was a dismal prospect indeed, but not as dismal as what Representative Wilde of Georgia had in mind. If Indians were allowed to "perpetuate" themselves, he said, "a hundred or a thousand fold the number of white men would not be born" as a consequence.[23] Such dire events did not have to happen, of course, and the preventive measures seemed clear enough, at least in theory. In practice, however, the agency of time was problematic even to the most determined exponents of progress, as the following passage from *White-Jacket* demonstrates:

> The Past is dead, and has no resurrection; but the Future is endowed with such a life, that it lives to us even in anticipation. The Past is, in many things, the foe of mankind; the Future is, in all things, our friend. In the Past is no hope; the Future is both hope and fruition. The Past is the text-book of tyrants; the Future the Bible of the Free. Those who are solely governed by the Past stand like Lot's wife, crystallized in the act of looking backward, and forever incapable of looking before.[24]

The Past is demonstrably dead, Melville would like to suggest; and yet the demonstration, in its very obsessiveness, would seem to suggest the reverse. The passage offers neat serial categories ("the Past" and "the Future"), but the stubborn presence of what ought to be bygone jeopardizes the very notion of seriality. In its giddy dissonances, the passage anticipates the equally schizophrenic paean to democracy in *Moby-Dick*. The fear, in both cases, is that the Future might not become the future at all. Starbuck's defeat at the hands of barbaric "sultanism" gives that fear a palpable shape. Of course, by 1851 America's future was hardly likely to be threatened by Indians, but the anxiety in *Moby-Dick* remains real. Indeed, what the book articulates seems to be the inverse of what Representatives Strother and Wilde prophesied—not what savages might do to America's future, but what America's future might be like after savages have been done in.

Americans had always worried about the future of the American Empire. If that empire had so far been time's beneficiary, would it not (like other empires) ultimately also be time's casualty? Americans liked to think of their empire as unlike any other in history, unexampled both in character and duration. Its duration, as it turned out, had everything to do with its character, for in order to escape the proverbial fate of empires, America had to be imagined as a very special case indeed: not just any empire but an "empire for liberty," "an empire of reason," "an empire of virtue," "an empire of love."[25] By the same token, any territorial conquest by this "noble young empire" would have to be distinguished from other less laudable imperialist exploits. The text most often cited during the Congressional debates on Indian Removal in the 1820s and 1830s was Vattel's classic *Law of Nations*, in which the Swiss jurist had argued for the legality of the North American settlements:

> Thus, though the conquest of the civilized Empires of Peru and Mexico was a notorious usurpation, the establishment of many colonies on the continent of North America may, on their confining themselves within just bounds, be extremely lawful. The peoples of those vast countries of land rather overran than inhabited them.[26]

Taking land away from the Indians constituted no territorial conquest, because Indian title "cannot be taken for a true and legal possession." For the same reason, Vattel added, "People have not, then, deviated from the views of nature, in confining the Indians within narrow limits."[27]

Those were reassuring words from an acknowledged authority. It was interesting, however, that those words had so often to be invoked, and that expansionists felt so urgently called upon to defend themselves from the charge of aggression. The acquisition of Texas occasioned this editorial, for instance, from the *New York Morning News*:

> It is looked upon as aggression, and all the bad and odious features which the habits of thought Europeans associate with aggressive deeds, are attributed to it. . . . But what has Belgium, Silesia, Poland or Bengal in common with Texas? . . . Rapacity and spoliation cannot be the features of this magnificent enterprise, not perhaps, because we are above and beyond the influence of such views, but because circumstances do not admit of their operation. We take from no man; the reverse rather—we give to man. This national policy, necessity or destiny, we know to be just and beneficent, and we can, therefore, afford to scorn the invective and imputations of rival nations.[28]

Such a frenzy of protest, of course, only affirmed what it denied. The vehemence of the *New York Morning News* inversely registered the fear that America had lost its character as an "empire of virtue" or an "empire of love." This would bode ill indeed for its future, for its claim as the champion of progress and the seat of permanence. What would be the fate of an empire founded upon "aggression," "rapacity," and "spoliation"?

Emerson, seeker with no Past at his back, would have known how to answer that question. The art of discontinuity, judiciously applied, clearly has its political advantages. If time were no more than a series of discrete units, if Past and Future were related only as disjunction, and if what ensues had no reference to what preceded, one could indeed be absolved from one's actions. Emerson and antebellum Americans wanted "the sense of an ending," as Frank Kermode calls it, the condition in which "an act could be without succession, without temporal consequence." But as Kermode also says, "acts without 'success' are a property of the *aevum*. Nothing in time can in that sense be *done*, freed of consequence or equivocal aspects."[29] Antebellum Americans, defending themselves from charges of aggression, rapacity, and spoliation, were especially haunted by the prospect of consequences, by the infinitude of action and reaction. Vengeance, mimetic repetition in time, dramatized that infinitude as infinite retribution. America's very future was endangered by it. Even worse, the instrument of vengeance was not to be the lordly savage (now happily on his way to extinction), but his servile counterpart, one apparently meek and jolly, but at heart as savage as the Indian himself.

"I tremble for my country," Jefferson wrote in 1782, "when I reflect that God is just: that his justice cannot sleep for ever." He was speaking of slavery. The slave uprisings in St. Domingo some ten years later seemed to confirm his fears. Jefferson foresaw "bloody scenes" for "our children certainly, and possibly ourselves." St. Domingo was only "the first chapter," he thought, and thinking about other chapters to come, he predicted, "we shall be the murderers of our own children."[30] David Walker, author of *An Appeal to the Coloured Citizens of the World* (1829), made the same prediction from the other side. America's "victims of oppression," he said, were daily calling upon "the God of Justice, to be revenged":[31]

> I tell you Americans! that unless you speedily alter your course, you and your country are gone!!!!!! For God Almighty will tear up the very face of the earth. . . . I hope that the Americans may hear, but I am afraid that they have done us so much injury, and are so firm in the belief that our Creator made us to be an inheritance to them for ever, that their hearts will be hardened, so that their destruction may be sure.[32]

Walker's *Appeal* was nationally denounced as "one of the most wicked and inflammatory productions that ever issued from the press."[33] On 28 June 1830 he was found dead, apparently of poison, near the doorway of his shop. To the horrified nation, however, his hellish predictions seemed to have come true in August 1831, when Nat Turner led about seventy slaves on a rampage through Southampton County, Virginia, killing some sixty whites, more than half women and children.

Such bloody episodes of vengeance were kept very much alive in the public memory in the decades before the Civil War. Nat Turner was "a symbol of wild retribution," Thomas Wentworth Higginson reported. So potent was his threat, or the memory of his threat, that even "the remotest Southern States were found shuddering at nightly rumors of insurrection." Abolitionists, playing upon Southern fears, regularly made "vengeance" their theme—to such an extent that they even sometimes joked about it. "The nigger has terrible capacities for revenge," which "ought to convince the skeptic that he is a man, not a baboon," an 1855 article ("About Niggers") in *Putnam's Magazine* suggested. Less playfully, black activist William Wells Brown invoked Nat Turner not only as the author of a "blood-thirsty and revengeful" insurrection but also as someone who "meditated upon the wrongs of his oppressed and injured people," and went on to issue this ominous warning: "Every iniquity that society allows to subsist for the benefit of the oppressor is a sword with which she herself arms the oppressed. Right is the most dangerous of weapons: woe to him who leaves it to his enemies."[34]

Vengeance as actual slave insurgence was horrible to contemplate. But increasingly, another kind of "vengeance" gained currency in the discourse about slavery. This vengeance also took the form of mimetic repetition, but in this case it came about, not in bloody revolt, not in the victim's imitation of his victimizer, but in familial reproduction, in the offspring's imitation of his parent. For Jefferson, the "unhappy influence" of slavery resided in just this sort of mimesis, one that turned the family itself into a vehicle of retribution:

> The whole commerce between master and slave is a perpetual exercise of the most boisterous passions, the most unremitting despotism on the one part, and degrading submissions on the other. Our children see this, and learn to imitate it; for man is an imitative animal. . . . The parent storms, the child looks on, catches the lineaments of wrath, puts on the same airs in the circle of smaller slaves, gives a loose to his worst of passions, and thus nursed, educated, and daily exercised in tyranny, cannot but be stamped by it with odious peculiarities.[35]

Slavery was its own retribution, then, as it enforced mimesis within the family, as it "stamped" the offspring, "an imitative animal," with the mark of the parent, in a kind of reproductive

penalty. Jefferson was not the only one to think of "vengeance" in intrafamilial terms. Harriet Beecher Stowe had
much the same idea in *Uncle Tom's Cabin* (1852). "It is perfectly outrageous,—it is horrid, Augustine! It will certainly
bring down vengeance upon you," Miss Ophelia assures her
slave-owning cousin.[36] And "vengeance," in Stowe as in Jefferson, works from within the family and inflicts its punish-
ment reflexively on the slave owner himself. This is no doubt
why we find, in *Uncle Tom's Cabin*, a character like Henrique,
little Eva's ungentle cousin. Henrique, aged twelve, is already
in the habit of striking his slave boy Dodo "across the face with
his riding-whip" and speaking to him in the following tones:
"There, you impudent dog! Now will you learn not to answer
back when I speak to you? . . . I'll teach you your place!"[37]
Henrique exemplifies precisely what Jefferson fears. An "imitative animal," he is already a juvenile copy of the brutal master, will grow up to be an adult copy, and will in turn produce
more copies of his own. Slavery, ensconced within the family,
reproduces itself with a vengeance.

By locating mimesis within the family, by imagining the
slave owner as someone who punishes himself in the mere act
of reproduction, Jefferson and Stowe come up with another
model of "vengeance," a circular model, in which the master
enslaves himself and genealogy is its own retribution. This
prospect is by no means pleasing, but there is something reas-
suringly tautological about it all the same. For if genealogy is
already its own retribution, and the master already his own
slave, any further act of vengeance would seem unnecessary.
Slave rebellion is not so much wrong as gratuitous here, because the master, especially such a one as Augustine St. Clare,
has assuredly been punished enough. And because that self-
punishing master is eternally reproduced through the family,
slave rebellion is eternally unnecessary. For Stowe especially,
retribution runs its course within the compass of a single individual, the master himself; any repetition in time would simply
reenact that spatial figure. As a self-contained unit, a model
of discrete closure—at once agent and victim of his own fate—
the self-punishing master is not unlike the self-victimizing In-

dian. Both are products of Jacksonian individualism, the ultimate institution of the discrete. But whereas the self-victimizing Indian is erased from history, the self-punishing master eternally remains. Vengeance as tautology, as the circular agency within a single person, displaces vengeance as reciprocity, as the action and reaction between persons, and preserves the master who so conveniently punishes himself. Stowe offers no bloody scenes of vengeance, only Uncle Tom.

Published just a year before *Uncle Tom's Cabin*, *Moby-Dick*, too, is a meditation on vengeance: on the deflection of it and the deterrence of it. Melville is fascinated, however, by the savage energy of the undeflected and the undeterred. And so he ends up parting company with Stowe after all. *Moby-Dick* will have no Uncle Tom, only Captain Ahab. Ahab believes in vengeance. He refuses to locate it, moreover, in a circuit of identity, in the reflexive self-punishment of the victimizer. For him, the dismembered and the dismemberer are mutually engendering but by no means identical. His "vengeance" is a question of relation, not to oneself but to someone else; it is also a question of action, inflicted on another and perhaps returned in kind by that other.[38] Such a model entails not the spatial containment of victim in victimizer, but the temporal reversal of positions between the two. In short, Ahab's syntax of vengeance invokes the agency of time not only to preserve both victim and victimizer but, more crucially, to constitute one as the potential of the other. The two will trade places in time. Change is possible, indeed logical, as far as Ahab is concerned. It will not be absolute change, of course—his world will always have two positions, victims and victimizers—but one can at least move from one position to the other. Against Stowe's closed circuit, Ahab offers instead a temporal sequence, a sequence of reversals operating in time and through time. What he says to the "clear spirit of clear fire" might have been said to Stowe as well: "There is some unsuffusing thing beyond thee . . . to whom all thy eternity is but time" (417). Claiming time as his medium and ally, he can invoke another temporal phenomenon, what he calls the "genealogies of these high mortal miseries" (386), to champion his cause:

Nor, at the time, had it failed to enter his monomaniac mind, that all the anguish of that then present suffering was but the direct issue of a former woe; and he too plainly seemed to see, that as the most poisonous reptile of the marsh perpetuates his kind as inevitably as the sweetest songster of the grove; so, equally with every felicity, all miserable events do naturally beget their like. . . . Mortal miseries shall still fertilely beget to themselves an eternally progressive progeny of griefs beyond the grave. (385)

It is altogether fitting that these thoughts should come from Ahab—and Melville is careful to attribute them to his "monomaniac mind"—for such a "genealogy," cheerless as it might seem, actually turns out to be the best hope for a doomed man. Not only does it affirm Ahab's sense of injury (his action is the "direct issue of a former woe" rather than the crazy dilatations of a monomaniac), it also offers him vicarious life beyond his own preordained death. Ahab might be killed off, but his wrong will never die out, because it will "beget" an "eternally progressive progeny of griefs beyond the grave." Individuals perish, their positions remain: Ahab dies only to give birth to a thousand other Ahabs. The model here is not the primacy of the self but the primacy of relation; not the discrete spatiality of Jacksonian individualism, but an interweaving sequel that "naturally beget[s] their like."

Ahab's "genealogy" represents an apparent tautology that refuses to be one. His syntax of vengeance—"to dismember my dismemberer"—turns out to be anything but circular. It activates, on the contrary, a temporal process, a process of reversals at once inevitable and interminable. Against and around this temporal menace, Melville would have to erect other spatial forms of defense. The most effective form, he discovers, turns out once again to be the form of the tautology, for nothing works better as a vehicle of containment, and nothing keeps Ahab's vengeance under tighter control. And tautologies are easy enough to come by. All Melville needs is five short words: "Ahab is for ever Ahab" (459). Those are Ahab's own words, defiantly spoken; ironically they are also the words that condemn him. From our standpoint, these words must stand as the very epigraph of negative individualism, the punitive logic centered on the autonomous self. That punitive logic, we can now see, is tautological almost by necessity: it begins and ends with the self, a self constituted here not only as the seat of agency but also as the circuit of discipline. The version Melville comes up with—"Ahab is for ever Ahab"—therefore operates as two related tautologies, both of which begin and end with Ahab, and condemn him in just that circularity. Both are vehicles of containment, mobilized to contain Ahab's syntax of vengeance, and we might speak of them, accordingly, as the syntax of fate and the syntax of self.

Fate begins, in Ahab's case, with the name itself. Such a name is clearly "not without meaning," as Melville might say, and it is just this meaning that dooms its unlucky bearer. Ishmael and Peleg allude to that meaning even before Ahab appears. In response to Peleg's remark that "Ahab of old, thou knowest, was a crowned king!" Ishmael replies, "And a very vile one. When that wicked king was slain, the dogs, did they not lick his blood?" (77). No nineteenth-century reader would have missed the meaning of such a name, and few of them would have been surprised by what happens to Ahab at the end. Ahab can only mean what his name says he means: he is characterized by that name, summarized by it, and doomed by it. As a bearer of meaning, at once unmistakable and immutable, Ahab is less a living thing, perhaps, than a legible sign. He is a personified name, a human receptacle invested with a signifying function. That signifying function is quite literally his fate: he lives in it and dies in it, since his whole life is really nothing more than a recapitulation of what his name has made abundantly clear at the outset. To be called Ahab is to inhabit a narrative tautology, in which the ending is already immanent in the beginning, and in which all temporal development merely reenacts what is in place from the very first.

Ahab, of course, has hoped for change. He has hoped that time will help him. He should have known better, for his own name ought to have taught him the futility of his hope. Personifying that name, Ahab can have only one narrative, not a narrative of vengeance, but a narrative of doom.[39] His story is

therefore (as Elijah says) "all fixed and arranged a'ready" (87),
already inscribed in the fate of his Biblical namesake. Ahab is
right, then, to say, "This whole act's immutably decreed.
'Twas rehearsed by thee and me a billion years before this
ocean rolled" (459). The passage of time ("a billion years")
brings no change, no prospect of vengeance, for time turns out
to be completely unavailing here. Its status is summed up in
the five words, "Ahab is for ever Ahab," a tautology that,
quite literally, puts time in its place, in the spatial confines of
the personified name. Ahab's story can only be a story of fate,
because personification is, in effect, a vehicle of predestination. Under its dictates, time counts only as duration, not as
potentiality. The circuit of identity between "Ahab" and
"Ahab" marks the circuit from immanence to permanence,
and affirms a timeless design, the design of "for ever."

Earlier, we spoke of personification as a procedure that spatializes time. In Ahab we see that procedure at work. Through
him we also see, perhaps more clearly than anywhere else, the
context as well as the function of such spatializations. For it is
just this procedure that authorizes the category of "fate" in
Moby-Dick: authorizes it, in a temporal landscape in which the
future appears, already inscribed, composed, demarcated, almost as a fact of geography. This is what Melville in *White-
Jacket* has called "the wilderness of untried things,"[40] a wilderness that materializes, apparently, when time is converted into
space. Signs and omens hail from this region; prophets make
their way into it, like so many venturous prospectors, mapping
its terrain, claiming it as virtual property. Prophecy in *Moby-
Dick* is a territorial enterprise. To be a prophet one must survey
the future, with an eye to ownership. And it is in the jealous
tones of a proprietor that Elijah accosts Ishmael: "Didn't ye
hear a word about them matters and something more, eh? No,
I don't think ye did; how could ye? Who knows it? Not all
Nantucket, I guess" (87).

What is odd is that Elijah's field of knowledge actually lies
not in the future but in the past: he pities Ishmael for having
heard "nothing about that thing that happened to [Ahab] off
Cape Horn, long ago, when he lay like dead for three days and

nights; nothing about that deadly skrimmage with the Spaniard afore the altar in Santa?—heard nothing about that, eh? Nothing about the silver calabash he spat into?"(87). Prophecy in *Moby-Dick* enlarges upon the past. But that too is what one should expect from a spatial ordering of time. Indeed, the future is knowable to the prophets only because it has been converted into a spatial category, part of a known design. Prophets are prospectors and colonizers because they are emissaries of the known, because their mission is to expand and assimilate, to annex the "wilderness of untried things" into the domain of the existing. They can function as prophets only by reducing the potentiality of sequence to the legibility of design, only by reading time as space.

In that regard Melville's prophets are perhaps less prophets of the future than spokesmen for their own age, for spatialized time was the very condition for Manifest Destiny. What Albert Weinberg calls America's "geographical determinism" operated by equating geography with destiny, an equation that, in conflating time and space—in harnessing time to space—at once recomposed time and incorporated it as a vehicle for spatial aggrandizement. The familiar strategy for antebellum expansionists was to invoke some version of "Providence," whose plans for the future happened to coincide exactly with America's territorial ambitions. American expansion in space and providential design in time turned out to be one and the same. In the famous words of John L. O'Sullivan, it was America's "manifest destiny to overspread the continent allotted by Providence for the free development of our yearly multiplying millions."[41] This manifest destiny had no spatial limits, for as another expansionist enthusiastically put it, America was bounded "on the west by the Day of Judgment."[42] For this hopeful soul, and for many others, spatialized time legitimized and empowered. Yet the same mechanism could just as easily victimize and destroy. For Indians too happened to be subjects of spatialized time. As much as America, they too were "destined"—destined, that is, "to melt and vanish." Representative Wilde of Georgia found that destiny only too manifest: "Jacob will forever obtain the inheritance of Esau. We cannot alter the laws of Providence, as we read them in the experiences of the ages."[43] Within the spatialized time of providential design, the fate of the doomed savage became legible as a text.

Spatialized time is also what *Moby-Dick* invokes to make Ahab's fate legible. Reading that fate, Melville's prophets turn Ahab too into a doomed figure, spatializing his temporal endeavor into a timeless script. Melville's "imperial folio," then, logically shares the same temporal economy with its imperial environment, for a structure of dominion is inseparable from a structure of time, as J.G.A. Pocock has reminded us.[44] Fate in *Moby-Dick* and Manifest Destiny in antebellum America are kindred constructs. Ahab and America, bearers both of a timeless destiny, mirror each other in familial likeness.

Of course, the relation here cannot be anything other than *mirroring*, for if Ahab and America are in one sense kindred, kindred in their timelessness, in another sense they are also diametrically opposed. The destiny that afflicts Ahab is, after all, nothing like the destiny that awaits America. It resembles rather the fate of those whose "doom" America dictates. But even here, America's destiny and Ahab's are not so much opposed as complementary. One exists as the companion to the other, the necessary condition for the other's possibility. Putting this another way, we might say that America and Ahab represent the two poles in a single narrative of spatialized time, a narrative that (not surprisingly) also has two contrary provisions: for sovereignty as well as for subjection, the doom of the one being no more than a measure of the other's fated ascendancy.

In this regard, Ahab too might be said to have a Manifest Destiny of his own. Because this was the nineteenth century, however, Manifest Destiny could also appear in guises other than the providential. The fixed disposition of the natural—the "identity" of a person, or a race—could serve equally well as a sign of doom. The naturalized category was more effective, in fact, as we will discover both in antebellum America and in *Moby-Dick*. In both cases, the narrative of fate is supplemented by a narrative of self, a naturalized vehicle that produces much the same outcome as its providential counterpart, for it too is a vehicle of predestination. It too dictates doom, as we can see all too clearly in the genesis of the Indian "character" and the narrative it underwrites. Whether described positively as showing "bravery and fortitude," "commanding energy and force of mind," "firmness, courage, and decision of character," or negatively as "intractable," "fixed and rigid,"[45] the Indian was represented as a creature stuck with such a timeless identity that his very immutability spelled his doom. Francis Parkman put this most dramatically:

> The Indian is hewn out of a rock. You can rarely change the form without destruction of the substance. Races of inferior energy have possessed a power of expansion and assimilation to which he is a stranger; and it is this fixed and rigid quality which has proved his ruin. He will not learn the arts of civilization, and he and his forest must perish together. The stern, unchanging features of his mind excite our admiration from their very immutability; and we look with deep interest on the fate of this irreclaimable son of the wilderness.[46]

For Parkman the naturalist, "immutability" of identity was a sounder and much more useful argument than the "immutable decree[s]" of fate. Naturalized and internalized, fate now operated within the self as a sort of internal mechanism of doom. Of course, for that doom to come about, Indians would need to be immutable—they would have to be posited as such even if they appeared otherwise—as the "mutable" Cherokees found out when they tried to use their "civilized" way of life as an argument against dispossession.[47] What seems clear, from the example of the Indians, is the extent to which "identity" might be a product of attribution. What seems also clear is the extent to which that process is itself "interest[ed]" in every sense of the word. Identity, for that reason, would seem never to be merely neutral or objective. Harnessed always to meanings and trajectories, its attribution might turn out to be just as fatal as denomination. To be called "immutable" is as good as to be named "Ahab."

Ahab, as it turns out, is not only named Ahab but also

called "immutable." In an uncanny parallel, he seems to have been fashioned out of just those attributes antebellum Americans bestowed on the Indian. In Ahab, Melville tells us, "There was an infinity of firmest fortitude, a determinate, unsurrenderable wilfulness, in the fixed and fearless, forward dedication of that glance" (111). "The path to my fixed purpose is laid with iron rails," Ahab himself says at one point (147). Elsewhere he is said to be "made of solid bronze, and shaped in an unalterable mould" (110). He commands an "iron soul" (438) and an "iron voice" (439); his face is "set like a flint" (369). To Parkman, the Indian seemed "hewn out of a rock"; to Melville, Ahab's very coat appears "stone carved" (438).

The startling correspondence here suggests, once again, not thematic correspondence—not a deliberate decision on Melville's part to make Ahab an allegory of the Indian—but rather the cultural genesis of Ahab and Indians as analogous "characters."[48] Both are generated by a common representational form of the self, one that produces not only literary meanings but also social meanings, and not only fictive casualties but also casualties of flesh and blood. I have referred to that representational form as personification: in a different register, we might also call it negative individualism. In the "persons" of Ahab and the Indians, we see what such a form can do, and why it might be useful. Personification, then, would seem to operate in a much broader domain than we ordinarily think. It is as much a social phenomenon as a literary one. It comes into play both in the "dooming" of Ahab and in the "dooming" of the Indians. It assigns analogous destinies to analogous selves.[49]

The tautology "Ahab is for ever Ahab" functions here not as the syntax of fate then, but as something altogether analogous to it, what we might call the syntax of self. At once subject and predicate, instrument and embodiment of his own misfortune, Ahab stands convicted the moment he is ascribed with a self, the moment he is bound, himself to himself, by "is for ever." The verb here can only be "is," only the present tense, for the syntax of self, like the syntax of fate, invokes a timeless regime, a circuit of identity. Following Lacan, we might say that such an identity is itself the mark of alienation, that it "symbolizes the mental permanence of the *I*, at the same time as it prefigures its alienating destination."[50] That unhappy fate is what afflicts Ahab, and what afflicted the Indians. "Identity," in both cases, would thus seem to be as much a sociopolitical category as a psychoanalytic one. Certainly it has its sociopolitical uses. Negative individualism, the punitive logic based on the autonomous self, cannot operate outside its province.

For the punitive logic must reside in the very identity of selfhood. As a self-contained unit, the self is the seat of agency, we have said, but, as we can also see, such a unit is no less the seat of penalty. Within its circuit of identity, as Ahab and the Indians embody it, the self encapsulates both cause and consequence, both injury and blame. Even as it generates a circuit of closure, the attribution of identity would seem also to generate, in the same process, a circuit of discipline, one that regiments the self, fashions it into the seat of "self-government." This it accomplishes not just by enclosure but equally by exclusion: by marking the self's boundary against a companion domain, that of the "extraneous," posited as outside the self. As we shall see, it is in tandem with this companion category, paradoxically, that the self bodies forth its most powerful punitive logic.

Starbuck gives voice to that logic when he advises Ahab, "let Ahab beware of Ahab; beware of thyself, old man" (394). In a sense, this is merely another way of saying what Ahab has already said about himself—"Ahab is for ever Ahab"—for Starbuck's injunction, too, centers on "Ahab," the all-encompassing, all-responsible individual self. What is striking about Starbuck's formulation, however, is what it manages to exclude, and, in the process of exclusion, where it manages to locate blame. According to Starbuck, Ahab must beware of himself, presumably because he is his own worst enemy. There is no mention here of Moby Dick, no mention of what has been done to Ahab, no mention, in short, of either adversary or antecedent. Relation and temporality alike are excluded in Starbuck's formula for selfhood. Portrayed as such, Ahab indeed has no one to fear but himself, and no one to blame but himself. His fate is a "consequence of [his] stubbornness," his refusal to "quit [his] present pursuits." If this sounds familiar, that is because we have heard it before, in Benjamin Lincoln's indictment of the Indians. Starbuck's indictment of Ahab follows the same logic. The instrument of indictment, in both cases, is the very figure of selfhood, a figure that both encloses and excludes: a tautology, finally, within whose confines one always is what one is.[51] Denied either potentiality in time or relation in space, denied any hope of change or any notion of injustice, the self must bear the full burden of its own condition. It must undertake to doom itself.

What we are witnessing is that most pervasive and persistent of phenomena: the phenomenon of blaming the victim. Starbuck dramatizes the connection between that phenomenon and the institution of "selfhood." It is no accident that the spokesman for "Nantucket market" should be a champion of the autonomous self, no accident that such a self should be exhorted as the seat of agency, and no accident, either, that the same self should be invoked as the grounds for damnation. Starbuck only advises Ahab, "beware of thyself," but he might also have said, "help thyself." The two mottoes go hand in hand. If the latter ushers in the self-reliant entrepreneur, the former dispatches the self-victimizing savage. There is no contradiction here: for self-reliance and self-victimization too are kindred, the freedom of the one making up the fate of the other, the penalty for one being the other's reward. To make the self the seat of agency is to invoke the agency of both.

Even in *Moby-Dick*, we see not just the spectacle of self-victimization but also the spectacle of self-reliance. We see it, quite graphically, in the whale, the proud owner of "thick walls" and "interior spaciousness," who lives "in the world without being of it" (261). We see it, less graphically, in the book named after the whale—or rather, we see it in Melville's image of the book. The image remains ideal, however, for Melville, his dream of freedom notwithstanding, is haunted always by its obverse. Ahab's death is, for that reason, not quite the last word in *Moby-Dick*, and certainly not the last word as Melville goes on to reconsider it in *Pierre*. In that book the doomed savage returns, in logic if not in person, but vengeful as ever. What triumphs in *Pierre* is what is defeated in *Moby-Dick*: genealogy as Ahab imagines it, genealogy as a sequel of reciprocal relations, as the reversal of positions and even the circulation of attributes. For Melville, that is utter nightmare. Something of that horror is already suggested in *Moby-Dick*, in the image of Tashtego, "the submerged savage," extending a "red arm and hammer" in his "death-grasp" to bring down a sky-hawk with "his imperial beak thrust upwards" (469). That image of reciprocity is negated, of course, by the final image of Ishmael, "orphan[ed]" by the catastrophe but surviving all the same as an autonomous self.[52] *Pierre*, whose protagonist is likewise "orphan-like"—indeed, an "infant Ishmael"—will come to very different conclusions.

5. *Knowing the Victim*

"WOULD that all excellent books were found-lings, without father or mother," Melville writes in "Haw-thorne and His Mosses" (1850).[1] It is a vain hope, of course, and nobody is more aware of its vanity than Melville himself, but he is not quite willing to stop hoping either. He wants books in general—other people's books—to be "foundlings," so that he might "glorify them, without including their osten-sible authors."[2] Closer to his heart, however, is probably the status of his own books; and here too he would have liked to see a few "foundlings" as well. It is good to be the author of "foundlings," and perhaps even to be a "foundling" oneself, for that forlorn condition, in Melville's inverted scheme of things, turns out to be the rarest privilege. So rare, in fact, that hardly anyone can claim to have known it. "No one is his own sire," Melville laments to Evert Duyckinck.[3] For him, that deplorable fact sums up the burden, the curse, and the goal of authorship. Not to be one's own sire is to be secondary and derivative: it is to be trapped within a "long line of de-pendencies" (67), in whose "manacled procession" (11) one appears as a mere "product" (67)—part of a genealogy—rather than as an original author and a creative individual.[4] It is not a fate Melville cherishes, and he refuses to be reconciled to it. His dream always is to be "his own sire," to write as a "found-ling" would write, and, through the act of writing, to achieve the distinction of being "without father or mother."

Orphanhood, under this new dispensation, is something of a utopian ideal. Without much exaggeration, we might call it the ideal of literary individualism. In one sense, what Melville wants is commonplace enough: his dream, to put it less fancifully, is simply the dream of originality. Yet there is something odd, all the same, about the analogy he invokes. According to him, originality is somehow comparable to a familial relation—or rather, to the absence of such a relation. To be original is to be "without father or mother," to be outside the province of kinship. A truly original author is related to nobody else and like nobody else. Such a definition of originality makes it at once a measure of where others have failed and an index to where Melville himself might succeed. "The world is forever babbling of originality; but there never yet was an original man" (259), he complains bitterly in *Pierre*. The world has "never yet" seen an original author because no one has dared to be "his own sire"—but (as the qualified negative suggests) Melville is not without hope. An original man might "yet" appear; the author of *Pierre* is one such candidate.

Melville's literary individualism—his desire to be "his own sire," to transcend kinship—obviously has some bearing on *Pierre*, a book equally obsessed with originality, and equally repelled by kinship. We might think of *Pierre*, in fact, as the fictionalization of a literary credo, the narrative enactment of an authorial fantasy. Like *Moby-Dick*, *Pierre* at once practices and thematizes a poetics, embodied and internalized in its protagonist as a way of being. And so Melville's ambition, not surprisingly, turns out also to be Pierre's. Where Melville dreams of becoming "his own sire," Pierre speaks yearningly of a "divine unidentifiableness, that owned no earthly kith or kin" (89). "I will no more have a father," he announces when he discovers (or thinks he discovers) his father's secret (87). Elsewhere he also speaks of his sense of being "doubly an orphan" (90), of "not own[ing] a mortal parent, and spurn[ing] and rend[ing] all mortal bonds" (106). His most memorable utterance, however, is reserved for that equally memorable occasion, the burning of his father's portrait, when he is heard to say: "Henceforth, cast-out Pierre hath no paternity, and no past. . . . therefore, twice-disinherited Pierre stands untrammeledly his ever-present self!—free to do his own self-will and present fancy to whatever end!" (199).

Like Melville, Pierre speaks in the voice of individualism.

He too thinks of orphanhood as a privilege and an achievement, not a condition of loss, but a feat of volition. Unlike Melville, however, for whom orphanhood cannot be anything other than a metaphor, Pierre is free to literalize that metaphor, to stage it and rehearse it, to execute it as policy and to test its limits. Orphanhood, for him, no longer figures only as a rhetorical trope, but beckons as an accessible object, one that dictates its narrative, its discipline, and (not coincidentally) its casualties. To the extent that such a narrative is the narrative of individualism itself, *Pierre* has a great deal indeed to tell us about that phenomenon—about its logic of individual endeavor as well as its logic of individual disposal, both of which the book melodramatically, and methodically, enacts.[5]

Melodrama aside, Pierre's career is more methodical than we might think. Even his desire for orphanhood has a certain contextual rationality to it, for that desire turned out to be something of a cultural preference in nineteenth-century America. With the destruction of the local farm economy, the collapse of the artisan and apprenticeship system, and rapid industrial growth—all of which hastened the breakdown of kinship ties and promoted the notion of individual autonomy—an orphanlike freedom was fast becoming a routine phenomenon.[6] Numerous Americans were benefiting from it, claiming for themselves the right to be unattached, unindebted, unbegotten—to be oneself, to own oneself, to make oneself. In the congregation of single, uprooted men and women in factory towns, metaphoric "orphans" were the rule rather than the exception. What Melville and Pierre celebrate as ideal was already the material reality for many others.

Against this background, against the emergence of the orphanlike individual in antebellum America, I would like to examine *Pierre*. Most frequently read as a psychological novel,[7] the book might also be read—with equal justice, I think—as a historical testimony, an intimate portrait of the most celebrated figure in nineteenth-century America: the "untrammeled . . . ever-present self" (199). *Pierre* will not strike most of us as the story of a self-made man, and yet self-making, in the broadest sense of the word, seems to unite author and protagonist, as one sets about to become "his own sire" and the other proceeds "not [to] own a mortal parent." Both of them would have harkened to Emerson, who, in the "Divinity School Address," has championed the very line of action they now adopt. Anticipating Pierre's desire to become a "heaven-begotten Christ," Emerson has urged his audience to become "a newborn bard of the Holy Ghost."[8] What that means, as he goes on to explain in "Self-Reliance," is a systematic rejection of kinship ties, a rejection even more resolute than Pierre's:

> O father, O mother, O wife, O brother, O friend, I have lived with you after appearances hitherto. Henceforward I am the truth's. Be it known unto you that henceforward I obey no law less than the eternal law. I will have no covenants but proximities. I shall endeavor to nourish my parents, to support my family, to be the chaste husband of one wife,—but these relations I must fill after a new and unprecedented way.[9]

Emerson does not specify what that "unprecedented way" is going to be. Pierre, in his "unprecedented situation" (283), would seem to be supplying the particulars. What makes *Pierre* more extreme (and more revealing) than either the "Divinity School Address" or "Self-Reliance" is just those monstrous particulars, for *Pierre* is, in many ways, a faithful execution of Emerson's counsel—to the point where it will try to enforce as action what Emerson proposes only in hyperbole. If "Self-Reliance" stands as a hymn to individualism, *Pierre*, in its literal-mindedness, will end up being a dirge. Self-making here can no longer be a unitary given, as with Emerson; it will unfold rather as procedure, as a sequence of positions and relations. And the self-made man that we meet will likewise be an evolving figure: he is both the self-made man in the process of being made and, by extension, a candidate for potential unmaking.

From this perspective, it is useful to think of Pierre, the "heaven-begotten Christ," as a not-so-remote ancestor of Jay Gatsby (also "a son of God," in F. Scott Fitzgerald's inspired description). Like Gatsby, Pierre seems to have sprung from what Fitzgerald calls a "Platonic conception of himself."[10] He too wants to be born again: born of himself and unto himself. His orphanhood is a vehicle of that "conception"; he hardly submits to it, it is what he wills. Like Gatsby, Pierre can arrive at an identity only by erasing his genealogy, only by declaring that both his parents are "dead henceforth to me!" (196). Free of kinship, he can then fashion himself into a transcendent entity, autonomous in space and time, an "untrammeled . . . ever-present self" (199).

Melville, in his ambition to be "his own sire," would seem to have something in common with Gatsby as well. Certainly there is something Gatsby-like in his poetics of individualism, in the fate he maps out for the autonomous self, as we have seen in *Moby-Dick*, and as we will see again in *Pierre*. The story of *Pierre*, however, is not meant to be the same story as its predecessor's, but rather the obverse. If it once again summons forth an "untrammeled, ever-present self," that self is now imagined not as a mechanism of doom, but as a nucleus of freedom. Self-making rather than self-victimization is what this book proposes to recount. Turning from *Moby-Dick* to *Pierre*, Melville turns from the negative pole of individualism to its positive term: from the burial ground of the self-victimized, to what Mary Ryan has called the "cradle" of the self-made.[11] *Pierre* both responds to *Moby-Dick* and enlarges upon it: "Leviathan is not the biggest fish;—I have heard of Krakens," Melville confides to Hawthorne.[12]

The last two words in *Moby-Dick*—"another orphan"— nicely serve as the transition from one book to the other. Surviving the wreck of the *Pequod*, the "orphan" from *Moby-Dick* lives on to become the protagonist in Melville's next book, where he gets to have his own story. Even Ishmael's name appears again: Pierre fancies himself, we are told, "driven out an infant Ishmael into the desert, with no maternal Hagar to accompany and comfort him" (89). *Pierre* glosses as structural correlation what appears in *Moby-Dick* merely as anecdotal conjunction. The "submerged savage" and the emerging "orphan," so briefly juxtaposed as the *Pequod* goes down, now appear in *Pierre* as a necessary couple, as the twin products of individualism: its necessary victim and necessary victor. Since

Pierre means only to celebrate the latter, it should have been a happy book, but it most assuredly is not. It winds up, instead, being yet another narrative of doom—which suggests that self-making and self-victimization are by no means two discrete processes, assignable to discrete individuals. Rather, they are functionally cognate, one complementing the other and sometimes becoming the other. Even worse, this complementarity, as we begin to see in *Pierre*, might turn out to be radically asymmetrical, dominated always by its negative term. If so, individualism must work primarily as a punitive logic: it ministers to the self-made far less often than it does to the self-victimized.

Victimization is, in any case, what preoccupies Melville and his hero:

> The family of the Glendinnings was imperiously called upon to offer up a victim to the gods of woe; one grand victim at the least; and that grand victim must be his mother, or himself. If he disclosed his secret to the world, then his mother was made the victim; if at all hazards he kept it to himself, then himself would be the victim. A victim as respecting his mother, because under the peculiar circumstances of the case, the non-disclosure of the secret involved her entire and infamy-engendering misconception of himself. But to this he bowed submissive. (179)

Pierre's "gods of woe" seem to work by much the same logic as "Fate" in *Moby-Dick*: both insist on the necessity of victims. Pierre, responding to that sovereign demand, voluntarily offers himself. The choice, as he sees it, is between victimizing his mother and victimizing himself. Opting for the latter, he bows submissive to his mother's "misconception." But, since this "misconception" actually suits what he wants, since it actually promotes his orphanhood, he is perhaps less of a victim than he suggests. Victimization, however, does seem to be an important issue in this book, and so, like its predecessor, *Pierre* too has a provision for "dismemberment." And the candidates for that fateful operation cannot be more symbolic: they include a relic of Pierre's father, the chair portrait ("dismember[ed]" [198] just before it is burned); and a relic of Pierre's

grandfather, an "ancient dismemberable and portable camp-
bedstead" (270). Such tokens of kinship must be dismembered, for only then can Pierre pronounce himself "doubly an
orphan" (90) and claim for himself an imaginary loss, "as
though both father and mother had gone on distant voyages,
and, returning, died in unknown seas" (90).

Death "in unknown seas" once again underscores the parallel between Pierre's parents and those on the *Pequod*. The
identical fate of the two, and the identity of the executory
instruments, points to an important continuity between
Moby-Dick and *Pierre*, a continuity shaped by the provision for
victimization in both books. Such a provision, as we have seen
in *Moby-Dick*, turns out to be central not only to the logic of
selfhood, but equally to the logic of nationhood. And so
Pierre, in its preoccupation with the "untrammeled" self, will
also end up bearing witness, however obliquely, to the presence of an "untrammeled" nation. In setting and in action,
the book cannot be further removed from the geopolitical
theater, and yet, as we shall see, even at home, even in the
domestic enclave, something like a generalized logic of "Manifest Destiny" would still seem to be at work. Human relations,
in an age of individualism, are perhaps doomed always to be a
frontier drama: of succession and possession, combat and dominion.

Some such logic no doubt accounts for the otherwise inexplicable frontier images in *Pierre*'s domestic landscape. Here,
in the sanctuary of home and family, we nevertheless encounter the "timber man of Canada" (86), the "resting traveler in
snows" (87), "Arctic explorers" (165), the "resolute traveler
in Switzerland" (284), and the "frontier man . . . seized by
wild Indians" (307).[13] Indeed, human relations in *Pierre* are
almost exclusively territorial relations. They have to do with
the "occupan[cy]" (50) of "region[s] of thought" (47) or "region[s] of [the] heart" (46), with alien "encroach[ment]" (49),
with the "dislodging" (50) and "displacing" (129) of one occupant by another. Pierre, for instance, informs Lucy that he
means to have "unchallenged possession of thee . . . for my
inalienable fief" (36). Being possessed, however, is what ac-

tually happens to him, for at the sight of Isabel, he himself is transformed into occupied terrain: "He felt that what he had always before considered the solid land of veritable reality, was now being audaciously encroached upon by bannered armies of hooded phantoms, disembarking in his soul, as from flotillas of specter-boats" (49). He rallies, however, and "with the hue-and-cry of his whole indignant soul, pursued them forth again into the wide Tartarean realm from which they had emerged" (138). For a while the thought of Lucy "dislodg[es] thence all such phantom occupants" (50). But that victory does not last, and presently Pierre finds himself once again under "vassalage to his original sensations" (52). At this juncture, Isabel's "sovereign power" (189) is such that "no veto of the earth" can "forbid her heavenly claim" (173) (although that does not stop Lucy, later in the story, from being an "untraceable displacing agency" [338]). In short, occupancy and dispossession, the drama of empire, also make up the domestic drama in *Pierre*.

In this geopolitical theater, love appears, appropriately enough, as a colonizing force. It is daily expanding its domain, daily exterminating the "wolves" and "panther[s]" of this world, as Melville explains in this astonishing passage:

> Time and space can not contain Love's story. . . . Love made not the Arctic zones, but Love is ever reclaiming them. Say, are not the fierce things of this earth daily, hourly going out? Where now are your wolves of Britain? Where in Virginia now, find you the panther and the pard? Oh, Love is busy everywhere. Everywhere Love hath Moravian missionaries. No Propagandist like to Love. The south wind wooes the barbarous north; on many a distant shore the gentler west wind persuaded the arid east. (34)

Melville is perhaps wrong to characterize as "gentle" the "west wind [that] persuaded the arid east" in the mid-nineteenth century. (The Opium War, after all, had just been waged and won by the British in 1842, making Hong Kong the first of the British colonies in China.) But his account of Love is certainly a good summary of the workings of imperialism. As "the world's great redeemer and reformer" (34), Love gets rid of the "wolves" and "panther[s]," not by brute force, but by "reclaim[ing]" them and assimilating them into its domain, by converting them out of existence. It is not for nothing that Love has both "emigrates" (34) and "missionaries" (34), for, like the great colonial powers whose mantle it inhabits, Love needs both kinds of "emissaries" (34)—the ones to do the occupying as well as the ones to do the converting—before it can accomplish its historic task of "reclaiming" the "barbarous."

The labors of imperialism might seem a peculiar metaphor for the labors of Love. Within the logic of *Pierre*, however, such a metaphor is not only appropriate, but inevitable. For to the extent that the book honors the autonomous self—to the extent that it imagines that self as a discrete entity, self-contained and self-possessed—it must also entertain the obverse of that logic: the self operating not as a field of possession but as a field of dispossession, not a field of sovereignty but a field of combat, encroachment, alien occupation. To push the point further, we might even say that, to invoke such a construct as the "self" is already to spatialize identity, to imagine a site, or a receptacle, for a collection of attributes—a site that can be demarcated, set apart from other sites, and owned, on that basis, as "property." The Lockean model of selfhood is perhaps inevitably a territorial one. And if this human cartography underwrites Blackstone's confident belief that the right of property is a "sole and despotic dominion," it must equally inspire the fear that this "dominion" would be usurped, encroached upon, appropriated by alien powers. A self owned by oneself might also end up being owned by somebody else. To make ownership the constitutive essence of selfhood is already to commit the self to a theater of eternal warfare, in which everyone, operating as a personified battlefield, is ceaselessly invaded and defended, possessed and dispossessed.

C. B. Macpherson, commenting on Hobbes's model of selfhood, makes just this point. A society of "possessive individualism," he argues, "permits and requires the continual invasion of every man by every other."[14] The self that inhabits such a society must be an "imperial" self then: in its defensive pose no less than in its appropriative venture, it must act like an imperial polity. From this perspective, there is nothing fortuitous about the presence of Manifest Destiny in *Pierre,* and nothing decorative about its allusions to empire. Those allusions describe, on the contrary, both the structure of its "untrammeled" self and the structure of the environment that dictates to the self its particular shape. The imperial trappings of Love, especially, have everything to do with the "internalization" of Manifest Destiny, with the constitution of the self as a "dominion," a terrain subject to sovereignty and expropriation both.

This does not completely explain the action of Love, however. For if the self does indeed operate as an empire, and if Love regularly sends out "emigrates" and "missionaries" to capture that empire, what do those agents actually do, and how are we to measure the success of their takeover attempts? Melville comes closest to giving an answer, I think, in the following passage, one that presents the empire of the self in graver peril than anything we have seen before:

> Sudden onsets of new truth will assail him, and overturn him as the Tartars did China; for there is no China Wall that man can build in his soul, which shall permanently stay the irruptions of those barbarous hordes which Truth ever nourishes in the loins of her frozen, yet teeming North; so that the Empire of Human Knowledge can never be lasting in any one dynasty, since Truth still gives new Emperors to the earth. (167)

Melville is speaking here, admittedly, not of Love but of Truth, and the invaders show up as "barbarous hordes" rather than as "emigrates" (34) and "missionaries" (34). Still, the paradigm of invasion and occupation is much the same here as in the earlier account of Love. What makes this passage especially interesting, for our purposes, is its dramatization of a previously undisclosed term, "Knowledge," held forth not only as a qualifying appendage to "Empire" but, to a large degree, as its governing attribute. For the self here turns out to be not just any "empire," but a rather special one. Melville calls it the "Empire of Human Knowledge." Such an empire is by definition short-lived, he tells us, because it is continually besieged and beset by the "barbarous hordes" of Truth, which will over-run its defenses just as surely as the Tartars overran the China Wall.

This might seem an odd account of the conduct of Truth, but even odder is the topography it maps forth, for what is suggested here is an implicit separation, and indeed an implicit opposition, between two terms not usually considered antag-onistic: Truth and Knowledge. If Truth is imagined as the in-vader, the self's enemy, Knowledge is imagined, strangely enough, as the self's defense. Knowledge is what fortifies the self, what makes it an empire in the first place. But there is also a sense that such knowledge can never be permanent, for Truth is always trying to reclaim it, always trying to turn it over to some other "new Emperors"—which is why the "Em-pire of Human Knowledge can never be lasting in one dy-nasty." In short (if we change the metaphor a bit), Knowledge seems to be the local property in a global economy of which Truth is the supreme dispenser, and as local property it is con-stantly subject to redistribution, with disastrous consequences for its original owner. The battle for Knowledge, then, is al-ways a battle between the incumbent and the aspiring, a pro-prietary battle at once ruthless and inevitable.

The logic of "knowing" in *Pierre*, being a geopolitical logic, presupposes not only its supremacy but also its territorial im-perative. We ordinarily associate such a model not with Mel-ville but with James (*The Golden Bowl* comes immediately to mind), but in *Pierre* something analogous is already in place.[15] It is just such a territorial imperative that compels Lucy to de-mand from Pierre his "unbounded confidence":

> "[C]ould I ever think, that thy heart hath yet one private nook or corner from me;—fatal disenchanting day for me, my Pierre, would that be. I tell thee, Pierre—and 'tis Love's own self that now speaks through me—only in unbounded confidence and in-terchangings of all subtlest secrets, can Love possibly endure. Love's self is a secret, and so feeds on secrets, Pierre. Did I only know of thee, what the whole common world may know—what then were Pierre to me? Thou must be wholly a disclosed secret

to me; Love is vain and proud, and when I walk the streets, and
meet thy friends, I must still be laughing and hugging to myself
the thought,—They know him not;—I only know my Pierre;—
none else beneath the circuit of yon sun." (37)

Lucy wants to know Pierre, to know him as "wholly a disclosed
secret." She cannot tolerate even "one private nook or corner"
unknown to her. Her metaphor spatializes Pierre, quite logically, I think, for it is only as a kind of human terrain that
Pierre can be thus surveyed and possessed by her. Not unlike
Elijah in *Moby-Dick*, Lucy has nothing but scorn for "what the
whole common world may know." She wants only that knowledge that will give her an exclusive title to her beloved, that
will enable her to say, "They know him not;—I only know my
Pierre."

Knowledge, as Lucy defines it and demands it, is obviously
a sign of proprietorship. Even more importantly, it is also a
sign of victory over rival claimants: what Lucy wants is not
only that she should know "my Pierre," but also that "they"
should "know him not." Like its more famous progeny in *The
Confidence-Man*, "unbounded confidence" operates here in
complementarity, by generating two opposed yet related positions: triumphant knowledge on the one hand, abject ignorance on the other. For the value of confiding lies ultimately
not in what it has to impart, but in whom it manages to exclude. It operates less as a substantive than as a dative: it is
always directed against someone else, someone denied confidence. Confidence constitutes itself, in fact, in the very act of
exclusion—the partners in confidence are partners precisely
because somebody else is in the dark. This complementary
logic makes inequity a structural requisite in the battle for
knowledge. It also makes "confidence" the property of an exclusive owner.

Lucy fails in her plea (at this point in the story) for just that
reason. Pierre cannot give her what she wants, because that
desired article, "unbounded confidence," is already in somebody else's possession. Mrs. Glendinning is the happy owner
of it. Between her and Pierre, Melville tells us, a "perfect con-

fidence" (5) prevails. Knowing her son perfectly, Mrs. Glendinning, not surprisingly, also finds him docile: "My dear boy—the fine, proud, loving, docile, vigorous boy!—the loftyminded, well-born, noble boy; and with such sweet docilities!" (20). Unfortunately for her, however, neither her son's "confidence," nor his "docilities," are meant to last. With Isabel's appearance, Pierre is immediately moved to stop confiding in his mother: to "parry, nay, to evade, and, in effect, to return something alarmingly like a fib" (50). He worries that he has become "a falsifyer—ay, a falsifyer and nothing less—to his own dearly-beloved, and confiding mother" (51). Still, he has no wish to make amends. Indeed, after his first lapse he will never again tell Mrs. Glendinning what she wants to know. Isabel's entrance, in short, has "give[n] eternal exit to all confidence between him and his mother" (96).

The son's action is felt equally keenly by Mrs. Glendinning. She knows what is being taken away from her, and pointedly demands it back:

> "I feel, I know, that thou art deceiving me;—perhaps I erred in seeking to wrest thy secret from thee; but believe me, my son, I never thought thou hadst any secret thing from me, except thy first love for Lucy—and that, my own womanhood tells me, was most pardonable and right. But now, what can it be? Pierre, Pierre! consider well before thou determinest upon withholding confidence from me. I am thy mother. It may prove a fatal thing. Can that be good and virtuous, Pierre, which shrinks from a mother's knowledge? Let us not loose hands so, Pierre; thy confidence from me, mine goes from thee." (96)

Mrs. Glendinning is of course making the same plea that Lucy has made earlier, a plea for "unbounded confidence." Unlike Lucy, however, she is asking for something she has once been privileged to enjoy. That privilege is now behind her. Mrs. Glendinning herself makes this ironically clear at her last meeting with her son: "Pierre, thou thyself hast denied me thy confidence, and thou shalt not force me back to it so easily" (185), she tells him. But the point, of course, is that Pierre has no desire to "force [her] back to it." Her reign, the reign of "a mother's knowledge," has already drawn to a close. As Melville says, "the Empire of Human Knowledge can never be lasting in any one dynasty" (167).

Mrs. Glendinning is, in this sense, as doomed as Ahab. Her destiny is as manifest as his. That destiny appears, in fact, in the shape of her own son, for even as Pierre evades his mother's knowledge, she becomes in turn a subject of his knowing. Knowing her, he condemns what he now perceives to be her true character. She is "no longer this all-alluring thing" she once was (89). She is "a noble creature, but formed chiefly for the gilded prosperities of life" (89), he sums her up with not a little contempt. He sees through even her love for him, for in "her most caressing love, there ever gleamed some scaly, glittering folds of pride" (90). In short, in "knowing" his mother, Pierre is already dismissing her, condemning her, denying all that she once was to him. Not accidentally, at this juncture he also announces that this experience "doth rob me even of my mother; thus doth make me now doubly an orphan" (90). Pierre speaks of being "robbed" of his mother, but since orphanhood is what he has always wanted—since his goal has always been "not [to] own a mortal parent" (106)—we can hardly credit him with the passivity he claims. And indeed, the son is an "orphan" only in his own mind, since Mrs. Glendinning is quite alive at this point. She is dead, however, as far as he is concerned. His knowledge of her has done her in. "Wonderful indeed," as Melville says, is "that electric insight which Fate had now given him into the vital character of his mother" (89).

Melville is right to speak of Pierre's insight as an "electric" insight, for power—electric power in the concrete, other forms of power in the abstract—is very much an issue here. For one thing, this electric insight has enabled the son to achieve something like a generational reversal: he has effectively reduced his mother from a parent to a product. As he explains, "not his mother had made his mother; but the Infinite Haughtiness had first fashioned her" (90). Mrs. Glendinning is no longer a mother, she has not even made herself. Instead she has been cast into the role of the "made": she is fashioned by

"Infinite Haughtiness." Her son, conversely, can now stop being her son: he has instead become her maker, the author of her true character. Pierre's "electric insight" is primarily an instrument of dominion, then. Pushing Melville's conceit a little further, we might even speak of this "electric insight" as an instrument of execution. It discharges its duty not only by transfixing its victim but also by fixing her, turning her into a still life, a frozen emblem of "Infinite Haughtiness," a damning attribute in human guise.

Using a different vocabulary, we might also speak of this procedure as the work of personification. For what fixes Mrs. Glendinning, what makes her dead to her own son, turns out to be her constitution as a personified attribute. Here she personifies "Haughtiness." Elsewhere (in a slight variation on the same theme) she personifies "pride." And in the rest of the story we continue to hear about her "curled and haughty beauty" (90), her "haughty temper" (179), her "haughty heart" (179). We are shown "the before unthought of edifice of his mother's immense pride;—her pride of birth, her pride of affluence, her pride of purity, and all the pride of high-born, refined, and wealthy Life, and all the Semiramian pride of woman" (89). In short, she becomes the receptacle of an attribute. Melville refers to this attribute as her "vital character" (89), but there is really nothing "vital" about it: it could have served as her epitaph. Pierre is quite right to credit "Haughtiness" with the power to "fashion" (90) and to "mold" (90) (not to say to "finish"), for personification is indeed the means by which he "makes" his mother—makes her into something he can both know and reject.

Like *Moby-Dick*, *Pierre* uses personification as a lethal weapon, one that creates "persons" out of attributes and dooms these "persons" on the basis of just those attributes. As a doomed person—or rather, a doomed attribute—Mrs. Glendinning is exactly analogous to Ahab. Like him, she is imaged as an ancient relic, and convicted as such.[16] She is lucky in not having a name like his—she escapes, at least, the fate of a personified name. However, as a personified attribute, she most certainly finds herself in his sad company. The two are alike not only genetically but also teleologically. Both are generated as bearers of attributes, and both must submit to the dictates of those attributes. Both must carry out, to the bitter end, the destiny that is already inscribed within themselves.

Abab and Mrs. Glendinning are overdetermined victims, for what eventually happens to them is really legible from the very beginning. Their narrative is the narrative of destiny. But if so, that narrative is logically also a narrative of selfhood, for as we have seen, "destiny" in the nineteenth century actually works better as a naturalized category, as the immutable dictates of "character." One's destiny is always oneself. And that, in fact, is what Mrs. Glendinning comes to realize. "Right one's self against another, that, one may sometimes do," she muses, "but when that other is one's own self, these ribs forbid" (131). She does not go on to say, "Mary is for ever Mary," but that fateful tautology might have been hers as much as Ahab's, for in her case too, as she freely admits, one's worst enemy is always "one's own self." Just like Ahab, Mrs. Glendinning is doomed by a manifest destiny, legible in what she is. No Elijah or Gabriel shows up to proclaim that destiny, it is true, but she has an even more formidable prophet in her own son, who, with every confidence, is already calling himself "doubly an orphan." What makes Pierre so sure is his reading knowledge of his mother. Because he knows her—because he has even made her into the personified attribute that she now is—he also knows that, in good time, she will become a "sad victim . . . in the ground" (286).[17]

Like *Moby-Dick*, *Pierre* inscribes a logic of victimization in the act of personification. The relation between those two processes is even more sharply focused here, for *Pierre* has now dramatized the mediating term between them. "Knowledge," that mediating term, is what personification permits, and what victimization requires. To become a "sad victim" one must first of all be known, and to be known one must be fashioned into a personified attribute. The knowable subject—the self that can be identified, summarized, and dismissed—is what occupies the common ground between personification and victimization: he is produced by the one, dispatched by the other.

Mrs. Glendinning shows how this works, but the fate of being known, of being personified and victimized, is by no means hers alone. Indeed, an even better example of that fate can be found in Lucy Tartan, who virtually begs to be known. "What secret thing keep I from thee? Read me through and through. I am entirely thine," she urges Pierre (40). And read her Pierre did: she is "fond, all understood" (129).

Lucy is a known quantum, just like Mrs. Glendinning. Unlike the older woman, however, she embodies not a specific instance of personification, but rather its operation in the abstract. She appears, that is, not as personified "Haughtiness," but simply as a "sign": "For the real Lucy, [Pierre], in his scheming thoughts, had substituted but a sign—some empty x—and in the ultimate solution of the problem, that empty x still figured; not the real Lucy" (181). As an unadorned sign, an "empty x," Lucy dramatizes the act of personification at its starkest and least ceremonious. Pierre has made her, in this case, not even into a personified attribute, but simply into an integer. In that skeletal form, we see the extent to which the making of Lucy is also the unmaking of her. For the constitution of Lucy as an "empty x" is of course what enables Pierre to "know" her, to dispose of her as sign, and to greet her with the following words: "Thou indeed art fitted for the altar; but not that one of which thy fond heart dids't dream:—so fair a victim!" (183).

Victimization, as it is performed on both Mrs. Glendinning and Lucy, involves not only the eventual subjection of the self but also the initial constitution of the self. Both women have to be given a knowable identity before they can be dispatched to their respective victimhood. *Pierre* would seem, from this perspective, to illustrate exactly Foucault's contention about the production of knowledge and the production of individuality in the nineteenth century. A knowable identity, Foucault suggests, is the mark of the Other, the mark of the supervised and the subordinated. Mrs. Glendinning and Lucy, attributed with their respective identities, known and victimized as such, demonstrate just that point. But to discern a Foucauldean dynamics in *Pierre* is not just to promote a particular interpretation of the book. It is also to restore to it a context and a history. Instead of reading *Pierre* as the highly idiosyncratic performance by a highly idiosyncratic author (as most of us are wont to do), we might read it instead as a social text, obsessed but no less representative. For the obsessed drama that emerges from the book—the drama of wanting to know and the plight of being known—ultimately registers a historical phenomenon: the emergence, organization, and deployment of knowledge as a technology of control, a technology at once consonant with and intrinsic to the institution of individualism.

Along these lines, it would be helpful to read *Pierre* in the company of Foucault's *Discipline and Punish*, or David Rothman's classic study of social control in America, *The Discovery of the Asylum*.[18] To my mind, however, the best background to *Pierre* is a rather unlikely text—the 1830 Reports on the Course of Instruction in Yale College, jointly written by James Kingsley and Jeremiah Day, president of Yale. This document, an effort to implement the doctrine of "superintendence," outlines a program of "college government" regulated by two terms Melville would have recognized: "mutual affection and confidence." The ensuing passage offers an interesting gloss to the drama of knowledge in *Pierre*:

> In the internal police of the institution, as the students are gathered into one family, it is deemed an essential provision, that some of the officers should constitute a portion of this family; being always present with them, not only at their meals, and during the business of the day; but in the hours allotted to rest. The arrangement is such, that in our college buildings, there is no room occupied by students, which is not near to the chamber of one of the officers . . .
>
> The tutor of a division has an opportunity, which is enjoyed by no other officer of the college, of becoming intimately acquainted with the characters of his pupils. It is highly important that this knowledge should be at the command of the faculty. By distributing our family among different individuals, minute information

is acquired, which may be communicated to the Board, whenever it is called for. [19]

In the "internal police" of Yale College in 1830, we encounter, oddly enough, many of the measures we are later to encounter in *Pierre*. Here too, knowing was a strategic necessity, and here too, "knowledge" required as its subject not the student body as a whole, but the student body as atomized units. Students had to be known as "individuals" and known "intimately," their "characters" had to be ascertained, every "minute information" about them collected and filed away. The production of knowledge, at Yale as well as in *Pierre*, was inseparable from the production of individuals, and both processes were central to what Jeremiah Day and James Kingsley aptly called a system of "internal police," a system that policed the "intimate." As Day and Kingsley saw it, this was what made Yale College a "family."

That *Pierre* too should locate its drama of knowledge within the family is all too logical. For the nineteenth-century family, as Day and Kingsley invoked it, was the primary site for the production of knowable identities, and therefore also the primary model for any secondary attempt at "internal police." What Jacques Donzelot calls "government through the family" in France seemed to have a solid parallel in America as well. [20] In the context of *Pierre* it is especially useful to examine the nineteenth-century family, for the operating terms in Melville's novel—knowledge, empire, and the self—also happened to be the terms antebellum Americans invoked when they discussed the character and function of the family. One such exposition, *Domestic Education* (1840), written by Heman Humphrey (a graduate of Yale and later the president of Amherst College), offers a particularly good example of how and why those terms might work together.

"Every family," Humphrey wrote, "is a little state, or empire within itself, bound together by the most endearing attractions, and governed by its patriarchal head." [21] The allusion to "empire" was not merely rhetorical here, for according to Humphrey, a rigorous "domestic policy" turned out to be essential for America's imperial longevity. Because the "bayonet of the Czar and the scimitar of the Sultan" were not America's to have, the nation must come up with an alternative instrument, one that would enable it not only "to make a single good subject," but also "to tame them and keep them in subjection." Toward that end Humphrey had this to propose:

> Children must be prepared to reverence the majesty of the laws, and to yield a prompt obedience to the civil magistrate, by habitual subjection to their parents. If they are not governed in the family, they will be restive under all the wholesome and necessary restraints of after life. . . . I repeat, therefore, that if it is important to secure a prompt obedience to the wholesome laws of the state, then is family government indispensably necessary.[22]

Family government and national government, for Humphrey, were one and the same. If the former served as an arm of the latter, the latter in turn served as a model. The two were, in any case, reciprocal, mutually entailed and mutually sustaining. Humphrey's reference to the family as an "empire within itself" made perfect sense, for not only was the family structured like an empire, it was also instrumental for the workings of empire. Its explicit duty was to reproduce within its domestic precincts the "wholesome laws of the state." Those wholesome laws were designed, of course, to govern the individual, the one who had to be made into a "good subject," and to secure that outcome the family was indeed "indispensably necessary," for the individual could not be governed more effectively anywhere else—indeed he could not be governed any other way. As Humphrey explained, "Without family government there will be very little self-government."[23]

As the seat of "self-government," the family would seem to be the disciplinary arm of empire. Here, the self was to be "tamed" and "subjected," as Humphrey said. Yet discipline was by no means the sole duty of the nineteenth-century family, nor was its association with empire always in Humphrey's sense. Henry C. Wright had a very different meaning in mind, for instance, when he coined the phrase "the empire of the mother." So did Horace Mann when he spoke reverently of "the empire of Home—the most important of empires," where the woman "must enrobe herself in the shining garments of Knowledge and Love."[24] For both Wright and Mann, as indeed for most authors of domestic literature in the 1850s, the family figured as an empire, not because it was meant to enforce the "wholesome laws of the state," but for the opposite reason. Refuge, rather than discipline, was what these advocates would like the family to represent. Against the heartless turmoil of the outside world, the "fluctating state of our population, the alterations in commercial affairs, the sudden and unexpected reversals of fortune," the family was to stand as a haven of love, purity, harmony. As the advertisers of suburban housing said, everyone should try to make "a little world of the home, where truthfulness, beauty, and order have the largest domain." In short, the family, in the domestic writings of the mid-nineteenth century, was charged also with the production of freedom: freedom from fluctuation, aggression, corruption. It was to be "a sanctum where the world has no right to intrude."[25]

Invoked simultaneously as a realm of control and a realm of freedom, an instrument of empire and a refuge of sentiment, the nineteenth-century family might seem hopelessly torn between two contrary representations. It would be a mistake, however, to try to choose between the two accounts, for the most significant fact about them, it seems to me, is precisely their doubleness. The discourse about the family cannot be anything but double, for the construct that it is made to subserve—the individual that it simultaneously disciplines and pampers—is itself a double entity. At once empire unto others and empire unto itself, self-made and self-governed, the autonomous self is, in its very constitution, already an animated polarity. The family, in administering to that self, is simply replaying its polarity on a different register. The family is thus especially useful as an index to individualism, for in the glaringly contrary accounts of its function, we see, magnified and foregrounded, the not always so glaring contradictions of individualism. In the double discourse about the family, both the freedom of the imperial self and the fate of the imperial subject find their suitable representations.

The discourse about the family has something to tell us about *Pierre* as well, for if this double discourse registered the contradictions of individualism, so too does Melville's book. Between its philosophical commitment to the "untrammeled" self on the one hand, and its structural need for "sad victim[s]" on the other, *Pierre* too is propelled by a double logic, an uneasy engagement with both the positive and the negative poles of individualism. Like the family it invokes as setting, *Pierre* also has two stories to recount, two destinies to map out for the autonomous self. We have been concerned, so far, primarily with the story of self-making—with Pierre's attempt to "own no earthly kith or kin" (89). But even the most cursory reading of the book must suggest that there is another story, one that proceeds not from Pierre, but from the "earthly kith or kin" he would like to disown. And if Pierre's freedom is measured by the banishment of that "kith or kin," his fate must be measured by the return of the same.

The very presence of "kith or kin" in *Pierre* would seem to suggest a negative pole of individualism in the book. If that is indeed true, the "self" Melville celebrates might turn out, after all, not to be a figure of freedom, not the untrammeled self of "Self-Reliance," but its hapless counterpart, the self to be "policed" and "known," "tamed" and "subjected." Jeremiah Day, James Kingsley, and Heman Humphrey—rather than Emerson—might prove to be the ghostly monitors in *Pierre*. In any case, it is in their spirit that I would like to return to the book, to the other story of individualism, of the self's "government." For Melville, that unhappy story can take only one form. If the self, in its freedom, has hoped to "own no kith or kin," in its subjection it is allowed nothing else.

In the rest of the chapter, I discuss Pierre's ordeal in just those terms: as the self's subjection in kinship. That ordeal, I further suggest, is not so much a thematic development as a structural necessity. The very logic of individualism demands it, for the imperial self cannot exist, after all, without an imperial casualty, its functional partner and identical twin.

Pierre cannot become the one without being related to the other, without being, in some sense, just like the other. If he has so far appeared different—if he has so far operated as an "untrammeled self," rather than as a "sad victim" like his mother, or like Lucy—the fate of the others will eventually catch up with him. It will show up, in fact, as a constitutive provision within himself, for what happens to them is already inscribed in him, in the structure of likeness that makes him their reluctant "kith or kin." Some intimation of this logic emerges early in the book, in an oddly graphic passage that supposedly portrays Pierre's father but ends up portraying Pierre himself, a portrait of bizarre kinship:

> There had long stood a shrine in the fresh-foliaged heart of Pierre, up to which he ascended by many tableted steps of remembrance. . . . this shrine was of marble—a niched pillar, deemed solid and eternal, and from whose top radiated all those innumerable sculptured scrolls and branches, which supported the entire one-pillared temple of his moral life; as in some beautiful gothic oratories, one central pillar, trunk-like, upholds the roof. In this shrine, in this niche of this pillar, stood the perfect marble form of his departed father; without blemish, unclouded, snow-white, and serene; Pierre's fond personification of perfect human goodness and virtue. (68)

"Personification," in this case, has the effect of constituting the self as a "perfect marble form." For the moment, this marble form is a receptacle for "perfect human goodness and virtue," but its reified status suggests that it might one day be reduced to "prostrated ruins" (69)—which is of course what happens soon enough. This fate, at first glance, would seem reserved only for the father. Unfortunately for Pierre, however, he turns out, on this occasion, to be all too literally his father's son. For he too is "of marble": he is the marble "shrine" that houses his father's "marble form." The son is really a chip of the old block. What unites the two is not just their material composition either, for their very structures of selfhood coincide. Like his father, Pierre seems to have inherited a reified shape—he is a "shrine," no less. But if so, the fate of "prostrated ruins" would seem equally to await him.

That fate, to put it another way, is simply the fate of personification itself. Neither Pierre nor his father can escape it, for personification, as I have tried to describe it, is the very process by which selves are constituted: a process that invests attributes as well as narratives within spatialized entities. The kinship between father and son resides in just that fact: both are personified into being, both are bearers of attributes, and (more pertinent here) both are receptacles for destinies. A more extreme version of this process we have seen earlier in Ahab, just as we have seen it in Mrs. Glendinning and in Lucy. Now we see it in Pierre himself. Nor is this the only instance when it happens to him, for Pierre appears regularly and quite literally as a human receptacle throughout much of the book. On this occasion he happens to be a marble "shrine"; elsewhere we hear about the "warm halls of [his] heart" (71), the "corners of [his] conviction" (71), his "life's muzzle" (107), the "many chambers" in his "noble heart" (156), and the "profoundest vault of his soul" (286). In each of these instances, Pierre appears not only spatialized but altogether reified. In that capacity, he resembles exactly those he would disown, for their destiny—the destiny of the reified, of prospective "ruins"—is no less his, and no less constitutive of his being. Personification, it seems, can fashion the self in only one way, and, with a logic at once imperial and impartial, it seems to spare no one. It permits only "kith or kin" in its domain.

Kinship—involuntary kinship, kinship as a structural dictate—obviously bodes ill for Pierre's future. His most significant (and most ominous) kinship, however, is not with his father, but with Isabel. More than anyone else, Isabel resembles Pierre, or rather, she anticipates him. As an orphan who "never knew a mortal mother" (114), and whose paternity remains unrevealed to the end, Isabel has already achieved what Pierre is still striving for. She does not need to devise a program, as Pierre does, of "spurn[ing] and rend[ing] all mortal bonds" (168), for she seems to have none to begin with. In her apparently unbegotten selfhood, we see the privileged term of individualism in its naturalized form. Not surprisingly, she also occupies the most enviable place in *Pierre*'s hierarchy of human positions. She is the unknown, unknowable figure in a book in which to be known is to be a victim. "Enigmatical obscurity" (136) seems to be the very ground of Isabel's being. She is "unfathomable" (153), the mistress of "wonderful enigmas" (138). Her "clew-defying mysteriousness" (137) approaches the "unravelable inscrutableness of God" (141). This is what Pierre notices, and what attracts him to her. "Oh! wretched vagueness—too familiar to me, yet inexplicable,— unknown, utterly unknown!" he complains ecstatically (41). Faced with this "dumb, beseeching countenance of mystery" (52), Pierre has only one desire. "But go on, and tell me every thing and any thing. I desire to know all, Isabel" (145), he says almost piteously at one point. He dare not dream of complete knowledge, however. Isabel is a "dark-lantern" (141), which he has "renounced all thought of ever having . . . illuminated to him" (141).

Isabel's lack of identity raises the hope that there might, after all, be a privileged position in *Pierre*, where one could be different, superior, unique, where one could indeed "own no earthly kith or kin." Yet, as the metaphor "dark lantern" suggests, Isabel's privilege is altogether transient, for a lantern, momentarily "dark," might nonetheless be lit in due course. Indeed, to be a "lantern" at all, Isabel would seem already to be some kind of human receptacle, some article of Pierre's making. In form if not in substance, she is no different from the other human receptacles—Mr. Glendinning's "marble form," for example—and her fate might not be as unique as we hope. As a "dark lantern," she cannot fail to invite what Mrs. Glendinning has already received in abundance: the agency of Pierre's knowledge, his all-powerful, all-annihilating "electric insight" (89).

The process of illumination begins, appropriately enough, with Pierre's discovery that, "against the wall of the thick darkness of the mystery of Isabel, recorded as by some phosphoric finger, was the burning fact, that Isabel was [Pierre's] sister" (170). Pierre's electric insight takes the form, in this case, of a "phosphoric finger," which reveals a "burning fact" about Isabel. What that "burning fact" amounts to, in plainer language, is simply a new identity for Isabel—she is now Pierre's sister—and the forging of this new selfhood permits her brother "to own her boldly and lovingly" (170). The pun "to own" is very much to the point here, for if by "owning" his sister Pierre means to acknowledge her, what he seems also to be doing is to possess her, to claim her as his own. He is able to do that because he now "knows" her to be his sister. In short, in illuminating Isabel, Pierre bestows on her an identity. Knowing that identity, he owns her as his sister and, in the same gesture, terminates her orphanhood. And so, Isabel's privileged existence quickly comes to an end. Unknown and unowned as the book begins, she ends up being known and owned by her "all-acknowledging brother" (113).

We have spoken earlier of the "internalization" of Manifest Destiny in *Pierre*: the constitution of the self as a site to be possessed and dispossessed. In Isabel's fate—the fate of a "dark lantern," destined to be lit up sooner or later by her brother's "electric insight"—we see the same logic at work. More so than any other character's, Isabel's "identity" here is clearly a construct, summoned forth only to provide a field of appropriation, only to promote the cause of an alien claimant and to facilate ownership by someone else.[26] The drama of empire, once again, has a domestic edition, as selves invade one another in battles no less fierce. What transpires between Pierre and Isabel, however, is more complicated than just a drama of appropriation, for inscribed in it is still another activity, one whose connection with empire might merit some scrutiny.

Isabel points to this activity when she expresses gratitude to Pierre for what he has done to her. "This strange, mysterious, unexampled love between us, makes me all plastic in thy hand" (189), she tells him. Somewhat later she puts the case even more dramatically: "Thy hand is the caster's ladle, Pierre, which holds me entirely fluid. Into thy forms and slightest moods of thought, thou pourest me; and I there solidify to that form, and take it on, and thenceforth wear it, till once more thou moldest me anew" (324). According to Isabel, then, Pierre seems to have been the most marvelous of reformers: he has taken his "plastic" sister into his hands, guided her and "molded" her, giving her a new "form" in the end. Nineteenth-century reformers would have recognized the language, and they would have envied Pierre for his accomplishments, for "molding" and "forming" the human character were their ambitions as well. In that endeavor they were especially encouraged by the "plastic" material they claimed to find among children. "We are then like plaster, prepared by the molder, soft and impressible, taking forms and images from every thing we may chance to touch," Samuel Goodrich wrote, uncannily anticipating Isabel's account of her own experience in Pierre's hands.[27] Pierre, predictably then, also thinks of Isabel as a "child of everlasting youngness" (140), and speaks repeatedly of her "singular infantileness" (140), the "artless infantileness of her face" (140), not to say her "angelic childlikeness" (140). As such evocations suggest, what unfolds between them is in many ways analogous to an encounter between the reformer and the reformed: between the desire to "form" and "mold" on one side, and the "childlike" "plasticity" on the other.

In itself, the logic of reform is not especially remarkable. What is remarkable here, however, is the partnership it seems to have entered into, and the ease with which it does so. For what Isabel embodies, in her malleable, alienable identity, is a strange (though by now not altogether unexpected) alliance—between the logic of empire and the logic of reform. In her dual capacity, as a sister to be "owned" and as a child to be "formed," she offers herself as the theater for both. She is the fantasy of the reformer: a "plastic" body capable of being "mold[ed] anew." She is also the fantasy of the colonizer: a human virgin land for him to "own." The duality of interests here, collected in Isabel's curiously accommodating person, points once again to the twin uses of the "self," to its functional centrality both in a geopolitical theater and in a social polity. For if Jacksonian expansionists operated by invoking the "self" as a strategic category—by constituting the Indians as personified Property—so too did nineteenth-century reformers. Singling out the individual as both problem and cure, both the seat of malaise and the vehicle of regeneration, antebellum reformers were among the ablest strategists in the institutionalization of the self.[28] In that capacity they seem remotely to supplement the expansionists, nourishing in America's civil society what the expansionists were busily producing on the frontier. Thus, it is something of a historical conjunction that we witness in Isabel's person. Here as elsewhere, the self is doubly useful, and doubly commodious: it has a part to play both in the frontier exploits of empire, and in its metropolitan governance.

It is doubly fitting, then, that Isabel should be made into an individual. "If sacred nature carefully . . . eggs round and round her minute and marvelous embryoes; then, Isabel, do I most carefully and most tenderly egg thee" (189), Pierre assures his new-found sister. It is a good thing that Isabel is "not of woman born" (114), because that only makes it easier for Pierre to "egg" her. In this oddly maternal occupation, Pierre seems to be perverting "sacred nature" itself; however, as we have seen, self-making in *Pierre* (and in nineteenth-century America) is not a matter of biology but a matter of personification. Pierre has made a few other "marvelous embryoes" before using that method, including Mrs. Glendinning the Haughty; Glendinning, Sr. the Perfect Marble Form; and Lucy the Empty x. Isabel, more "tenderly" conceived, will fare better than they do, but her status, both genetic and structural, is finally no different from theirs. In her case, the personifying machinery is even more visibly on display. She appears, for instance, as the "glorious child of Pride and Grief, in whose countenance were traceable the divinest lineaments of both her parents" (173). And she has other "parents" as well. Earlier, her face has struck Pierre as "the fair ground where Anguish had contended with Beauty, and neither being conqueror, both had lain down on the field" (47).

With so many allegorical "parents" hovering above her head, all claiming her to be their "child," Isabel can hardly stay an orphan for long. But if so, the advantages that inhere in that position would also cease to be hers. This happens almost immediately, in fact, for Isabel stops being a privileged figure the moment she is personified, the moment she is made to embody a set of attributes. As a freshly minted individual, she becomes just like everybody else. In fact (as we shall see), she becomes worse than some others, for what were once her privileges will now be appropriated, owned, and put to use by some other person. She is a living proof of Melville's contention that the self's empire can "never be lasting in any one dynasty" (167). True to the logic of Manifest Destiny, she is destined to be succeeded. By a kind of rotational logic, her successor, the person who will supplant her and dispossess her, turns out to be none other than Lucy Tartan, known previously as a "fair victim" (183).

Lucy, we might recall, has earlier been deposited by Pierre, along with Mrs. Glendinning, in "the profoundest vault of his soul" (286). Unlike the older woman, however, Lucy refuses to stay there. In her ability to emerge from vaults, she seems to have more in common with Poe's heroines than with Melville's. Her inconvenient appearance here certainly makes things complicated. What Lucy brings with her, when she emerges from the vault, is what looks like the resurrected specter from *Moby-Dick*: vengeance as mimesis, as the imitation of victimizer by victim, and the reproduction of victimizer in victim.

For Lucy, in an uncanny fashion, seems to have reproduced Isabel in herself by imitating her former usurper. Like Isabel (whose "artless infantileness" [140] and "angelic childlikeness" [140] have so impressed Pierre), Lucy now stages her reappearance with an "artless, angelical letter" (311). Isabel has previously called herself "poor Bell" (154, 156–59); Lucy now calls herself "poor Lucy" (310). And if Isabel has once seemed "enigmatical," "mysterious," "inscrutable," it is Lucy's turn now to exude "mysterious, inscrutable divineness" (317). Her "inconceivable conduct" utterly "amaze[s] and confound[s]" Pierre (317), to the point where he finds himself "a prey to all manner of devouring mysteries" (315). Every time he turns his thought to Lucy, he is "remastered" by her "enigmatical" resolve, her "secret and inexplicable motive" (315, 317).

Lucy has, in short, become a second Isabel. She has indeed reclaimed Isabel's terrain, and she has done so by reclaiming Isabel's identity. Retribution in *Pierre* ultimately means reattribution, a reversal of positions through the reassignment of attributes. This too is what one should expect from a geopolitical model of human relations, which, even as it imagines the self as property, must also imagine the takeover of that property. Lucy, in her vengeful return, in her vengeful assumption of Isabel's identity and territory, is merely inflicting on her rival the other face of the Lockean self. Having "made" herself anew, having embraced the positive term of individualism, she now freely extends to Isabel the obverse—the negative term of individualism that will be Isabel's unmaking. The one thing left, to make Lucy's vengeance complete, is a new bond of "confidence" with Pierre, both to imitate and to outdo Isabel's earlier bond with him. Such a creation will make Isabel the "unknowing" party, the equivalent of the former Lucy. This is exactly what Lucy proposes.

"She will never know—for thus far I am sure thou thyself hast never disclosed it to her what I once was to thee. Let it seem, as though I were some nun-like cousin immovably vowed to dwell with thee in thy strange exile" (309–10), Lucy suggests in her "artless, angelical letter." The "she" who "will never know" is of course Isabel, and Lucy is quite right to insist on this as the terms of her revenge, for within *Pierre*'s logic, there is no worse fate than "not knowing." Lucy understands this all too well, for she herself, once upon a time, was in that position. Now she is ready to put someone else there. Lucy does not explicitly counsel deceit—she settles for the euphemism "let it seem"—but her point is clear enough. What she hopes to gain from this perpetual "seeming" is equally clear: "Our mortal lives, oh, my heavenly Pierre, shall henceforth be one mute wooing of each other; with no declaration; no bridal; till we meet in the pure realms of God's final blessedness for us . . . when, there, thy sweet heart, shall be openly and unreservedly mine. Pierre, Pierre, my Pierre!" (310). Secrecy on earth will entitle the lovers to a paradise of flaunting conjugality. Lucy's goal remains unchanged—she still hopes to possess "my Pierre"—but she has now found a way to make the pronoun truly operative. The trick is to make Isabel the new casualty of "confidence," to make her both known and unknowing. Lucy's fabricated cousinship does just that.

Isabel, of course, likes Lucy's arrival not at all. She senses danger right away, and she senses as well the exact nature of that danger: "Either thou hast told thy secret, or she is not worthy the commonest love of man! Speak, Pierre,—which?" (313). Pierre replies, quite truthfully, that "The secret is still a secret" (313). What he goes on to say, however, is not so reassuring. Lucy is still in the dark, he tells Isabel: "she knows [the secret] not" (313). And yet, "without knowing the secret, she yet hath the vague, unspecializing sensation of the secret—the mystical presentiment, somehow, of the secret" (313). Isabel has every reason to worry, for Lucy really knows what she needs to know. She knows enough, in any case, to mount an attack, and, "hour by hour, to be somehow inexplicably sliding between" Pierre and Isabel (337). In this domestic staging of Manifest Destiny, it is Lucy's turn now to dispossess Isabel, to subject her former rival to "some untraceable displacing agency" (338). "All words are arrant skirmishes; deeds are the army's self" (333), Isabel has once observed; if so, Lucy's deeds would seem to bespeak the most powerful of armies. Imitating Isabel, she comes to know Isabel; and knowing Isabel, she "displac[es]" what she knows.

The model of human relations in *Pierre* can only be a model of compulsory rotation, for privileges, always unequally distributed here, must also be continually circulated, in their very inequality, among rival claimants.[29] Lucy's usurpation of Isabel's privilege is, from this perspective, altogether a structural given, hardly to be wept over. More worrisome for Pierre, however, is his own fate, for if a rotational logic is indeed in place, it must eventually affect him as well. The negative term of individualism spares no one. It seems only a matter of time before Pierre, too, will come to be imitated by Lucy, and usurped by her. Lucy herself says as much: "I have still more thought of thine own superhuman, angelical strength; which so, has a very little been transferred to me" (309). What is "transferred" from Pierre to Lucy is in fact not just "a very little," for she now possesses such quantities of "superhuman love" (311) and "superhuman beauty and glory" (311) that the original owner is himself overwhelmed. His "heavenly fire" (107) is now reproduced in her, as "sterling heavenliness" (327). She is a "rapt enthusiast" (324), just as Pierre has once been an "Enthusiast to Duty" (106). Indeed, she has absorbed so much of his "heavenly manner" (327) that she even assumes the same architectural form. Pierre's heart has once been a "shrine . . . of marble" (68); Lucy now appears as "the temple of God, and marble indeed were the only fit material for so holy a shrine" (328).

Lucy has thus become not just a second Isabel, but also a second Pierre. What she does to Isabel, she will eventually (and inevitably) do to Pierre as well. Soon enough, she addresses the following words to the person who has previously made her a "fair victim" (183): "Now, when still knowing nothing, yet something of thy secret I, as a seer, suspect. Grief—deep, unspeakable grief, hath made me this seer. I could murder myself, Pierre, when I think of my previous blindness" (309). As a newborn "seer" who "could murder" herself for her "previous blindness," Lucy suggests an interesting sequel to that somewhat sketchy figure at the end of *Nature*: "the blind man . . . gradually restored to perfect sight."[30] Emerson would have applauded her ocular exercise—he would have seen the point of it—for he himself is famously the apostle of the transparent eyeball. But Lucy, in making herself an Emersonian heroine, also reveals something about the complementary logic of an Emersonian triumph. One exercises one's "perfect sight," apparently, only by subjecting someone else to one's "electric insight" (89). Of course, Lucy is only doing to Pierre what he has once done to her. She has once been "fond, all understood" to him (129); now it is her turn to be his "seer."

Lucy is not the only seer in the book, however. Plotinus Plinlimmon, owner of a "steady observant blue-eyed countenance" (291) and a "blue-eyed, mystic-mild face" (292), anticipates her and the "clear mild azure of her eye" (329). Indeed, Plinlimmon offers an interesting example of what a "seer" might do:

> Any way, the face seemed to leer upon Pierre. And now it said to him—*Ass! ass! ass!* This expression was insufferable. . . . What was most terrible was the idea that by some magical means or other the face had got hold of his secret. "Ay," shuddered Pierre, "the face knows that Isabel is not my wife! And that seems the reason it leers." (293)

All-leering and all-knowing, the omniscient face here reduces Pierre to the abjection of the known. Plinlimmon is the transparent eyeball turned on its head—or rather, the transparent eyeball turned inside out, the organ of vision externalized as the organ of supervision. Knowledge, in Melville as in Foucault, is both the instrument and the form of power. In his leering gaze, Plinlimmon dramatizes the seer as overseer.[31]

Yet ultimately it is not Plinlimmon but Lucy who proves to be the greater "seer" in *Pierre*. For what Lucy embodies, as she becomes a second Isabel and a second Pierre, as she initiates a rotational logic, is an altogether different, and infinitely more powerful, form of "supervision": not monitoring from without the self, but monitoring from within the self. Lucy is the all-seeing, ever-present rival, the hateful specter that turns daily existence into daily combat. She is hateful, but she is also necessary. The logic of individualism cannot do without her. Where the self figures as property, the figure of the rival claimant is not only logical but constitutive. A geopolitical model of selfhood requires the menacing presence of the other—it must necessarily posit the other as menace—for only the intimation of a perpetual threat can keep the self perpetually vigilant, and perpetually "governed."

In fact, in her ability to assume a new identity and to occupy a new position, Lucy is merely enacting the celebrated dream of individualism, the dream of mobility. From Isabel's perspective, that dream is a nightmare. The fate of displacement complements the freedom to advance. Yet, as we can also see, such a "fate," far from being an unfortunate by-product of individualism, turns out to be its functional provision, an indispensable part of its system of "internal police." For the self needs no better monitor than such a fate, held in intimate abeyance. Like Manifest Destiny, supervision too can be internalized. It works, in this case, as a rotational logic, unmistakable in others and all too probable in oneself. The very thought of such a logic—the very thought that privileges will be distributed and redistributed, territories lost and won—is enough to keep the self "supervised," in every sense of the word. The logic of mobility, both in what it promises and in what it threatens, is thus the best form of "self-government."[32]

In her success as a rival claimant, Lucy destroys, once and for all, the hope that there might be a privileged figure—a figure of difference—within the structure of individualism. Difference inheres, it seems, only in positions, not in the occupants of those positions. Indeed, the occupants take on each other's identities as positions change hands. Individualism, hardly precluding interchangeability, needs the latter to operate, to produce and reproduce "individuals." This is what dooms Pierre, what defeats his hope to be "without kith or kin," and what dictates to him a familiar fate. Formerly a uniquely "incomprehensible fiend" (184), he is bound to become like the others—which is to say, "all understood." And just as he has once summed up and pronounced upon his mother, he is bound, in his turn, to be summed up and pronounced upon. Not without some justice, his publisher calls him a "swindler" (356); Glen and Fred call him a "liar" (357). A known quantum, Pierre ends up enacting the same familiar story—everybody else's story.[33]

Kinship governs *Pierre*, and nothing says it more forcefully than the two portraits at the gallery, the "Cenci" and "the Stranger"—the former, an intended copy of the original, and the latter, an unexpected copy of the chair portrait. Together, in their voluntary and involuntary filiations, the two portraits affirm a world of likeness, a world of kinship and only kinship. Pierre's dream of "own[ing] no earthly kith or kin" fails, of course. But so does Melville's dream of becoming "his own sire." Originality is at once an article of faith and a practical impossibility even within the terms of individualism. In Melville's case, this parodox is especially ironic, for contrary to his dream, he winds up enacting a rather unoriginal story himself, one that underscores the kinship between him and his fictive creations. Like Ahab, like Mrs. Glendinning, and like Pierre himself, Melville has the misfortune of being made into a "known character." The following review of *Moby-Dick*, from the *United States Magazine and Democratic Review*, shows this process at work:

> Mr. Melville's vanity is immeasurable. He will either be first among the book-making tribe, or he will be nowhere. He will center all attention upon himself, or he will abandon the field of literature at once. From this morbid self-esteem, coupled with a most unbounded love of notoriety, [came] all his declamatory abuse of society, all his inflated sentiment, and all his insinuating licentiousness.[34]

This is clearly an example of what has sometimes been called the rise of "symptomatic reading" in the nineteenth century, a mode of reading that increasingly focused on the character of the author as a subject of speculative diagnosis.[35] More generally, however, we might also take it as an example of personification in the nineteenth century, an example of the production of knowable subjects. For "Melville," liberally endowed with attributes on this occasion, had indeed been fashioned into a "person," a figure with an identity. The reviewer of the *United States Magazine and Democratic Review* knew him entirely, and knew entirely, too, what to do with his book.

Damning as this instance of personification might seem, it was nothing compared with what greeted Melville after the publication of *Pierre*. That book, a compendium of "crazy sentiment and exaggerated passion," "might be supposed to emanate from a lunatic hospital," the *Boston Post* observed. The New York *Day Book* went even further. "A critical friend who read Melville's last book, *Ambiguites*," it reported, "told us that it appeared to be composed of the ravings and reveries of a madman. We were somewhat startled at the remark; but still more at learning, a few days after, that Melville was really supposed to be deranged, and that his friends were taking measures to place him under treatment. We hope one of the earliest precautions will be to keep him stringently secluded from pen and ink." That sentiment was echoed by the *Southern Quarterly Review*: "The sooner this author is put in ward the better. If trusted with himself, at all events give him no further trust in pen and ink, till the present fit has worn off."[36]

Like Mrs. Glendinning the Haughty, Melville was well on his way to becoming Melville the Madman. The author himself was in danger of being turned into a personified attribute. That prospect ought not to surprise him too much, though, for what his own fate suggests is simply a radical continuity between the literary and the social, between the logic of individualism in *Pierre* and that in antebellum America. In both cases, the constitution of a field of knowledge—which is also to say, a field of individuality—turns out to be the very grounds for subjection. Attribution of character, then, is not only what a writer does, it is also what is done to him in an age of individualism, as it seems to be done to everyone else. From this perspective, the authorial practice in *Pierre*—the practice of personification— seems not so much a deliberate choice on Melville's part as the very environment he inhabits.

Melville, of course, still dreams of authorial freedom and authorial exemption. Summoning tautology once again to his aid, he allows Pierre to say at one point, "I render no accounts: I am what I am" (325). This expression of hope is echoed even more forcefully in Isabel's final words, "All's o'er, and ye know him not!" (362). What remains for Melville to do is simply to translate both those hopes into the reality of *The Confidence-Man*: into an unknowable world, a world of authorial unaccountability.

6. *Personified Accounting*

> When charmed by the beauty of that viper, did it
> never occur to you to change personalities with him?
> to feel what it was to be a snake? to glide unsuspected
> in grass? to sting, to kill at a touch; your whole beau-
> tiful body one iridescent scabbard of death? In short,
> did the wish never occur to you to feel yourself ex-
> empt from knowledge, and conscience, and revel for
> a while in the care-free, joyous life of a perfectly in-
> stinctive, unscrupulous, and irresponsible creature?[1]

"Exempt[ion] from knowledge," according to Mark Winsome,
is the great advantage rattlesnakes have over human beings.
Those magical words would have electrified everyone in *Pierre*,
but among the indifferent crowds on the *Fidèle*, only the cosmopolitan is there to listen. The "knowledge" from which the
snake is exempt is presumably self-knowledge, but, recalling
Melville's previous book, we might imagine the snake as being
exempt from knowledge of another sort: a variety that, to
some, would seem an even greater affliction, a variety (en-
countered earlier in *Pierre* and at Yale College) that at once
supervises and individualizes, producing a "subject" both as a
field of inquiry and as a field of dominion.

With *Pierre* alive in the background, the snake's exemption
from knowledge must count as a privilege indeed. But its good
fortune goes even further, for in being "exempt from knowledge" it is entitled to a corollary benefit: exemption from
"conscience." Doubly exempt, the snake would seem to offer
yet another model of freedom, the newest, most bizarre, but
perhaps also the most efficient. The reptile is perfectly "carefree," Winsome tells us, "perfectly instinctive, unscrupulous,

and irresponsible." Winsome, quite rightly, connects this freedom with the snake's accountability—or rather, with the nonexistence of that problem for the snake. "Is a rattle-snake accountable?" (163), he asks at one point. But for him, the question is clearly rhetorical. The answer is never for a moment in doubt.

But if the answer is a decided no, it is not (as the cosmopolitan wickedly suggests) because the snake has a "permit of unaccountability to murder any creature it takes capricious umbrage at" (164), but because the very category of "accountability" has been preempted where the snake is concerned. The snake cannot be blamed for what it does, because it is merely doing what is "instinctive"—or, as we tend to say these days, it is merely "being itself," merely enacting its natural disposition. In killing its victims, it is just being a snake. There is no distinction, in other words, between what the snake does and what it is, between its action and its character. This identity of being and doing is what exonerates the snake, and what Winsome singles out as its supreme privilege. The snake is to be envied, he says, in that its "whole beautiful body [is] one iridescent scabbard of death." Form and function, in the rattlesnake, are one and the same. Its lethal beauty makes up a reflexive instrument, merging being and doing into a circuit of identity.

As a model of reflexity, the snake is hardly a unique invention, either in Melville or in antebellum America. Like the whale, like Ahab, like Stowe's self-punishing master and America's self-victimizing savages, the snake too makes up a self-contained unit, a figure of closure. Like the others, it too is a child of individualism, a reptilian member. Although the reflexive form of the snake is not new, the functional network into which Melville inserts it is. For the snake, in its customary circuit of closure, is nevertheless the site for an uncustomary operation, a new way of deploying two strategic categories: the inherent and the extraneous, the former justifying axiomatic admission, the latter guaranteeing axiomatic dismissal. This, it seems to me, is the controlling logic in Winsome's account of the snake, in his evocative portrait of its "whole

beautiful body one iridescent scabbard of death." The image is
evocative, but even as it evokes it also dismisses. In its circularity of reference, in its apposition of "beautiful body" and
"one iridescent scabbard of death," the image not only underscores the identity of the snake by turning it back upon itself,
it also excludes what might otherwise have jeopardized that
identity. It excludes, for instance, the figure of the victim. As
the receiving end of the "scabbard of death," a figure neither
beautiful nor iridescent, the victim would have seriously qualified the "charm[ing]" picture of the snake. For this reason, no
doubt, he fails to appear. Winsome shows only a solitary
snake, reveling in its own "carefree, joyous" existence. The
victim is extraneous in every sense of the word.

The snake is unaccountable (to return to our initial point)
because it somehow manages to leave out the victim from its
account of itself. Using a different set of terms, we might also
speak of such "unaccountability" as a mode of "negative accounting." The convergence of the moral and the economic
here is not altogether fortuitous, for the snake's moral neutral-
ity is ultimately predicated on a particular kind of economics,
what we might call an economics of selfhood, a process of accounting and discounting instituted within the self. The snake
is unaccountable because its reptilian self effectively works as
an ontologized accounting house, a site of exchange that not
only asserts the equivalence between being and doing, but also
"discounts" the latter in the name of the former. Imagined as
a constitutive province of selfhood, action ceases to count as
action and becomes simply an extension of being, even as the
actor ceases to count as an actor and becomes simply an "instinctive" agent. The snake is exonerated on just those
grounds: its action has been discounted, absorbed, and absolved by its economy of being.[2] But if so, such an economy
must necessarily discount the victim as well, the recipient of
the snake's action. Because that action no longer counts, the
recipient too must be seen as something other than an injured
party. He cannot claim to have been "victimized" in any
proper sense of the word. Indeed, "victimization" can have no

meaning here except as a structural requisite. It is simply another mode of being, one complementary to that of the snake.

Such an economy of selfhood—in this case, an economy of discounting—obviously makes for a rare kind of freedom. Profiting from it, the snake might have said, "I render no accounts: I am what I am." Those words, of course, are not really the snake's; they were Pierre's.[3] But if the snake could talk, that no doubt is what it would have said, for nothing better describes its enviable situation. In this improbable line of descent, from a "superhuman" hero to a reptile no less superhuman, we see a crucial link between Melville's last two novels. The dream of individualism in *Pierre*, the dream of an "untrammeled self," of the self's transcendent freedom, seems to have survived well beyond the unhappy ending of that book. It reappears (and flourishes) in *The Confidence-Man*, for here, in Melville's newly minted economy of selfhood—embodied by a snake, no less—the untrammeled self can indeed "be itself" and "render no accounts" in that process.

But as we also know, individualism usually has more than one story to tell. Unaccountability is only half the story, the snake's half. It is not the story of the victim, the snake's casualty and companion. Here, quite another principle prevails. For if the snake is rendered unaccountable by an ontologized economy, one that discounts its action, such an economy can work, paradoxically, only in conjunction with something that is its obverse: an economy that counts everything, that constitutes the self, in fact, as a site of reckoning. We ordinarily refer to this as the principle of "individual accountability." Within the terms of this book, we might also call it "personified accounting," the production of "persons" out of an economic practice. This alternate principle, in any case, is what complements the snake's—which is why its champion is once again Mark Winsome. Finally addressing the figure he has previously ignored, the figure of the victim, he invokes just this principle of individual accountability to exonerate the snake yet again. "Whoever is destroyed by a rattle-snake," he says, "it is his own fault" (163).

Mark Winsome is, of course, not a sympathetic character,

hardly a spokesman for Melville.[4] Yet a crude summary of
Moby-Dick would not have sounded very different from Winsome's adage. Ahab's fate would have been recognizable in this
account: "Whoever is destroyed by the whale, it is his own
fault." *The Confidence-Man* might be said, in this regard, to be
a descendant of *Moby-Dick*, as much as it is a descendant of
Pierre. Melville's last novel acknowledges (and revises) both
these predecessors, for his ambition here is not only to gesture
toward the freedom of the unaccountable but also to safeguard
that freedom—by locating accountability elsewhere, in a discrete and manageable site. In other words, if the logic of the
"untrammeled self" now prevails, in a way that has not been
possible in *Pierre*, so too must the logic of self-victimization,
in a way also not possible in *Moby-Dick*. *The Confidence-Man*
succeeds, in fact, precisely because it is able to summon both
its predecessors, both the terms of Pierre's freedom ("I render
no accounts: I am what I am"), and the terms of Ahab's subjection ("Ahab is for ever Ahab"), to yield a double logic, the
logic of individualism at its most efficient and most mind-bog-
gling: a logic of complementary license and control, complementary discounting and accounting.

This new achievement—a new ability to discount what he
has previously been forced to concede—permits Melville to
speak lightly of his erstwhile worries. The "doctrine of future
retribution" (56), that hideous idea from *Moby-Dick*, is now
simply a casual subject, indifferently entertained by the agent
of the Black Rapids Coal Company. Ahab's menace is a menace no more, it seems, and nothing proves it more forcefully
than Melville's candor in his choice of chapter titles. "The
Metaphysics of Indian-hating" could not have appeared in any
book other than *The Confidence-Man*. The phrase would have
made an excellent subtitle for *Moby-Dick*, of course, but only
here can it actually appear on record. The Indian-hater can
appear on record now, because like the rattlesnake, he too
turns out to have a "charmed" existence, he too is "exempt
from knowledge," and really has nothing to fear. "There can
be no biography of an Indian-hater par excellence, any more
than one of a swordfish, or other deep-sea denizen," Melville

tells us (131). Indeed, the "career of the Indian-hater par excellence has the impenetrability of the fate of a lost steamer" (131). The Indian-hater is "impenetrable" because his hatred cannot be fathomed: he is someone whose "hate . . . is a vortex from whose suction scarce the remotest chip of the guilty race may reasonably feel secure" (130). Such a "vortex" obviously recalls the apparition at the end of *Moby-Dick*, the "concentric circles that . . . round and round in one vortex, carried the smallest chip of the *Pequod* out of sight."[5] But the "suction" of the Indian-hater would seem to be even greater. He is the more powerful vortex, one suspects, because in hating Indians he is merely being himself: he hates Indians because he is an Indian-hater. Like the rattlesnake, only more spectacularly so, he too is reflexively unaccountable, and reflexively innocent, his action being likewise absorbed by ontology, in a tautological circuit of being and doing.

Still, if the Indian-hater is the newest and most deadly vortex, he is not, significantly, *only* a vortex. In a dumbfoundering reversal of figurative logic, Melville also compares his "impenetrability" to "the fate of a lost steamer" (131). This makes the Indian-hater an extreme case of mixed metaphor, but the peculiar effect here stems, I think, not just from the act of mixing metaphors, but from the kinds of metaphor garnered for that operation. At once "vortex" and "lost steamer," the Indian-hater effectively occupies both ends of an operational field. He is both agent and object, both the force that destroys and the casualty of that destruction. This might seem incomprehensible, but it is hardly fortuitous, and it most certainly is not due to any carelessness on Melville's part. For the Indian-hater's glaring contradiction turns out (as we shall see) to be something of a necessary contradiction. Far from being disruptive, it is functional, even constitutive. The Indian-hater cannot exist without this contradiction, for that in fact is what he is: not a substantive but a relation, a principle of internal difference. For our purposes, we might call his condition an "oxymoronic" economy of selfhood.

As a human oxymoron, the Indian-hater manages not only to be both vortex and lost steamer but, even more curiously, to be both hater and lover. John Moredock, for instance, is "an example of something apparently self-contradicting, certainly curious, but, at the same time, undeniable: namely, that nearly all Indian-haters have at bottom loving hearts" (134). "Hat[ing] Indians like snakes," they are "to all but Indians juicy as a peach" (122). The phenomenon is only "apparently" self-contradicting, as Melville says, and only "apparently" bizarre, we might add, for in being oxymoronic, the Indian-hater is in fact well within a venerable American tradition. Seen within that tradition, he is, quite simply, the hero of individualism, the imperial self: a self so encompassing that it encompasses even opposites. Whitman has celebrated just such a self in these famous lines in *Song of Myself*: "Do I contradict myself? / Very well then I contradict myself, / (I am large, I contain multitudes.)"[6] A self so "large" is bound to be full of contradictions, to be oxymoronic almost by definition. The Indian-hater certainly fits the pattern. It is crucial that he should neither merely hate nor merely love, but do both at once, for his identity resides not in either term, but in the discrete complementarity of their opposition. He is the locus of internal difference, a human oxymoron in dramatic relief.

But if the Indian-hater personifies a contradiction, it is not solely for the benefit of becoming a "loving hater." Hating alone is not enough for him, he must "act upon a calm, cloistered scheme of strategical, implacable, and lonesome vengeance" (130). Such a course of action should logically make him heir to Ahab, the spirit of "vengeance," but it surprisingly does not. The fact that it does not, that the "avenger" is no longer a new Ahab, suggests a masterful inversion of terms in *The Confidence-Man*, one that allows Melville to settle, once and for all, the vexing problem of vengeance and the even more vexing problem of victimization. This I take to be the burden of "The Metaphysics of Indian-Hating," a chapter most felicitously titled, for what transpires here is indeed "metaphysics," an ontological sleight of hand that completely rewrites the relation between vengeance and victimization.[7] From this operation, an "avenger" (132) emerges unlike anything we have seen before, an avenger allied not with Ahab, the vengeful savage, but with his enemy, the Indian-hater, the "vanguard of conquering civilization" (126). What boggles the mind is, once again, the impossible conjunction—the fact that the victimizing "conquer[or]" and the victimized "avenger" turn out to be one and the same. But that, ultimately, is no more than what we might expect, for being a human oxymoron, the Indian-hater is always able to encompass polar opposites. Just as he is both "vortex" and "lost steamer," both a "snake" to Indians and a "peach" to everyone else, he is both "conquer[or]" and "avenger," both the one to inflict the injury and the one to clamor for revenge. In his remarkable metaphysics of being, the "retributive spirit" (133) that once accrued to the victim as a consequence of victimization now accrues to the "conquer[or]" as a postulate of ontology.

The Indian-hater is all the more remarkable as an "avenger" because it is unclear what he is avenging. John Moredock, to be sure, has his personal grievance, but Indian-haters as a group do not. Indeed, "Indian rapine having mostly ceased through regions where it once prevailed, the philanthropist is surprised that Indian-hating has not in like degree ceased with it" (125). There is no correlation, in other words, between provocation and reaction, between what was done to the Indian-hater and what he does in return—for he is not doing anything "in return," nothing having been done to him in the first place. His "vengeance" is "impenetrabl[e]" (131), because it has no reference to any prior event, but stems, quite simply, from his "self-contradicting" (134) character, which makes him a proleptic victim precisely because he is a proven conqueror.

Of course, to be an "avenger" in this context, where vengeance is understood to be unoccasioned, is to play some funny tricks with definition. The "avenger" in "The Metaphysics of Indian-hating" is the white whale parading as Ahab, we might say, an Ahab with no lost limb, an avenger who never was a victim. Such an "avenger," avenging a wrong he never suffered, is really no different from a simple "conqueror"—but that too is the point. For if the Indian-hater is oxymoronic, he is just as surely tautological: his double identity as "conqueror" and "avenger" turns out to be a single identity after all, for definitions aside, there is really no difference between the two. Internal difference, in his case, gathers always into a circuit of identity. This point of convergence, where oxymoronic divisions collapse into tautological equivalence, is unquestionably the single most important feature in the Indian-hater. It makes him an exemplary figure, and makes his model of selfhood a model of metaphysical wonder, both within the confines of *The Confidence-Man* and (as we shall see) beyond it.

That self, to put the point another way, is simply another site of exchange—in this case, another site of discounting. Like the rattlesnake, the Indian-hater is constituted by an internal economy, by the exchangeability between being and doing. Also like the snake, he invokes that exchangeability to discount his action. Discounting is especially effortless for him, because his self, in its contradictory largesse, is also uniquely suited to work as an instrument of dismissal. Because such a self "contain[s] multitudes," as Whitman says, because it is the sum and measure of all things, it can afford, on the strength of what it contains, to rule out what it chooses not to admit. "I don't believe it," Dr. Johnson says of the Lisbon earthquake (136), invoking the "I" for just that purpose. The incident is cited, with evident approval, by the cosmopolitan, by way of explaining why he himself does not believe in the phenomenon of Indian-hating. The analogy is apt, for Dr. Johnson and the cosmopolitan are kindred not only in their imperial disbelief but, more to the point, in their imperial selfhood, in their ability to invoke a sovereign "I," to equate "I believe" with "what is." As the arbiter of reality, the self is free not only to underwrite but also to nullify. It credits and discredits, counts and discounts.

What is discounted in the imperial self, in this case the Indian-hater's, is once again the victim. That unsightly creature has no place here, for the Indian-hater, in offering himself as both "conqueror" and "avenger," has once again obviated the category of "victim." His selfhood, in its oxymoronic amplitude, not only collapses two antithetical terms into a single identity, it also, in the same measure, removes any grounds for an adversarial relation. The victim can have no independent reality here, he cannot claim even to exist, for he has already been absorbed and appropriated by the imperial self, his position incorporated to become part of that self's constitutive duality. What might have existed as a relation between persons is once again ontologized to become an internal structure within the self. The Indian-hater stays innocent, much as the rattlesnake does, by preempting the very category for which he might be held accountable. His method, in fact, turns out to be still more marvelous than the snake's, for if the snake absolves itself in ontology, by "being itself," the Indian-hater extends the reign of ontology to eliminate even the need for absolution. He need not absolve himself because he has no victim to speak of, because the latter has become truly a non-entity, at once unremarkable and inconceivable.

There is no Ahab in *The Confidence-Man*, or anybody remotely resembling Ahab. The victim has become utterly faceless, utterly inconsequential here: he figures merely as the "he" in Mark Winsome's casual remark, "it is his own fault" (163). Winsome is referring to "whoever is destroyed by a rattlesnake" (163), but his adage would have applied just as well to those destroyed by the Indian-hater. It would have applied even better to those duped by the confidence man. Nobody embodies "their own fault" more vividly than these unsavory characters. Less victim than culprit, they are taken in only because they are greedy, gullible, moronic. What befalls them is no more than a measure of what they are. They are what we might call "deserving victims." In a different vocabulary, we might also call them accountable selves, accountable because, by a kind of internalized bookkeeping, each of them has traded his sin for his penalty, each of them stands as a balance sheet of matching receipt and return.

Such a model of selfhood (as my own rhetoric suggests) is obviously an economic one, and it is a tribute to Melville's prescience that he is able to enlist its service. For if *The Confidence-Man* remains typically Melvillean in its commitment to the autonomous self, it is nonetheless unique in being able to imagine that self in economic terms—to imagine it, in fact, as a personified site of accounting. The individualism that animates the book is a rather special version, a market version that has the power to "discount" its victims. It also has the power to "account for" them, which really comes to the same thing, for to be "accounted for," to be constituted as the ground of one's undoing, is in effect to be discounted as well. What market individualism offers, then, is something like a self-consuming figure, a victim sufficient unto himself and trading within himself, consuming his own fault and being in turn consumed by it. Such a construct is obviously central to *The Confidence-Man*, but Melville can hardly claim to have invented it. Indeed, this figure exists both outside and prior to the book, for he is altogether a necessary invention in nineteenth-century America. The market economy cannot do without him.

The Confidence-Man is generally taken as a transcendent critique of the market economy.[8] I propose to examine a different relation between the two, a relation not of transcendence but of kinship. What unites the book and the market, I suggest, is an economic model of selfhood, what I have tried to describe as a model of personified accounting. Melville's novel needs this construct, but the market needs it even more. For the "individual" that the market solicits—the autonomous figure who serves as the putative origin of demand and the consenting party in contract—can be an "individual" only to the extent he is constituted as an economy in himself. Only an economic model of selfhood can make him the autonomous entity that he is supposed to be. Producing in order to consume and selling in order to buy, he internalizes the market as the self's constitutive principle. He is an entire economy collapsed into one person: he expends himself, regulates himself, and contains himself.

But if the market produces the individual as a self-contained economy, it can also account for him within that enclosure. Being an autonomous unit, such an individual must look to himself to explain whatever is happening to him; he is a human calculus, and the sole calculus, of both penalty and reward. In other words, even as the market consecrates the subjective sovereignty of the individual, it is free, by the same token, to exclude any consideration of the nonsubjective. The market is ultimately a form of "economic subjectivism," we might say.[9] Its pivotal figure is always the individual, whose subjective choices, in their aggregate form, regulate the very law of supply and demand. But in granting the individual the freedom to be subjective—in making him a free agent, free to do what he wants—the market also relieves itself of any need to account for the transactional relations among subjectivities. Contract pays "no attention," after all, as Walter Benn Michaels says, "to the equity of the exchange as perceived by anyone other than the contracting parties."[10] If so, to make the individual the originary ground for contract is to make exchange axiomatically equitable. Market transactions are by definition acts of free choice, negotiated by free agents under the freedom of contract. There can be no unfairness here, for the mere fact that there are two contracting parties in exchange is already proof that such exchange is equitable.

Like the rattlesnake and the Indian-hater, then, the market recognizes no victim, for injustice is a noncategory here, just as the victim is a nonentity. Where freedom is the axiomatic property of the individual, inequity too is axiomatically impossible. Tracing the triumph of what he calls a "subjective theory of contract," Morton Horwitz writes,

> Where things have no "intrinsic value," there can be no substantive measure of exploitation and the parties are, by definition, equal. Modern contract law was thus born staunchly proclaiming that all men are equal because all measures of inequality are illusory.[11]

What makes market individualism especially useful to Melville as a model, more useful than the rattlesnake or the Indian-hater, is its ability not just to erase the victim (which the other two can also do), but to do so through the agency of contract—by replacing the victim with the category of the "contracting party."[12] The victims of the confidence man appear in just this guise, and they hardly invite sympathy. For if contract is indeed an expression of subjective desire, these victims' folly of contract can only be an expression of their own foolish wants. They do not, after all, have to be victims; indeed they would not have been if they had only been different. Even as Melville replaces the victim with the contracting party, he also projects, around each of them, a world in which choice is apparently possible, in which the presumed availability of another position makes one responsible for the position one is in. [13] In this he might have learned something from the market as well.

For the market also has two positions to offer. As a model of exchange—of two bargaining positions in a functional complementarity—it must constitute the individual as a double entity, fit to occupy either position. In the immediate context of exchange, that individual is both buyer and seller. Within the terms of our discussion, we might also think of that individual as a "subject" in a double sense: he is both the "subject" of freedom, whose action is discounted by his being, and the "subject" of accountability, whose fate is measured by "his own fault." There will always be subjects and subjects in a market economy, and indeed, the efficacy of the market lies precisely in the maintenance of those two categories, at once permanent and permeable, the passage from one to the other being both incentive and threat. The market needs both winners and losers, and it generates them ceaselessly. Only the continual production of both categories can allow it to constitute itself as a field of exchange and a field of mobility, where positions are circulated and recirculated, fortunes made and unmade.

The double logic of the marketplace—its ability to fill and refill two positions, to produce and reproduce two kinds of subjects—is especially instructive to Melville, for this mobile complementarity is just what he needs. *The Confidence-Man*, in this respect, is less a representation of nineteenth-century economics than a formal rehearsal of its workings. Like the market itself, the book operates by generating polarities: the wise and the gullible, the verbally adept and the verbally inept, those who make dupes of others and those who are duped. Even as it institutes these polarities, however, it also destabilizes them, again in the manner of the market, suspending them in a circulatory economy, a field of perpetual reversals. The word that Melville uses to bring about this double operation is obviously "confidence." Nothing better registers his indebtedness to the market—to the lesson afforded by its mobility and polarity—than this single word in its contrary valencies.

What, after all, does it mean to "have confidence" in someone else? When Black Guinea laments his sad fate in the beginning of the book ("Oh, oh, good ge'mmen, have you no confidence in dis poor ole darkie?" [13]), he is demanding confidence from others and offering himself as the recipient of it. This usage governs a number of subsequent encounters: to the good merchant (16), the sophomore (23), the charitable widow (37), the old miser (64), the sick man (70), and the cripple (86), the confidence man similarly demands confidence, and receives it. So far, the syntax of confidence seems to identify the donor of confidence as the victim, and the recipient of confidence as the con man. Yet what are we to make of the instance when the man with the weed, turning fondly to the good merchant, declares, "I want a friend in whom I can confide" (17)? On this occasion, contrary to the formula we have just derived, the one who offers confidence turns out to be the confidence man himself, while the victim stands as the recipient. Lest this appear as a single aberration, in the second half of the book it quickly establishes itself as the rule. The cosmopolitan has plenty of confidence, and he is bent on giving it away. To Charlie Noble, for instance, he confesses that the latter's character has impelled him "to throw myself upon your nobleness; in one word, put confidence in you, a generous confidence" (155). In the same mode he exclaims to Egbert (obligingly playing Charlie): "Charlie, I am going to put confidence in you" (172). On those occasions, offering confidence is the name of the game. Offering confidence, of course, is what has previously made dupes and victims of others, but when the confidence man does it himself, the effect is quite the reverse. Confidence can go either way, it seems; but it always goes where the confidence man wants it to.

The crucial point, though, is not the confidence man's deviousness, which we all know, but the apparent syntactical reversibility of the word "confidence" itself. Alternatively a liability and a benefit, something to demand and something to resist, confidence generates two opposing syntaxes of meaning, the effect of which is to break down not so much its polarities as the substantive difference between the two. In other words, there will always be a winner and a loser in the confidence game: those polarities will always remain. What changes radically, what reverses itself in successive encounters, is what constitutes a winner or a loser. Receiving confidence is what the winner sometimes does, but it hardly guarantees that outcome, for in the next instance the same move might make one a victim. Confidence appears to be a highly mercurial substance; it produces drastically different effects. Yet, above and beyond its local reversals, confidence continues to honor the syntax itself—continues to divide people into duper and duped, and will always do so. Those divisions persist, not because of any intrinsic difference among those divided, but because the very syntax of confidence requires divisions, requires the complementary genesis of duper and duped, winners and losers.

If "confidence" enacts the two operative terms of the marketplace—its polarity as well as its mobility—what it ends up revealing, in a rather dramatic way, is an *asymmetrical* relation between those two terms, an unequal partnership between what might have appeared equal allies. That asymmetrical relation, as Jean Baudrillard describes it, is what characterizes all ideological processes; it entails, quite simply, the binary production of a joint pair of terms: a privileged term in need of legitimation, and an "alibi" term generated to serve that need.[14] That certainly seems to be what is happening here. "Mobility" is the alibi term, we might say, and, taking our cue from Baudrillard, we might also say that an "alibi" it will always remain. For even as the market constitutes itself as a field of mobility—even as it dramatizes mobility to downplay its obverse, polarity—what it continually, unfailingly reproduces is nonetheless polarity, its privileged term. Mobility, the supposed antidote to polarity, turns out to be no more than its excuse, for mobility hardly challenges polarity, but merely reinscribes it, in a ceaseless reconstitution of its segregated province.

Always present, if only in different guises, polarity might turn out to be the single most enduring fact in a market economy, even as it stands as the single most enduring fact in *The Confidence-Man*. Nor does it always need an alibi. In a different register, polarity can come forth openly, even conspicuously, as an appeal in itself. This form of polarity—displayed, instrumental, unapologized for—is what animates the word "confidence" in its semantic (rather than syntactic) career, and what makes it yet another example of the unaccountable. For what, after all, is "confidence"? Because the invocation of the term promotes, in most cases, a pecuniary transaction, confidence, in the crudest sense, seems to signify money. Money is what changes hands as confidence changes hands—that much is clear and indisputable—and yet something less tangible, harder to account for, seems to have changed hands as well. When the sick man pays three dollars for six boxes of the Omni-Balsamic Reinvigorator (70), and the cripple pays two for four boxes, what they have actually lost is just a petty sum of money—"two or three dirty dollars," as one character says—and yet the loss somehow seems greater, not so easy to calculate.

The mystery surrounding the word "confidence"—our sense that it is both tangible and intangible, both a specific thing and somehow more than just that thing—is perhaps only to be expected: for "confidence," to operate as such, must constitute itself not as a substantive, but always as a relation between two terms, itself undefined, and perhaps forever undefinable. Whether it is health for the sick man, or profits for the investor, the appeal of confidence is the appeal of something as yet unrealized, something all the more alluring for being offered strictly as a projected *difference* from things as they are. Confidence operates by a "constitutive discrepancy" within itself.

Always more than what it is, it ceaselessly negotiates between its actual and virtual referent, between what it signifies at any given moment, and what it signifies in potential. Like the word "charity," which the deaf-mute writes on his slate and to which he adds successive predicates ("Charity thinketh no evil," "Charity suffereth long, and is kind," "Charity believeth all things," "Charity never faileth"), "confidence" also lends itself to an infinite number of predicates but equates itself with no particular one. It exists, in short, always as a "more than," a projected relation between two terms, related by a principle of internal difference.

The internal difference within "confidence" makes it a commodity almost exactly as Marx defines the term. Commodification, Marx observes in his well-known discussion of the fetishism of commodities, is the process by which a product of labor comes to acquire what he calls a "two-fold character." The product exists both as an object of utility, something that we handle and use, and as an exchange value, something that circulates in the market. In other words, the commodity, in its very constitution as commodity, in its very entry into exchange, is already divided within itself. It is both itself and other than itself, both tangible and intangible, both a material object and an abstract figure. This internal "division of a product," according to Marx, is what generates its fetishism, what turns it into a kind of "social hieroglyphic." It is "something transcendent," "enigmatical," and "mysterious," with "qualities at once perceptible and imperceptible by the senses."[15] Within the terms of our discussion, we might also say that the commodity, as commodity, is already something unaccountable.

By this criterion, Melville's "confidence" certainly seems to work as a kind of commodity. Its "two-fold character," however, is even more complicated than Marx describes, for its internal difference, as we have seen, is a *projective* difference between an incomplete present and an unrealized future. This projective division makes confidence not just any commodity, but a peculiar one mapped along the temporal axis, a commodity constituted by a market relation across time. Confidence is a "promising" commodity. It operates by promising something as yet to come, something expected to be better than things as they are—something defined, in short, strictly as a difference between present and future.

What we are witnessing in *The Confidence-Man* is what we might call the commodification of time, the incorporation of the future into the structure of commodity. Melville's enactment of this drama is all too logical, for the nineteenth century, as Morton Horwitz describes it, was the century in which the very definition of "contract" was revised in order to incorporate time into the structure of exchange. "Futures contracts," executory instruments that focus on expectation damages rather than on specific performance, flourished in the speculative "futures" market of the nineteenth century. For Horwitz, this new, future-oriented definition of contract completed the erosion of objective values in a market economy and marked the demise of the equitable model of the eighteenth century.[16]

Within the pages of *The Confidence-Man*, the commodification of the future is no less important, for this alone enables the confidence man to do his business. He is operating along these lines, as a salesman of the future, when he tries to sell a young boy, what he calls a "new-born man-child," to the Missouri bachelor. This new-born man-child, he openly admits, is at the moment "not all that could be desired." In spite of this drawback, however, the article is still worth buying, because he happens to be the owner of potential merits, "points at present invisible, with beauties at present dormant" (105). What the confidence man is trying to sell, then, is not the young boy as he is, and not even the adult he is going to become, but the projected discrepancy between the two. Because the presumably wonderful adult is the owner of "points at present invisible," he can be apprehended (and marketed) only as a virtual object, a function of the presumptive difference between present and future. What the P.I.O. man is trying to sell is neither a man nor a child but a "man-child," a commodity whose market value lies in its future promise.[17]

What is interesting, of course, is that this promising com-

modity also happens to be a human commodity. What is even
more interesting is that this commodity turns out to be no different from something we do not usually think of as a commodity at all: the promising individual all of us aspire to become. Indeed, what is shocking about the man-child is that,
in his person, the promising individual is altogether indistinguishable from the promising commodity. To put the case
even more shockingly, we might say that the man-child becomes a promising individual only in the process of becoming
a commodity, for his very structure of selfhood—the very
"promise" that constitutes his being—is itself a commodified
form, a form of the salable future. If *The Confidence-Man* is
animated by a market individualism, that individualism
works, we can now see, not only by putting the individual in
the market but, even more crucially, by putting the market in
the individual. The market here is truly a "placeless market,"
as Jean-Christophe Agnew suggests.[18] Confined to no particular site, it is everywhere and nowhere, and, on this occasion,
it seems to have set up shop in each and every individual, turning each into an internalized economy. There is no distinction, finally, between the self and the commodity, for both
stem from the same structure, and both work, as we shall see,
toward the same end. The two converge at precisely the point
where time becomes an organic part of the market, and where
its incorporation into the self produces that self as promising
commodity.

The confidence man, however, is not the only one with
such an interesting man-child to sell. Robert Rantoul, Jr., a
popular writer and speaker in antebellum America, seems to
have been engaged in much the same business when he urged
the "Workingmen of the United States of America" to look to
the future, to discern in themselves "something higher and
better":

> There is a peculiarity implanted by its Maker in the human
> mind, never to rest satisfied with its present condition. How high
> soever its present attainments, it presses on with an undiminished
> ardor for something higher and better: it forgets the things which

are behind, and looks forward with immortal aspirations to those which are before. [19]

The ideal workingman, as Rantoul described him, is clearly a model of individualism: self-made and self-improving, never quite what he is, always on his way to "something higher and better." Within the terms of *The Confidence-Man*, we might also call such a creature a "man-child," for like Melville's human commodity, Rantoul's promising individual is no less the owner of "points at present invisible [and] beauties at present dormant" (105). He too is a child of commodified time, a salable future personified into human shape. To say this is not simply to mock the central tenet of Jacksonian individualism, but rather to contextualize it, to trace its provenance and correspondence within a wider-ranging process—in this case, the analogous production of selves and commodities. But if Melville's man-child casts a lurid light on the familiar doctrine of self-improvement, Rantoul, in his turn, has something to tell us about *The Confidence-Man* as well. For the promising self that Rantoul is trying to market is offered not to some Missouri bachelor, but actually to the owner of that self. Consumer and product are all one in this peculiar kind of marketing. This is a clever invention indeed, and it makes for an impressive kind of economy. The cleverness is not lost on Melville either, and so, in *The Confidence-Man* too, we will witness another form of marketing, one analogous to Rantoul's, and considerably more efficient than what is practiced on the Missouri bachelor.

That surly figure is not always needed, for the confidence man, like Rantoul, is also capable of a reflexive kind of marketing. He also can produce a buyer in the same motion as he produces a commodity, and effect an exchange between the two. From the sick man who invests in "the genuine medicine, and the genuine me" (71), to the miser who invests to make his "everlasting fortune" (87), what the confidence man sells to most of his victims is in fact a promising version of the victim's own self. Each of them is a buyer of his own "man-child." This situation, odd as it might sound, is actually only logical: to the extent that the promising self is a commodity, the most eager buyer of that commodity must be the prospective owner himself. But if so, to own a self, especially a promising self, is necessarily also to be a buyer, for in order to "have" promise one must continually "buy" the idea of it. A promising self is a commodity whose ownership must be continually renewed— whose ownership can be guaranteed only by endless acts of purchase. As a circuit of reflexive exchange, the promising self stands as a utopian marketplace, one that completes both its production and its consumption, both its buying and its selling, all within the compass of a single individual. This neat arrangement is possible because the promising self, in his internal division, can be made to function as both parties in exchange, both the buying agent and the bought object. The consummate consumer is also a consummate commodity. Ceaselessly commodified, he ceaselessly buys promising versions of himself.

Such marketing marvels are by no means the exclusive province of the confidence man, or Robert Rantoul, Jr. In their company we find no less a figure than President Lincoln, who was also something of an expert in that genre of marketing. Determined to show Southerners that the North had no class fated "always to remain laborers," Lincoln has announced, we might recall, that "The man who labored for another last year, this year labors for himself, and next year he will hire others to labor for him."[20] In this scenario, the man-child grows up in three stages: he begins as a hired hand, develops into the self-employed laborer, and ends up being the employer, who "hire[s] others to labor for him." Blessed with such a trajectory, the promising individual is never simply himself: the prospect of better things to come is already inscribed within him. What Lincoln neglected to discuss, of course, was the mechanics of such miraculous progress. What must one do to bring about this metamorphosis, and transform oneself from an employee to an employer in just three years? Had he been quizzed on that point, Lincoln might have answered, as the P.I.O. man does when he feels called upon to explain a similar metamorphosis in his man-child, with the following analogy:

> The second teeth follow, but do not come from, the first; successors, not sons. The first teeth are not like the germ blossom of the apple, at once the father of, and incorporated into, the growth it foreruns; but they are thrust from their place by the independent undergrowth of the succeeding set. (107)

Such a model most certainly takes care of the mechanics of self-improvement. Indeed, by its logic, self-improvement becomes strictly an autotelic phenomenon: it is social in manifestation but ontological in genesis, not so much an endeavor as a given. Just as the second set of teeth cannot fail naturally to succeed the first set, so the employer cannot fail naturally to succeed the employee. Mobility is a developmental law, a provision within every self. Defined in those terms, it requires neither effort nor proof, for simply to be—in the P.I.O. man's morphology of being—is already to be destined for better things.

What the dental model offers is yet another version of the promising self, a self imagined, in this case, as a self-contained theater of mobility, a time capsule programmed to release "something higher and better." For such a self, a self so happily promising, anything would seem possible. In fact, of course, not everything is possible, or at least, not everything is acceptable, for the point of the dental model is to prove that the self can only get better. Getting better is its right and prerogative, its duty and destiny. The paradox here is a self ascribed with such a promising future that the promise, gratifying as it is, ends up becoming its fate. If the dental model is offered to make self-improvement an innate privilege, its practical effect is to make self-improvement a moral obligation. The issue, then, is not that a self is able to better itself, but rather, that it is granted no other alternative, that it cannot be conceived except in terms of a "normal" career of advancement. The promising self is not only free to better itself but destined to better itself, not only promising but bound to account for its promise.

The apparent contradiction here, between promise as a measure of freedom and promise as a measure of obligation, is finally no contradiction, for the promising self turns out to be divided not only in constitution but also in usage. Its structural division, between what it is and what it is to become, is matched by a corresponding division in function—between what it is free to do and what it is obligated to do. Such a division, as I have tried to describe it, is simply the constitutive doubleness of individualism itself. Lincoln, understandably, mentions only one side of this division—the positive side, the self as the locus of freedom. But to do so, to speak only of the self's freedom to better itself, is already to mobilize a logic of obligation. For if everyone is indeed free to become an employer, if self-improvement is to be had for the choosing, one would have no excuse for not taking advantage of that opportunity. As Rantoul says, where "advancement in life courts us to accept it . . . nothing can snatch it from our grasp but some unpardonable vice inherent in our own character."[21] And so, even as Lincoln celebrates the freedom of opportunity—or rather, because he celebrates that freedom—he also inscribes a logic for assigning blame, for the promising self whose career he cites with so much approval is cited perhaps less to describe than to prescribe. Offered as an ontological given, it operates as a normative postulate: it is what everybody is supposed to be, and what everybody ought to be. In that double character it is unassailable, for nothing can disprove the validity of Lincoln's model, since the exceptions are, by definition, self-explanatory exceptions, carrying within themselves the measure of their own failure. The employee who remains an employee has only himself to blame.

What we are witnessing here is the other side of individualism, its negative side: what happens when the self, the repository of individual promise, fails to make good what is invested in him. In that event the self-contained economy becomes a site of imbalance and malfunction, one that fails to exchange its inscribed promise for projected gains. A defective model such as that obviously should be corrected, and correction can come only in the imposition of penalty. The promising self is a necessary postulate, then, both within an economy of reward and within an economy of penalty, and he serves as the locus of accountability in both. He is more necessary perhaps to the latter than to the former, for if he figures in the former simply as the axiomatic recipient of reward, in the latter he normalizes the dispensation of penalty, makes it natural and right.[22] Internally accountable, he produces and consumes "his own fault," as deserving victims always do.

The Confidence-Man—a book dedicated to self-consuming victims, "victims of Auto da Fé"—is hardly likely to overlook this punitive aspect of the promising self. And so the P.I.O. man's promising man-child turns out to have a promising twin, someone who also has a future inscribed in him. What that inscribed future does to the promising self, however, is quite another story:

> What avails, then, that some one Indian, or some two or three, treat a backswoodsman friendly-like? He fears me, he thinks. Take my rifle from me, give him motive, and what will come? Or, if not so, how know I what involuntary preparations may be going on in him for things as unbeknown in present time to him as me— a sort of chemical preparation in the soul for malice, as chemical preparation in the body for malady. (129–30)

The promising self here turns out to be a promising Indian. Structurally, this nascent savage is exactly analogous to the man-child: where the man-child is the owner of "points at present invisible" (105), the Indian is the owner of "things as unbeknown in present time." Unlike the man-child, however (whose promise is the promise of future good behavior), the Indian is promising because he has a "chemical preparation in the soul for malice." As the receptacle of that interesting concoction, the Indian cannot fail to fulfill his chemical destiny. He is bound to become evil, and if he has not so far revealed any of it, he can be trusted to do so in time.

A chemical Indian makes a promising self, but he is even more promising in the vegetable form. In an earlier metaphor, we are told that, with the passage of time, every Indian will grow to become just like Mocmohoc, that paragon of treachery: "But are all Indians like Mocmohoc?—Not all have proved such; but in the least harmful may lie his germ" (129).

Like the "chemical preparation for malice," the organic "germ" here also works as a projective category, and it works even better. From dormancy to maturity, the "germ" of malice follows a developmental path essentially known and charted. The time it takes to reach its destination is simply its growth period, so to speak, a period more or less computable, indeed already computed. Packed in this germlike form, time is once again incorporated, as projective property, into the province of the self. What its incorporation offers, in this instance, is a new and utterly ingenious way to measure the self's accountability. For the Indian is now accountable, not only in the sense that he can be counted on to turn evil but also, more literally, in the sense that he can be expected to do so within a calculable time, the period between the germination of malice and its maturation.

Accountability here takes on a quantitative literalness. But the literalization of accountability makes the Indian "accountable" in yet another sense: accountable—responsible and indeed punishable—for the malice whose germ he carries. Because the future of that "germ" is so clearly marked out, because one can even calculate how long it would take for that germ to attain full bloom, the Indian's potential malice is as good as real. Just as the Indian-hater can "avenge" himself as a proleptic victim, so the Indian himself can be punished as a proleptic victimizer, the seat of germinating malice. The incorporation of time into the self is crucial for the logic of penalty, we can now see, for what results is a self "accountable" not only for wrongdoings already accomplished but also for wrongdoings he can be counted on to commit. Along with the "futures market" and the "futures contract," there is also such a thing as "trying the remote future."[23] The promising Indian shows how it works.

The nascent savage thus enacts a very different career from that of his promising twin, the man-child. While the latter proceeds to "something higher and better," the former proceeds to his sad but just deserts. Neither the structural kinship between the two nor their disparate destinies are to be wondered at, for these two are the necessary partners within the double logic of individualism. Manifest Destiny, another experiment with the Future, required their joint production. What is striking in this context, however, is the absolute congruence between the imperialist structure of selfhood in Manifest Destiny and the capitalist structure of selfhood in individual accountability.[24] Both fashion the individual into a self-contained economy that, even as it encapsulates penalty, encapsulates as well its cause. The self-victimizing savage of Manifest Destiny and the self-consuming victim of the marketplace turn out also to be identical twins.

In a different context, we might think of the promising Indian as an extreme case of the autonomous self—so extreme, in fact, that he ends up being the casualty of what is usually construed to be the grounds for freedom. He is the promising self turned into the deserving victim. But even to use the word "turn," in this context, is already an imprecision, for no "turning" is really needed for the former to become the latter, since the two are cognate and complementary in every sense, mutually engendered and mutually contained. If we don't usually think of the promising self in punitive terms, if we habitually dissociate ourselves from deserving victims when we imagine ourselves to be promising selves, that only shows how well market individualism has succeeded in its charge—in rendering the victim accountable and discountable. Generalizing further, we might even say that the very notion of freedom that underwrites the promising self—his freedom of opportunity and mobility—is already, in its very conceptualization, a discriminatory category, embedded in a structure that requires deserving victims. For such freedom counts as "freedom" only because it manifests itself in some particular persons, only because it is not everyone's to evince.[25] Jefferson's phrase, "Empire for Liberty," makes perfect sense then, for freedom can easily accompany, and indeed often does accompany, an "empire," the "sole and despotic dominion" of discrete individuals. Elizabeth Fox-Genovese and Eugene Genovese were not thinking specifically of that phrase, but they might well have been when they wrote, "Only in America could the antithesis between democracy and freedom appear as other than intrinsic."[26]

In any case, it is with the promising Indian in mind that I now return to his twin, his better half, the happy half. This lucky creature we have already met in a number of guises—in Melville's man-child, for instance—but he is most conspicuous in a particular kind of discourse, one especially relevant, I believe, to *The Confidence-Man*: the discourse of nineteenth-century reform. Like Melville's Indian-hater, the antebellum reformer also happened to be a fond advocate of the promising self. (William Ellery Channing, for example, talked about the "germs and promises"[27] in an individual, just as the Indian-hater talks about the "germ" of malice.) Unlike the Indian-hater, however, the reformer was nothing if not benevolent. He invoked the promising self, not as an economy of penalty, but as an economy of reward. Emerson, in an essay called "Man the Reformer," points to just such an economy, one that exchanges virtue for benefit, as the "spring and regulator in all efforts of reform." Reform works, according to him, because there is an "infinite worthiness in man" answering to "the call of worth."[28] The man who employs his "infinite worthiness" in this gainful fashion is

> a free and helpful man, a reformer, a benefactor, not content to slip along through the world like a footman or a spy, escaping by his nimbleness and apologies as many knocks as he can, but a brave and upright man, who must find or cut a straight road to everything excellent in the earth, and not only go honorably himself, but make it easier for all who follow him to go in honor and with benefit.[29]

What is interesting about Emerson's portrait of the reformer is that he is clearly someone who has "advanced" in life. He apparently practices what he preaches, and, "not content to slip along through the world like a footman," he has turned himself instead into the most laudable kind of entrepreneur: he has traded virtue for the most edifying, as well as most gratifying, kind of reward. Having made it himself, he is now ready to help others do the same thing, "in honor and with benefit."

"Benefit," for Emerson as for most antebellum reformers, is no less to be emphasized than "honor." Indeed, in Emerson's formulation, "benefit" is virtually the equivalent of "honor," which makes perfect sense, because where the self is conceived as a self-enclosed economy, every virtue might be expected to carry a value, or a "benefit." Robert Rantoul, Jr., always anxious to prove the "preeminent worth of moral cultivation,"[30] is even more emphatic about where this "benefit" comes from, and how it figures in the scheme of things. "When we speak of the beneficial effect of [moral] education on the pecuniary circumstances of the next generation, we are far from intimating that there are not other interests involved of much more momentous importance," he says. "Heaven forbid that morality should ever be . . . debased to a sordid calculation of profit and loss." Still, the fact remains that, for him, "the humblest laborer" in the field of morality "will reap, in his own personal share of the benefit, an adequate remuneration for all his toil."[31]

Merrily trading his moral labor for his "adequate remuneration," the "self" that nineteenth-century reformers invoked was perhaps less a human being than a personified attribute, a principle of accounting personified into human shape. Historians have referred to antebellum reform as "systematic subjectivism" and "perfectionist individualism," because the reformers' social vision was inseparable from premises about the self, about its agency, identity, and accountability.[32] Under the tutelage of the reformers, we might even argue, the self-governing, self-improving individual was standardized and institutionalized. The "self" offered here, moreover, was not just any self, but one created specifically in the image of the market, a self imagined as the scene of commerce between virtue and reward. From this perspective, it is by no means absurd that, in *The Confidence-Man*, the man with the weed should propose to quicken reform with the "Wall street spirit" (35). He hardly needs to propose it, in fact, for it was already in existence. In the very model of selfhood it invoked, reform was already Wall Street's ally.[33]

The Confidence-Man, true to *its* Wall Street ally, therefore has its own reform program as well. The reformer in *The Confidence-Man* is of course the confidence man himself. He is a reformer, not only because he regularly talks like one, and not only because he is always reforming himself, but, more crucially, because he is able to "mold" others (to use the favored word of nineteenth-century reformers) into a new shape, into something that they themselves fail to recognize. Much more so than the transfer of money (which does not always take place), reforming the victim marks the triumph of the confidence man. Two chapter titles nicely summarize the procedure: from chapter 15, "An old miser, upon suitable representations, is prevailed upon to venture an investment," and from chapter 16, "A sick man, after some impatience, is induced to become a patient." As we can see, both titles record a three-part drama, chronicling the victim's change of heart, which is what happens over and over again. At the outset, the victim is staunchly resistant: he is indifferent, suspicious, unyielding. An involved dialogue ("suitable representations") then follows. And finally, at the last stage, the victim comes around, sets aside his mistrust, and, in succumbing to the confidence man, is himself transformed into a different creature.[34] In one way or another, the good merchant, the sophomore, the charitable widow, the old miser, the sick man, the cripple Thomas Fry, the Missouri bachelor, and the barber all undergo this sort of "reform."

Contradicting himself, becoming something other than what he used to be, the victim of the confidence man becomes a human oxymoron even as he suffers himself to be reformed. His structure of selfhood seems no different from the manchild's, no different from the Indian-hater's, and no different from that of the Whitmanesque self who boasts: "Do I contradict myself? / Very well then I contradict myself, / (I am large, I contain multitudes.)" The only difference between him and them is the fact of his victimization. But here too the difference is perhaps less a difference than a complementarity, or even an exchange of sorts: it is almost as if the victims were the tradeoffs for such untrammeled selves as Whitman celebrates. And even the victims remain, in some sense, the untrammeled self. For the central event in each of these episodes, these reform encounters, is after all the production of individual freedom. Each victim, as he comes into contact with the confidence man, is given the freedom of choice. Freely choosing and freely damning himself in his choice, he is the untrammeled self who chooses to become a victim.

If this sounds wrong, it is because we do not tend to associate "choice" with victimization. What *The Confidence-Man* dramatizes, however, is the extent to which the latter is compatible with the former—or perhaps even inscribed in the former. For it is their freedom of choice, after all, that makes the victims in *The Confidence-Man* deserving victims. Free agents all of them, they enter into their fateful dealings only because they choose to, and having thus chosen they must stick by their bargain. The notion of choice invariably subjectivizes the act of exchange then; it removes the burden of accountability away from the process of transaction and invests it instead in the "choice" entertained by the transacting individual. That individual is, accordingly, an accountable self. Internally calculable, and internally regulated, he owes his victimization not to the confidence man but to himself. Exercising his freedom of choice out of his own greed, ignorance, and imbecility, he gets what he bargains for.

The centrality of choice in *The Confidence-Man*, then, is really no more than a corollary of the market individualism that animates its pages. The effect, in any case, is to localize accountability, encapsulate it and stage it as a personal drama. But even as the book foregrounds this personified economy, what it authorizes, in the obscure background, is a general economy that (like the rattlesnake's) turns out to be one whose "accountability is not by nature manifest" (164). The existence of such an alternate economy is all too logical, for, being the double logic that it is, market individualism must serve not just to manage the accounted but also to license the unaccountable. As each victim consumes "his own fault," each of them, in his internal circulation, also affirms the presence of an inscrutable supervisory order: "something transcendent," "enigmatical," and "mysterious." Those are the words that Marx uses to describe the mystery of the commodity form, and their applicability here is not altogether accidental. For to the extent that Melville is able to fashion his characters into units of accountability, he is also able to claim for himself the obverse privilege of freedom, of being unaccountable. He can now operate as a principle of transcendence, mysterious in its executions, infallible in its logic, an Invisible Hand invisibly dispensing just deserts.

And so, the spirit of Adam Smith presides not only over the marketplace. It presides here as well. In the freedom and un-accountability of the Invisible Hand, Melville has finally found a model of freedom that suits him, a model after which he can fashion his own authorial hand. This explains, I think, the book's peculiar opaqueness, in which its author appears as both inscrutable and irresponsible.[35] Here, Melville is in the habit of making oddly discrete and contradictory pronounce-ments. Like the market, with its legendary freedom of choice, *The Confidence-Man* rejects nothing, questions nothing, and displays its abundance in segregated harmony. The triumph of the discrete allows Melville to contradict himself, and to do so frequently—one is almost tempted to say, flauntingly. In chap-ter 14, for instance, he defends inconsistent characters by in-voking the authority of the real. "In real life, a consistent character is a *rara avis*," he says, and an author is to be com-mended, not censured, for producing inconsistent characters, since he is merely being "faithful to facts" (58). Such rever-ence for "reality" (58) quickly evaporates, however, when Melville proceeds, in chapter 33, to defend other characters, those who cause us to exclaim, "How unreal all this is!" (157). We have no right to object, Melville tells us, for why should we expect from "a work of amusement" this "severe fidelity to real life" (157)? Real life is "dull," after all, and a good writer should know better than to stay "true to that dullness" (157). Clearly, "real life" in chapter 33 is not what it used to be in chapter 14.[36] Which is closer to what "Melville" really be-lieves? There is no way of telling, for "Melville" is simply not available for our enlightenment. Or rather, he is too available. He appears in too many shades and forms of ideas. He cancels himself out, as R. W. B. Lewis suggests, in his very plenitude of utterance.[37] He is at once manifest and unaccountable.

Vanishing behind his profusion of sentiments, "Melville" vanishes, even more thoroughly, behind his anonymity of speech. Authorial language in *The Confidence-Man* is, quite simply, indistinguishable from the language of the characters. To take just one example, Melville's keyword in chapter 14, "nature," is taken up in chapter 16 by the herb doctor, who turns it into a magical incantation: "Nature is health. . . . Get nature, and you get well. Now, I repeat, this medicine is nature's own" (69). And when the herb doctor vanishes, the verbal legacy remains, to pass on to his successor, the P. I. O. man, who echoes Melville not only in thought but even in metaphor. Melville has invoked the caterpillar-butterfly to justify his inconsistent characters, who may be, "at different periods, as much at variance with itself as the caterpillar is with the butterfly into which it changes" (58). The P. I. O. man now excuses the boy with a bad record with the happy thought that "he may have been a caterpillar, but is now a butterfly" (108). As the same words circulate among author and characters, "Melville" too is everywhere and nowhere. He says nothing for which he might be held accountable. In his blank cadences we cannot even detect a human source.

But the disjunction between speech and speaker is true not only of the author, but of everyone else. In this most bedeviling of books, what a person says has little to do with who he is—or rather, because he tends to say drastically different things at different times, because he is capable of eloquence and inanity in the same breath, it is impossible to tell who he is from what he says.[38] "Indeed, our sentiments agree so, that were they written in a book, whose was whose, few but the nicest critics might determine" (137), the cosmopolitan fondly assures Charlie Noble. That is the plain truth, as it turns out, for speech in *The Confidence-Man* has almost nothing to do with the speakers: it is an autonomous phenomenon, not a communicative device. Characters speak not because they want to, but because they happen to be around. Indeed, throughout the book, there is a certain arbitrariness in the assignment of speech, a certain indifference, on Melville's part, to the vehicle of utterance. Like the "interchangeable parts" writ large in the American system of manufactures, Melville's characters too are produced as interchangeable speakers.[39] This allows the good merchant to speak out on the subject of truth, and Charlie Noble, the small-time con man, to embark on an involved and often passionate discussion of Polonius. From the first scene till the last, disembodied voices are made to deliver oblique comments on the action of the story. All in all, we have the eerie sense that speech imposes itself on a character—rather than issuing from him—and that in the long run, it makes little difference who this character is. Characters are interchangeable. They are no more than the medium in which words circulate.

"In discipline, the elements are interchangeable," Foucault writes, since persons are individualized "by a location that does not give them a fixed position, but distributes them and circulates them in a network of relations."[40] By this description, *The Confidence-Man* would certainly count as a disciplinary model. Discipline here operates, I suggest, largely through the complementary genesis of discrete realms: the realm of the accounted and the realm of the unaccountable, the realm of interchangeable speakers, and the realm of autonomous speech. Nowhere is this more evident than in the five interpolated stories. We tend to discuss these stories as set pieces, more or less complete in themselves, often without considering who is telling them. That fact is indicative in itself. The story of China Aster, for instance, is related by Egbert, for altogether questionable motives. "The Metaphysics of Indian-hating" appears under the auspices of Charlie Noble. The human agencies of these stories do not bear reflecting upon, and indeed we do not reflect upon them, for the stories themselves encourage our oversight, disowning their human agents almost as soon as they come into being, acknowledging their indebtedness to no one.

At every point, Melville identifies the storyteller only to render that fact immaterial. Because storytellers rarely get to use their own words, their status as storytellers becomes virtually a parody of the term. The good merchant, for instance, does not really get to tell the story of the unfortunate man, for Melville has decided that, "as the good merchant could, perhaps, do better justice to the man than the story, we shall venture to tell it in other words than his, though not to any other effect" (50). Charlie Noble, teller of the John Moredock story, similarly defers to the authorship of Judge Hall, choosing, apparently out of modesty, to "render the judge upon the colonel almost word for word" (123). And finally, Egbert surrenders his authorship to the China Aster story with this explanation: "I wish I could do so in my own words, but unhappily the original story-teller here has so tyrannized over me, that it is quite impossible for me to repeat his incidents without sliding into his style" (177).

In the most systematic fashion, *The Confidence-Man* dramatizes the disjunction between speech and speaker—or even (as Egbert says) the "tyranny" of speech over speaker. People do not use words; words use them. The receding authorship in the three stories makes it impossible to say just who the story-tellers are—and in the long run, it does not matter. The discrete segregation and mutual imperviousness between speech and speaker make words utterly free, utterly unaccountable. They go nowhere, illustrate nothing, and refer to nothing but themselves.[41] If one could speak of the Invisible Hand as the ultimate capitalist fantasy, *The Confidence-Man*, in its inhuman, superhuman reign of words, would seem to enact that fantasy at its most extravagant, and most fantastic. Absolutely autonomous and absolutely harmonious, words eclipse their human speakers to shadow forth a transcendent order, at once relentless and inscrutable. In their crisscrossing paths, their repetitions and mutations, they make up a coldly hermetic universe. We see a number of words in close circulation, miraculously perpetrating their lives, passing from one character to another without much regard to who they are. Words like "confidence," "nature," "invention," and "original genius" inscribe trajectories more enduring than any human character. The latter comes alive (if that is indeed the right expression) only when he bodies forth one of those words, but even then, even during the brief moment when he is quickened into speech, he remains an appendage to what he says, attached to it and overshadowed by it. Involuntary ventriloquist, he lends himself to a design unintended by him, to a machinery more mysterious than anything he can know.

In that regard he is not unlike the inhabitant of Adam Smith's utopia, a world of "natural liberty," where everyone is "free to pursue his own interest his way" because he is guided, after all, "by an invisible hand to promote an end which was no part of his intention."[42] Smith was, of course, much heartened by such a prospect. In *The Confidence-Man*, though, we see something of its cost. To be "human" means very little here, for human characters in this book are not so much human beings as ciphers of an Invisible Hand. "You can conclude nothing from the human form" (193), the cosmopolitan tells the barber. But if that is indeed the case, it is due not to the complexity of that "human form" but to its stark simplicity, its reduction to a mere "form" governed by a single term. Commenting on just this phenomenon, Paul Brodtkorb writes:

> With few exceptions, humanity in this book is reduced to dupers and duped, many figures being both, so that characters come to seem interchangeable to the point where style itself gets confused, as antecedents of personal pronouns become so vague they must be repeated in parentheses.[43]

This is what accountability finally means in *The Confidence-Man*: everyone here is either a duper or a duped (or both at once), for those two labels alone sum up all human beings, and account for all human transactions. Measured always by one term, segregated always by it, characters in *The Confidence-Man* inhabit a universe not only divided but relentlessly reductive in its division. Such characters resemble personifications more than anything else. Inert signs, they bespeak a fixed meaning, body forth a rigid landscape. They become "persons" only when they allow themselves to be divided into dupers and duped. Their very personhood articulates that polarity: they are constituted by it, and cannot be conceived otherwise.

What is enacted here is not altogether unfamiliar, for the

drama of polarity in *The Confidence-Man* really does no more than rehearse the double logic of market individualism itself. The logic that produces winners and losers is the same logic that produces dupers and duped. In the pathetic shapes in Melville's book, however, we see something perhaps not quite so obvious in the marketplace: the extent to which personhood is generated by its own reduction. Shorn of the entangling complexity of relations and antecedents, bound by a single attribute, the self here becomes a principle of individuality only as it becomes abstracted, only as it fits itself into a "human form." It is their reduction to "form," indeed, that allows us to judge the book's characters, to hold them accountable, as Melville clearly asks us to do. By his taxonomic logic, they need only one label. It makes no difference that one is duped in his "sophomorean" "speculations" with the "superfluity in [his] pocket" (42), and that another is duped in an agonized attempt to regain his health, to be "something else to others than a burdensome care, and to myself a droning grief" (69). Whatever difference between them—in degree of need, desperation, or helplessness—is eclipsed by their categoric identity, their categoric accountability. Nothing else matters: dupes is what they are, and being duped is what happens to them.

As a circular construct, the accountable self finally accomplishes what Melville has, in book after book, gone in search for. Here, in the shadow of the marketplace, he has finally found a form of individualism that works for him: one that produces perfectly enclosed figures, one that works, in fact, as a perfect tautology. *The Confidence-Man* thus delights in tautologies, abounds with them; for like the market that encompasses it and inspires it, this too is the home of circular axioms. "And though indeed the dread of tautology be the continual torment of some earnest minds, and, as such, is surely a weakness in them . . . yet not to dread tautology at times only belongs to those enviable dunces," Melville has written in *Pierre* (227). Now, in *The Confidence-Man*, he is able, openly and with hardly any misgivings, to embrace what he dreads. We only have to look at the titles of chapters 14, 33, and 44 to get a sense of Melville's triumph: "Worth the consideration of those to whom it may prove worth considering," "Which may pass for whatever it may prove to be worth," and ". . . which will be sure of receiving more or less attention from those readers who do not skip it." Something seems to be said in the course of a tautology, but nothing is, for what is offered here is, quite literally, words, and nothing but words. This is what happens, of course, when words are utterly unaccountable, when they refer to nothing but themselves. Forever circulating, and forever circular, language here finally becomes what Melville has always wanted it to be: a self-enclosed universe, untouched by the barbaric world, untouchable to barbaric readers.

Yet, if *The Confidence-Man* represents a triumph for language, the triumph is hardly without a cost. For even as words luxuriate in their freedom, they must submit, in the same measure, to a corresponding reduction. They must become no more than material signs, no more than curious ciphers on a page. Radically self-contained, they are also radically self-imprisoned. That is how words function in a tautology, and, in some sense, that is how words function in *The Confidence-Man*. For if tautology engages language in its freedom and autonomy, it also dictates, at the same time, the utter futility of that language, its reduction to a senseless display of letters. Imperial in its freedom, inane in its reduction, language in *The Confidence-Man* paradoxically repeats, in its very triumph, the double logic of the individualism that is its model and inspiration.

From that reduction to futility, Melville himself is not exempt. He seems, in fact, to be aware of it, and nothing better demonstrates that awareness than his narrative apparatus, an assembly of stylized gestures at once effusive and pointless. Over and over again, Melville sets out with an avowed purpose, pursues it with exemplary zeal, but always ends up dramatizing the phoniness of it. This pattern is especially evident when he undertakes to deceive us, for he always manages not to. When the man with the weed meets the sophomore, we are told that "at the time, he was leaning over the rail at the boat's side, in his pensiveness, *unmindful of* another pensive figure near—a young gentleman with a swan neck" (21, italics mine). This is obviously not true, because the man with the weed is very mindful indeed of the other pensive figure. But Melville is nothing if not charitable in his account—and, even more important, he is charitable in vain. The same ineffectual charity he demonstrates once again when the man with the big book, looking "fatigued," drops down on a partly vacant settee and strikes up a conversation with his "chance neighbor, who happens to be the good merchant" (46). The latter is no "chance neighbor," as we well know, but Melville is once again too charitable to report otherwise—although, once again, he is not too charitable to allow us to see through his charity.

More decorative than functional, the very strategies for deception in *The Confidence-Man* have a pointlessness to them. Melville goes through the motions of deception, ceremoniously and ostentatiously, but the motions are pure motions emptied of efficacy, less application than display. We cannot help noticing them, but even as we notice them we also dismiss them from our attention. It hardly matters, after all, whether the confidence man meets his victims by design or by "chance," because this has no bearing on what we think about him. And it certainly does not matter whether the two porters carrying a large trunk "accidentally or otherwise swung their burden against" the deaf mute (3). Nothing can be more inconsequential than this bit of equivocation. Few of us share Melville's charitable uncertainty, but then we hardly care. The "truth" of the matter is immaterial, and so are the tactics deployed to convey or evade that truth. In their autonomy and inconsequence, their freedom and futility, such "tactics of indirection"[44] rehearse the very logic that the tautologies enact.

Freedom and futility sum up Melville's fateful triumph as well. He has finally found a poetics that serves his need, one that makes him transcendent and unaccountable, one that licenses excess even as it reinscribes excess as control. It is a triumph for him, and yet—such is the irony of individualism—

the very terms of his triumph would seem also to be the terms of his undoing. For no matter how skillful his attempt, how faithful his execution, the fact remains that the market is already doing what he is trying to do: doing it better, more thoroughly, and with an unaccountability even harder to scrutinize than Melville's own enigmatic performance. His authorial exercise, gratifying as it might seem, turns out also to be pointless. In that pointlessness, as in the repeated, resented instances of failure in his earlier books, Melville betrays his own status as a double entity, constituted by an individualism that is invariably and necessarily double. It makes sense, in any case, that *The Confidence-Man* should be his last novel, for having summoned forth a regime of unaccountability, all that is left for him to do is to witness it in silence: witness it as it carries on its accounting and discounting, in a space much wider than the pages of his book. Melville is right, then, to say at the end of *The Confidence-Man*, that "Something further may follow of this Masquerade" (217). Something does.

Notes

◆   ◆   ◆

Chapter 1
Nation, Self, and Personification

1. "Hawthorne and His Mosses," in *Moby-Dick*, ed. Harrison Hayford and Hershel Parker (New York: Norton, 1967), 544.

2. All four quotations are from *Moby-Dick*, 378–79.

3. Second Inaugural Address, 4 March 1805, in *A Compilation of the Messages and Papers of the Presidents, 1789–1897*, ed. James D. Richardson (New York: Bureau of National Literature, 1897), 1: 367. My argument here parallels Myra Jehlen's discussion of the "primacy of place" in American thought; see *American Incarnation: The Individual, the Nation, and the Continent* (Cambridge: Harvard University Press, 1986), 1–75.

4. *Young Hickory Banner*, 15 October 1846. Quoted in Albert Weinberg, *Manifest Destiny: A Study of Nationalist Expansionism in American History* (Baltimore: The Johns Hopkins University Press, 1935), 119.

5. For an important discussion of "Reification and American Literature," see Carolyn Porter, *Seeing and Being: The Plight of the Participant Observer in Emerson, James, Adams, and Faulkner* (Middletown, Conn.: Wesleyan University Press, 1981), 23–53. My emphasis here is somewhat different from Porter's: I am concerned less with the reified consciousness (Porter's focus) than with the genesis of contextless autonomy in the reifying process.

6. Sacvan Bercovitch, *The American Jeremiad* (Madison: University of Wisconsin Press, 1978), 55.

7. Michael Paul Rogin, *Subversive Genealogy: The Politics and Art of Herman Melville* (Berkeley: University of California Press, 1985); James Duban, *Melville's Major Fiction: Politics, Theology, and Imagination* (Dekalb: Northern Illinois University Press, 1983). Also see Hershel Parker, "Melville and Politics: A Scrutiny of the Political Milieux of Herman Melville's Life and Works" (Ph.D. diss., Northwestern University, 1963).

8. The phrase is Umberto Eco's; see "Looking for a Logic of Culture," in *The Tell-Tale Sign: A Survey of Semiotics*, ed. Thomas A. Sebeok (Lisse, the Netherlands: The Peter de Ridder Press, 1975), 9–19.

9. Melville to John Murray, 25 March 1848, in *The Letters of Herman Melville*, ed. Merrell R. Davis and William H. Gilman (New Haven: Yale University Press, 1960), 70; "Hawthorne and His Mosses," in *Moby-Dick*, 541–42.

10. Melville to Nathaniel Hawthorne, 16 April (?) 1851, in *Letters*, 124.

11. Defining the "imperial self" as a function of individual consciousness, Anderson has argued, in passing, that " 'Manifest Destiny,' and the imperialist fantasies of the end of the century have, I think, been exaggerated by historians." See *The Imperial Self: An Essay in American Literary and Cultural History* (New York: Vintage, 1972), 17. I would reverse Anderson's observation and argue that the literary "imperial self" has everything to do with America's "Manifest Destiny."

12. *Mardi, and a Voyage Thither* (Evanston and Chicago: Northwestern University Press and the Newberry Library, 1970), 368. *Moby-Dick*, 378; *Pierre* (Evanston and Chicago: Northwestern University Press and the Newberry Library), 167.

13. Melville to Nathaniel Hawthorne, 17 (?) November 1851, in *Letters*, 142.

14. *Moby-Dick*, 261.

15. William Blackstone, *Commentaries on the Laws of England: A Facsimile of the First Edition of 1765–1769*, vol. 2, *Of the Rights of Things* (Chicago: University of Chicago Press, 1979), 2.

16. Jefferson to James Madison, 27 April 1809, in *The Writings of Thomas Jefferson*, 20 vols. (Washington, D.C.: The Thomas Jefferson Memorial Association, 1904), 11–12: 277.

17. Claude Halstead Van Tyne, *The American Revolution, 1776–1783* (New York: Harper, 1905), 333.

18. See, for example, the chapters "The Imperial Logic," and "More Freedom and More Empire," in William Appleman Williams, *Empire as a Way of Life* (New York: Oxford University Press, 1980), 55–102.

19. *New York Morning News*, 27 December 1845. Quoted in Weinberg, *Manifest Destiny*, 145.

20. *Congressional Globe*, 28th Congress, 2nd session (1845), Appendix, 178.

21. "Mexican War," *United States Magazine and Democratic Review* 22 (1848): 120.

22. "Hawthorne and His Mosses," in *Moby-Dick*, 546.

23. Rogin's phrase is from *Fathers and Children: Andrew Jackson and the Subjugation of the American Indian* (New York: Vintage, 1976), 167. Most theorists of imperialism would exclude antebellum America from consideration, since imperialism is most often defined as "the international practices and relations of the capitalist world during the distinct stage of mature capitalism that emerged in the last quarter of the 19th century." See Harry Magdoff, "The Logic of Imperialism," *Social Policy* 1 (1970): 20–29. Following this criterion, Walter Lafeber, for instance, has chosen 1860 as the beginning of American imperialism in *The New Empire: An Interpretation of American Expansion, 1860–1898* (Ithaca, N.Y.: Cornell University Press, 1963). I am interested, however, less in the international operation of empire than in its domestic articulation. My discussion is informed by the fol-

lowing: R. W. Van Alstyne, *The Rising American Empire* (New York: Norton, 1974); Yehoshua Arieli, *Individualism and Nationalism in American Ideology* (Cambridge: Harvard University Press, 1964); Martin Green, *Dreams of Adventure, Deeds of Empire* (New York: Basic Books, 1979); Reginald Horsman, *Race and Manifest Destiny* (Cambridge: Harvard University Press, 1981); Frederick Merk, *Manifest Destiny and Mission in American History* (New York: Knopf, 1963); Richard Slotkin, *The Fatal Environment: The Myth of the Frontier in the Age of Industrialization, 1800–1890* (New York: Atheneum, 1985); Walter Russell Mead, *Mortal Splendor: The American Empire in Transition* (Boston: Houghton Mifflin, 1987); Weinberg, *Manifest Destiny*; Williams, *Empire as a Way of Life*.

24. See, for example, *The Great Republic: A History of the American People*, ed. Bernard Bailyn et al. (Lexington, Mass.: D. C. Heath, 1977), 1: 425–565; *The National Experience: A History of the United States to 1877*, 4th ed., ed. John M. Blum et al. (New York: Harcourt Brace Jovanovich, 1977), 187–91, 197–201.

25. See, for example, Sean Wilentz, *Chants Democratic: New York City and the Rise of the American Working Class, 1788–1850* (New York: Oxford University Press, 1984).

26. *The Great Republic*, 458–60.

27. Horace Mann, "Twelfth Annual Report" (1848), in *Annual Reports on Education* (Boston: Lee and Shepard, 1872), 668.

28. Ronald Walters, *American Reformers: 1815–1860* (New York: Hill and Wang, 1978), 4–5.

29. Fred Somkin, *Unquiet Eagle: Memory and Desire in the Idea of American Freedom, 1815–1860* (Ithaca, N.Y.: Cornell University Press, 1967), 11–54. The portentous phrases, all of which are by Lyman Beecher, are from "The Perils of Atheism to the Nation," in *Lectures on Scepticism* (Cincinnati: Corey & Fairbank, 1835), 78, 106, 108.

30. Mann, "Twelfth Annual Report" (1848), 668.

31. Theophilus Fisk, "Capital Against Labor. An address delivered at Julien Hall before the mechanics of Boston on Wednesday evening, May 20, 1835," in *Social Theories of Jacksonian Democracy: Representative Writings of the Period 1825–1850*, ed. Joseph L. Blau (New York: Bobbs-Merrill, 1954), 201.

32. *A Charge on the Rise of the American Empire* (1776), rare book in the Huntington Library. Quoted in R. W. Van Alstyne, *The Rising American Empire*, 1.

33. *The Federalist Papers* (New York: New America Library, 1961), no. 14, 104; "America in 1846," *United States Magazine and Democratic Review* 18 (1846): 61.

34. *The Great Republic*, 410.

35. "The Great Nation of Futurity," *United States Magazine and Democratic Review* 11 (1839): 427.

36. *White-Jacket, or, The World in a Man-of-War* (Evanston and Chicago: Northwestern University Press and the Newberry Library, 1970), 150–51.

37. *A Treasury of American Folklore*, ed. B. A. Botkin (New York: Crown Publishers, 1944), 276.

38. The "perfectly closed system" Lukács is referring to is the increasingly rationalized and mechanized industrial process, "a process mechanically conforming to fixed laws and enacted independently of man's consciousness and impervious to human intervention." But his description seems exactly to fit the spatial and temporal economy of Manifest Destiny. See *History and Class Consciousness*, trans. Rodney Livingstone (Cambridge, Mass.: MIT Press, 1971), 89.

39. Here I would like to acknowledge Joseph Frank's seminal essay, "Spatial Form in Modern Literature." My own application of the term is somewhat different, but Frank's essay is important in foregrounding the logic of space in literary form. Frank's essay is reprinted in *The Widening Gyre: Crisis and Mastery in Modern Literature* (New Brunswick, N.J.: Rutgers University Press, 1963). For a useful bibliography on space and narrative, see *Spatial Form in Narrative*, ed. Jeffrey R. Smitten and Ann Daghistany (Ithaca, N.Y.: Cornell University Press, 1981), 245–63.

40. Ralph Waldo Emerson, "The Young American" (1844), in *Nature, Addresses, and Lectures* (Cambridge, Mass.: Riverside, 1883), 345, 350.

41. Quoted in Eric Foner, *Free Soil, Free Labor, Free Men: The Ideology of the Republican Party before the Civil War* (New York: Oxford University Press, 1970), 27.

42. George Henry Evans, "To the People of the United States," *Working Man's Advocate*, 6 July 1844, in *The Reform Impulse, 1825–1850*, ed. Walter Hugins (Columbia: University of South Carolina Press, 1972), 92.

43. Harriet Martineau, *Society in America* (1837; rpt. Garden City, N.Y.: Doubleday, 1962), 168.

44. Henry C. Carey, *Principles of Political Economy*, 3 vols. (1838; rpt. New York: Augustus M. Kelley, 1965), 1: 339.

45. For a discussion of the notion of "harmony" in spiritualist reform, see Walters, *American Reformers*, 167–69.

46. Homi K. Bhabha, "Signs Taken for Wonders: Questions of Ambivalence and Authority Under a Tree Outside Delhi, May 1817," *Critical Inquiry* 12 (Autumn 1985): 153. Bhabha is talking about British colonial rule in India. I find his terms equally applicable in this context.

47. Instructions to Generals William Carroll and John Coffee from John H. Eaton, secretary of war, 30 May 1829, in *The Age of Jackson*, ed. Robert V. Remini (Columbia: South Carolina University Press, 1972), 64.

48. Francis Parkman, *The Conspiracy of Pontiac*, 2 vols. (1851; rpt. Boston: Little Brown, 1909), 1: 3, 238. Horace Greeley is mentioned in James Parton, *Life of Andrew Jackson*, 3 vols. (Boston: Houghton Mifflin, 1860), 1: 401.

49. Rogin, *Fathers and Children*, 166.

50. James Hall, *Sketches of History, Life, and Manners in the West* (Philadelphia: H. Hall, 1835), 19.

51. For a more comprehensive account of the ideology of "progress," see Ernest Tuveson, *Millennium and Utopia: A Study in the Background of the Idea of Progress* (Berkeley: University of California Press, 1949), esp. chap. 2–4. See also Slotkin, *Fatal Environment*, esp. chap. 3, "The Frontier Myth as a Theory of Development," 33–47.

52. Mann, "Twelfth Annual Report" (1848), 676. One account of industrial barbarism is Rebecca Harding Davis, "Life in the Iron Mills," *Atlantic* 7 (April 1861): 430–51.

53. Theodore Parker, *A Sermon of The Dangerous Classes in Society* (Boston: C. & J. M. Spear, 1847), 9.

54. For a fuller account of the city missions, see Carroll Smith Rosenberg, *Religion and the Rise of the American City: The New York City Mission Movement, 1812–1870* (Ithaca, N.Y.: Cornell University Press, 1971). For a discussion of nineteenth-century "colonial attitude" toward domestic slums, see Mark Seltzer, "*The Princess Casamassima*: Realism and the Fantasy of Surveillance," in *American Realism: New Essays*, ed. Eric Sundquist (Baltimore: Johns Hopkins University Press, 1982), esp. 101–103. For a discussion of the same phenomenon in late nineteenth-century America, see June Howard, *Form and History in American Literary Naturalism* (Chapel Hill: University of North Carolina Press, 1985), 70–103.

55. Foner, *Free Soil*, 16, 17.

56. *The Collected Works of Abraham Lincoln*, ed. Roy F. Basler, 9 vols. (New Brunswick, N.J.: Rutgers University Press, 1953–55), 3: 478; 2: 364.

57. For an account of the contradictions between liberal individualism and equality, see, for example, J. R. Pole, *The Pursuit of Equality in American History* (Berkeley: University of California Press, 1978), esp. chap. 5, "The Constitutional Aegis and the Emergence of Individualism," 112–47.

58. On a global scale, Karl Polanyi also sees a parallel in the management of colonized natives and the management of industrial workers; see *The Great Transformation: The Political and Economic Origins of Our Time* (Boston: Beacon Press, 1957), 157–79.

59. Maureen Quilligan, *The Language of Allegory: Defining the Genre* (Ithaca, N.Y.: Cornell University Press, 1979), 27–33.

60. Clifford Geertz, "Ideology as a Cultural System," in *The Interpretation of Cultures* (New York: Basic Books, 1973), 193–233. Also see Hayden White, *Tropics of Discourse: Essays in Cultural Criticism* (Baltimore: Johns Hopkins University Press, 1978), 51–134; Richard Slotkin, "Myth and the Production of History," in *Ideology and Classic American Literature*, ed. Sacvan Bercovitch and Myra Jehlen (Cambridge: Cambridge University Press, 1986), 70–90. Paul de Man does not connect figuration with ideology, but his insistence on rhetoric as an anti-intentionalist category, his refusal to read figuration as the "inventions, the products of a highly particularized individual talent," actually supports Geertz's view of figuration as cultural

activity. See his *Allegories of Reading: Figural Language in Rousseau, Nietzsche, Rilke, and Proust* (New Haven: Yale University Press, 1979).

61. J. Hillis Miller, "The Two Allegories," in *Allegory, Myth, and Symbol: Harvard English Studies 9*, ed. Morton Bloomfield (Cambridge: Harvard University Press, 1981), 365.

62. Walter Benjamin, *The Origin of German Tragic Drama*, trans. John Osborne (London: NLB, 1977), 166.

63. Paul de Man, "The Rhetoric of Temporality," in *Interpretation: Theory and Practice*, ed. Charles S. Singleton (Baltimore: Johns Hopkins University Press, 1969), 190, 207, 206.

64. Joel Fineman, "The Structure of Allegorical Desire," in *Allegory and Representation: Selected Papers from the English Institute, 1979–1980*, ed. Stephen Greenblatt (Baltimore: Johns Hopkins University Press, 1981), 32.

65. J.G.A. Pocock, *The Machiavellian Moment: Florentine Political Thought and the Atlantic Republican Tradition* (Princeton: Princeton University Press, 1975), 53.

66. Nina Baym has commented on the lack of enthusiasm for allegory among antebellum readers, in *Novels, Readers, and Reviewers: Responses to Fiction in Antebellum America* (Ithaca, N.Y. Cornell University Press, 1984), 91–93. This might be true of literary allegory in a rather specialized sense, but social allegory—as a way of personifying agency—was certainly the dominant mode of discourse in nineteenth-century America.

67. C. S. Lewis, *The Allegory of Love: A Study in Medieval Tradition* (London: Oxford University Press, 1936), 59. The connection between allegory and empire is also borne out in Pocock's discussion of Dante, and Stephen Greenblatt's discussion of Spenser. See Pocock, *Machiavellian Moment*, 50–55; Greenblatt, *Renaissance Self-Fashioning: From More to Shakespeare* (Chicago: University of Chicago Press, 1980), 157–92.

68. Benjamin, *Origin*, 183–84. Here, I am representing Benjamin's idea about allegory but not his sentiment. Benjamin admires allegory.

69. Angus Fletcher, *Allegory: The Theory of a Symbolic Mode* (Ithaca, N.Y.: Cornell University Press, 1964), 23.

70. Benjamin, *Origin*, 184. For the relation between allegory and reification, also see Quilligan, *Language of Allegory*, 139–40.

71. Fletcher, *Allegory*, 66.

72. In a discussion of personification in the eighteenth century, Steven Knapp has also suggested that personification might reflect a broader "philosophical, theological, and indeed political interest in a certain ambivalent notion of the self." See *Personification and the Sublime: Milton to Coleridge* (Cambridge: Harvard University Press, 1985), 4.

73. Alexis de Tocqueville, *Democracy in America*, ed. J. P. Mayer and Max Lerner, trans. George Lawrence (New York: Harper & Row, 1966), 343.

74. *Liberty Hall and Cincinnati Gazette*, 21 May 1825. Quoted in Somkin, *Unquiet Eagle*, 57.

75. Weinberg, *Manifest Destiny*, 59, 66, 49; Charles J. Ingersoll, *Recollec-*

tions, Historical, Political, Biographical, and Social (Philadelphia: J. B. Lippincott & Co., 1861), 21.

76. Weinberg, *Manifest Destiny*, 190.

77. Ibid., 202.

78. Parke Godwin, "Annexation" (1854), in *Political Essays* (New York: Dix, Edwards & Co., 1856), 165, 169.

79. Abraham Lincoln, Second Annual Message to Congress, 1 December 1862, in *Writings of Abraham Lincoln*, ed. Arthur Brooks Lapsky (New York: Collier & Son, 1906), 6: 195–96.

80. Not surprisingly, Lincoln also believed in the harmony of interests between capital and labor. See Foner, *Free Soil*, 20.

81. Martineau, *Society in America*, 191.

82. Jameson is speaking in particular of "Freudian allegory," but his remark seems equally applicable here. See "Criticism in History," in *Weapons of Criticism*, ed. Norman Rudich (Palo Alto, Calif.: Ramparts Press, 1976), 41. Also pertinent to my discussion is Jameson's suggestion (in the context of Wyndham Lewis), that "the use of national types projects an essentially allegorical mode of representation." See *Fables of Aggression* (Berkeley: University of California Press, 1979), 90.

83. D. W. Mitchell, *Ten Years in the United States* (London: Smith, Elder and Co., 1862), 326.

84. John Locke, *The Second Treatise of Government* (New York: Bobbs-Merrill, 1952), 17.

85. Karl Marx, *Capital*, trans. Samuel Moore and Edward Aveling, 3 vols. (New York: International Publishers, 1967), 1: 168.

86. Thomas Skidmore, *The Rights of Man to Property!* (1829; rpt. New York: Burt Franklin, 1964), 357–58.

87. Russel Lawrence Barsh and James Youngblood Henderson, *The Road: Indian Tribes and Political Liberty* (Berkeley: University of California Press, 1980), 45; Ronald N. Satz, *American Indian Policy in the Jacksonian Era* (Lincoln: University of Nebraska Press, 1975), 3.

88. John Quincy Adams, *Oration Delivered at Plymouth* (Plymouth, Mass.: J. Avery, 1820), 15–17.

89. Hall, *Sketches*, 128, 133.

90. "Remarks on National Literature" (1823), in *The Works of William Ellery Channing* (Boston: American Unitarian Association, 1877), 125.

91. Jackson to Secretary Graham, 8 July 1817, in *The Correspondence of Andrew Jackson*, ed. John Spencer Bassett, 7 vols. (Washington, D.C.: Carnegie Institute of Washington, 1926–33), 2: 304.

92. Rogin, *Fathers and Chidren*, 181. See also Barsh and Henderson, *The Road*, 46.

93. Andrew Jackson, Second Annual Message, 6 December 1830, in *The State of the Union Messages of the Presidents, 1790–1966*, 3 vols. (New York: Chelsea House, 1967), 1: 335.

94. Orestes A. Brownson, "Social Reform: An Address Before the Soci-

ety of the Mystical Seven in the Wesleyan University," 7 August 1844, in Hugins, *The Reform Impulse*, 251–52.

95. Timothy Dwight, *Travels in New-England and New-York*, ed. Barbara Solomon, 4 vols. (Cambridge: Harvard University Press, 1971–83), 4: 236.

96. Michel Chevalier, *Society, Manners and Politics in the United States* (1839; rpt. New York: Burt Franklin, 1969), 334–35; Robert Rantoul, Jr., "The Education of a Free People" (1839), in *Memoirs, Speeches, and Writings*, ed. Luther Hamilton (Boston: John P. Jewett, 1854), 135.

97. Thomas Jefferson to James Madison, 27 April 1809, in *Writings*, 11–12: 277. For a more sympathetic explication of Jefferson's remark, see Adrienne Koch, *Power, Morals, and the Founding Fathers* (Ithaca, N.Y.: Cornell University Press, 1961), 23–49.

98. Lyman Beecher, *Lectures on Scepticism* (Cincinnati: Corey and Fairbank, 1835), 35, 99, 103; Theodore Parker, *The Three Chief Safeguards of Society* (Boston: Wm. Crosby and H. P. Nichols, 1851), 8, 13, 14, 12, 8.

99. William Ellery Channing, *Self-Culture* (Boston: James Munroe & Co., 1839), 10–11.

100. *Manual of Self-Education* (1842), in *Antebellum American Culture*, ed. David Brion Davis (Lexington, Mass.: D.C. Heath, 1979), 70.

101. I am responding here to Angus Fletcher's point that allegory is "abstract in Whitehead's sense, when he says that abstraction is 'the omission of part of the truth.' " See Fletcher, *Allegory*, 29, n. 8. I would suggest that allegory works not only by omission but also by attribution.

102. See John L. Thomas, "Romantic Reform in America, 1815–1865," *American Quarterly* 17 (Winter 1965): 656–81; Clifford S. Griffin, *Their Brothers' Keepers: Moral Stewardship in the United States, 1800–1865* (New Brunswick, N.J.: Rutgers University Press, 1960), esp. chap. 3; Paul E. Johnson, *A Shopkeeper's Millennium: Society and Revivals in Rochester, New York, 1815–1837* (New York: Hill and Wang, 1978).

103. Robert Rantoul, Jr., "Remarks on Education," in *Memoirs, Speeches, and Writings*, 82.

104. Mann, "Twelfth Annual Report" (1848), 669.

105. Horace Mann, "Means and Objects of Common School Education," in *Lectures on Education* (Boston: Ide & Dutton, 1855), 17.

Chapter 2
Author as Monarch

1. Melville to John Murray, 25 March 1848, in *Letters of Herman Melville*, ed. Merrell Davis and William H. Gilman (New Haven: Yale University Press, 1960), 70.

2. Melville to John Murray, 28 January 1849, in *Letters*, 76.

3. Melville to John Murray, 25 March 1848, in *Letters*, 70.

4. Ibid., 70.

5. Richard Brodhead, "*Mardi*: Creating the Creative," in *New Perspec-

tives on Melville, ed. Faith Pullin (Edinburgh: University of Edinburgh Press, 1978), 29–53.

6. *Mardi, and a Voyage Thither* (Evanston and Chicago: Northwestern University Press and the Newberry Library, 1970), 368. All further references to this edition will be included in the text.

7. Raymond Williams, *Keywords: A Vocabulary of Culture and Society* (New York: Oxford University Press, 1976), 72–74. The standard critique of the notion of "creativity" is Pierre Macherey, *A Theory of Literary Production*, trans. Geoffrey Wall (London: Routledge & Kegan Paul, 1978), esp. 66–68. See also Jerome McGann's critique of Coleridge's "ideology of poetry and the power of the creative imagination," in *The Romantic Ideology: A Critical Investigation* (Chicago: University of Chicago Press, 1983), 95–107. For a critique of the notion of creativity in the sciences, see Paul Feyerabend, "Creativity—A Dangerous Myth," *Critical Inquiry* 13 (Summer 1987): 700–11.

8. Given Melville's almost sacred sense of authorship, Max Weber's discussion of "calling" as a point of convergence between the religious and the economic is especially relevant. See *The Protestant Ethic and the Spirit of Capitalism*, trans. Talcott Parsons (New York: Charles Scribner, 1958), 79–92.

9. William Blackstone, *Commentaries on the Laws of England: A Facsimile of the First Edition of 1765–1769*, vol. 2, *Of the Rights of Things* (Chicago: University of Chicago Press, 1979), 2.

10. It was customary in the seventeenth and eighteenth centuries to speak of "liberty" as a kind of "property." Some recent arguments that defend property as the basis for liberty are Lawrence Becker, *Property Rights: Philosophic Foundations* (London: Routledge & Kegan Paul, 1977), 75–80; Jean Baechler, "Liberty, Property, and Equality," and John W. Chapman, "Justice, Freedom and Property," both in *Property. Nomos 22: Yearbook of the American Society for Political and Legal Philosophy*, ed. J. Roland Pennock and John W. Chapman (New York: New York University Press, 1980), 269–88, 289–324; John Gray, "Individual Liberty, Private Property and the Market Economy," in *Liberalism* (Minneapolis: University of Minnesota Press, 1986), 62–72.

11. According to Madison, property includes not just "a man's land, or merchandize, or money" but a much broader range of things. He argues, for instance, that "a man has property in his opinions and the free communication of them," that he "has a property of peculiar value in his religious opinions, and in the profession and practice dictated by them," that he "has property very dear to him in the safety and liberty of his person," and that he "has an equal property in the free use of his faculties and free choice of the objects on which to employ them." In short, property is the all-inclusive category of which "liberty" is a subset. See "Property and Liberty," in *The Complete Madison*, ed. Saul K. Padover (New York: Harper, 1953), 267.

12. C. B. Macpherson, *The Political Theory of Possessive Individualism: Hobbes to Locke* (London: Oxford University Press, 1962), 142. As Mac-

pherson points out, the idea of "exclusion" is central even to the most radical exponents of property rights. See his discussion of the Levellers, 107–159. Alan Ryan, discussing "Kant and Possession," also argues that, in Kant's thinking, "An individual's title does not however stem from his use of property; to have a right is to have the right to exclude others." See *Property and Political Theory* (Oxford: Basil Blackwell, 1986), 82.

13. Arthur W. Calhoun, *A Social History of the American Family*, 3 vols. (New York: Barnes and Noble, 1917–19), 1: 75.

14. Timothy Walker, "Defence of Mechanical Philosophy," *North American Review* 33 (1831): 125.

15. Thomas Ewbank, *Report of the Commissioner of Patents* (1849), in *Antebellum American Culture*, ed. David Brion Davis (Lexington, Mass.: D. C. Heath, 1979), 366.

16. Richard Poirier, *The Renewal of Literature: Emersonian Reflections* (New York: Random House, 1987), 165. In the same discussion, Poirier also suggests that "literature might be considered a form of technology disguised as an attack upon it," and that, for that reason, it is "a form of cultural and imaginative imperialism"—an assertion that must make many of my statements seem tame and circumspect. Also relevant here is David Simpson's remark that Transcendentalism is "the literary and philosophical correlative of the mythology of Manifest Destiny"; see *The Politics of American English, 1776–1850* (New York: Oxford University Press, 1986), 231.

17. Gérard Genette, *Figures of Literary Discourse*, trans. Alan Sheridan (New York: Columbia University Press, 1982), 53. Genette is speaking, more specifically, of the "passion to name" in rhetorical taxonomy, but his remark seems to describe Melville's activity as well. See also the section on "Naming: Propriety, Property, Possession," in Mark Taylor, *Erring: A Postmodern A/theology* (Chicago: University of Chicago Press, 1984), 40–46. Interestingly, most of the names here are Polynesian, a fact perhaps not unrelated to the expansionist spirit of the namer. In this context, we might want to examine the logic of naming in *Mardi* against the background of what Walter Herbert calls the "civilized-savage polarity" in *Typee*. See *Marquesan Encounters: Melville and the Meaning of Civilization* (Cambridge: Harvard University Press, 1980), 149–91, as well as James Duban's suggestive discussion in *Melville's Major Fiction: Politics, Theology, and Imagination* (Dekalb: Northern Illinois University Press, 1983), 11–30.

18. The phrase is Derrida's. He is speaking of a more complex issue, what he calls the "constitutive erasure of the proper name" within a classifying system. But his aphorism seems to me to summarize the fate of names in *Mardi*. For Derrida's discussion of the "battle of proper names," see *Of Grammatology*, trans. Gayatri Chakravorty Spivak (Baltimore: Johns Hopkins University Press, 1976), 107–18.

19. Boston *Post*, 18 April 1849. For this and other nineteenth-century reviews, I am drawing upon the Melville Collection at the Newberry Library.

20. Milton Stern's wry remark sums up the mode of causality in *Mardi*: "Melville wants to talk about death, so someone dies." See *The Fine Hammered Steel of Herman Melville* (Urbana: University of Illinois Press, 1957), 84.

21. Walter Benjamin, *The Origin of German Tragic Drama*, trans. John Osborne (London: NLB, 1977), 184, 188.

22. Here I am recapitulating Walter Benjamin's and Angus Fletcher's point about the absolute power of the allegorist. See Benjamin, *Origin*, 182–84; Fletcher, *Allegory: The Theory of a Symbolic Mode* (Ithaca, N.Y.: Cornell University Press, 1964), 20–23, 135–46.

23. This was formulated, significantly, by the Levellers, the radical exponents of property rights. See Macpherson, *Possessive Individualism*, 137.

24. John Locke, *The Second Treatise of Government* (New York: Bobbs-Merrill, 1952), 4.

25. Locke is clearly worried about the uses to which "liberty" might be put—worried enough, in fact, to want to separate "liberty" from its illegitimate kindred, "license." His nervous distinction between these two terms (*Second Treatise*, 5) might be considered a kind of proleptic criticism of Melville: "But though this be a state of liberty, yet it is not a state of license; though man in that state have an uncontrollable liberty to dispose of his person or possessions, yet he has not liberty to destroy himself, or so much as any creature in his possession, but where some nobler use than its bare preservation calls for it." Melville, of course, can always reply that he is destroying the "creature[s] in his possession" for "some nobler use."

26. Benjamin, *Origin*, 183, 217.

27. See, for example, Stern, *Fine Hammered*, 69–70.

28. In this context, it is interesting to consider Claude Lévi-Strauss's account of the disclosure of names as an act of betrayal among the Nambikwara. See *Tristes Tropiques*, trans. John Weightman and Doreen Weightman (New York: Atheneum, 1974), 278–79. See also Ishi's refusal to disclose his name in Theodora Kroeber, *Ishi in Two Worlds: A Biography of the Last Wild Indian in North America* (Berkeley: University of California Press, 1961), 126–28.

29. Lévi-Strauss describes two operations at work in naming: "The choice seems only to be between identifying someone else by assigning him to a class, or under cover of giving him a name, identifying oneself through him. One therefore never names: one classes someone else if the name is given to him in virtue of his characteristics and one classes oneself if, in the belief that one need not follow a rule, one names someone else 'freely,' that is, in virtue of characteristics of one's own." See *The Savage Mind*, trans. George Weidenfeld (Chicago: University of Chicago Press, 1970), 181. The narrator obviously belongs to the second category.

30. Edwin Eigner, *The Metaphysical Novel in England and America: Dickens, Bulwer, Melville and Hawthorne* (Berkeley: University of California Press, 1978), 77.

31. Brodhead, "*Mardi*: Creating the Creative," 39. This is also Charles Feidelson's more general point in *Symbolism and American Literature* (Chicago: University of Chicago Press, 1953), 166–75.

32. Eigner, *Metaphysical Novel*, 26.

33. Terry Castle, "The Spectralization of the Other," lecture at Rutgers University, April 1987.

34. Gayatri Spivak's point—that "the project of imperialsm" is always to refract "what might have been the absolutely Other into a domesticated Other that consolidates the imperialist self"—is especially pertinent here. See "Three Women's Texts and a Critique of Imperialism," *Critical Inquiry* 12 (Autumn 1985): 253.

35. In this context, what Bakhtin calls Dostoevsky's "polyphony" usefully contrasts with Melville's monotony. See *Problems of Dostoevsky's Poetics*, trans. R. W. Rotsel (Ann Arbor: University of Michigan Press, 1973), passim.

36. Foucault has also commented on the constitutive nature of appropriative processes. "Neither the relation of discourse to desire, nor the processes of its appropriation," he writes, "is extrinsic to its unity, its characterization, and the laws of its formation. They are . . . its formative elements." See *The Archaeology of Knowledge*, trans. A. M. Sheridan Smith (New York: Harper & Row, 1972), 68.

37. Macpherson, *Possessive Individualism*, 221, also emphasizes the connection between ownership and appropriation.

38. Boston *Post*, 18 April 1849; *Southern Literary Messenger*, May 1849.

39. The *Athenaeum* celebrates the perseverance of the critic as a way of commenting on the dullness of *Mardi*: "Among the hundred people who will take it up, lured by their remembrances of *Typee*, ninety readers will drop off at the end of the first volume, and the remaining nine will become so weary of the hero . . . that they will throw down his chronicle ere the end of its second third is reached—with Mr. Burchell's monosyllable by way of comment. The Critic, of course, is the one intrepid mariner who holds on to the end. With ourselves such persistence was at once a duty, and in some measure a service of hope" (24 March 1849). The *Examiner*, on the other hand, identified the critic with the common reader: "Here [the narrator] dwells with his allegorical maiden, Yillah, till the reader, not always seeing clearly the intention, gets tired of the allegory; and even the all-wise critic, somewhat sharing the reader's dulness in that respect, thinks it safest to say as little as may be about the profundities of allegorical meaning which appear to be involved" (31 March 1849). The New York *Tribune* simply pointed to the abused good nature of the critic as a measure of *Mardi*'s effrontery: "We have seldom found our reading faculty so near exhaustion, or our good nature as critics so severely exercised, as in an attempt to get through this new work by the author of the fascinating *Typee* and *Omoo*" (10 May 1849).

40. New York *Saroni's Musical Times*, September 1849.

41. Melville to John Murray, 1 January 1848, in *Letters*, 68.

42. Melville to John Murray, 25 March 1848, in *Letters*, 71.
43. Melville to John Murray, 28 January 1849, in *Letters*, 75.
44. Melville to John Murray, 1 January 1848, in *Letters*, 68.
45. Melville to Richard Bentley, 5 June 1849, in *Letters*, 85–86.
46. Boston *Post*, 18 April 1849; *Athenaeum*, 24 March 1849; New York *Tribune*, 10 May 1849.
47. Walter Ong, "The Writer's Audience is Always a Fiction," *PMLA* 90 (1975): 9–21.

Chapter 3
Author as Subject

1. Melville to Lemuel Shaw, 6 October 1849, in *Letters*, 91.
2. Melville to Richard Henry Dana, Jr., 1 May 1850, in *Letters*, 106.
3. Melville to Evert Duyckinck, 14 December 1849, in *Letters*, 95.
4. *Redburn, His First Voyage. Being the Sailor-boy Confessions and Reminiscences of the Son-of-a-Gentleman, in the Merchant Service* (Evanston and Chicago: Northwestern University Press and the Newberry Library, 1969), 211. All further references to this edition appear in the text.
5. Walter Herbert relates Melville's "psychology of a failed patrician" to his adoption of the "civilized-savage polarity" in *Typee*; my discussion of Melville's appropriative subjectivity in many ways parallels this argument. See Herbert, *Marquesan Encounters: Melville and the Meaning of Civilization* (Cambridge: Harvard University Press, 1980), 149–91. Melville's uneasy relation to the social meanings embedded in the Gansevoort–Melville family history is, of course, Michael Rogin's more general point in *Subversive Genealogy: The Politics and Art of Herman Melville* (Berkeley: University of California Press, 1985).
6. The extreme subjectivity displayed in poems such as "Lady Lazarus" and "Daddy"—a subjectivity that takes over everything, including the Holocaust—vividly illustrates, to my mind, what Fredric Jameson calls the "centered subject of the age of reification." See *The Political Unconscious: Narrative as a Socially Symbolic Act* (Ithaca, N.Y.: Cornell University Press, 1981), 160. This chapter is informed by Jameson's account of the "authorial" as an instance of the "centered subject," and the "textual determinants" it engenders.
7. Macherey, *A Theory of Literary Production*, trans. Geoffrey Wall (London: Routledge & Kegan Paul, 1978), 53.
8. Two attempts to read *Redburn* and *White-Jacket* allegorically are Carolyn L. Karcher's discussion of *Redburn* and *White-Jacket* as an "allegorical exposé of slavery," and James Duban's treatment of Redburn's rambles through Liverpool as an allegorical rendition of "Christ's agonizing procession along the Via Dolorosa." See Karcher, *Shadow Over the Promised Land: Slavery, Race, and Violence in Melville's America* (Baton Rouge: Louisiana State University Press, 1980), 28–61; Duban, *Melville's Major Fiction: Poli-*

tics, Theology, and Imagination (Dekalb: Northern Illinois University Press, 1983), 39–46. I differ from these critics in my emphasis on allegory as a particular kind of signifying universe, a universe of "manifest subjectivity" (as Walter Benjamin suggests), rather than as a representation of themes.

9. The phrase appears in Benjamin's discussion of the German *Trauerspiel*, a genre characterized by the "display of manifest subjectivity." In the *Trauerspiel*, Benjamin argues, "subjectivity, like an angel falling into the depths, is brought back by allegories, and is held fast in heaven." See *The Origin of German Tragic Drama*, trans. John Osborne (London: NLB, 1977), 233–35.

10. C. S. Lewis, *The Allegory of Love: A Study in Medieval Tradition* (London: Oxford University Press, 1936), 30.

11. *White-Jacket* (Evanston and Chicago: Northwestern University Press and the Newberry Library, 1970), 75.

12. In its circular, unvarying universe, *Redburn* follows the same "anti-progressive" pattern Stanley Fish detects in *The Pilgrim's Progress*. See *Self-Consuming Artifacts* (Berkeley and Los Angeles: University of California Press, 1972), 224–64.

13. Edwin Honig refers to this allegorical device variously as "threshold emblem" or "threshold symbol," in *Dark Conceit: The Making of Allegory* (New York: Oxford University Press, 1966), 71–73. Maureen Quilligan refers to the same device as the "threshold text," in *The Language of Allegory: Defining the Genre* (Ithaca: Cornell University Press, 1979), 51.

14. The change of gender here—the tyrant and usurper is of course female—seems to me a clear instance of Melville's misogyny. For other even more obvious instances, see Wilson Walker Cowen, "Melville's Marginalia" (Ph.D. diss., Harvard University, 1965), passim.

15. Critics disagree among themselves about the exact number of Redburns in the book. See, for example, Lawrance Thompson, *Melville's Quarrel With God* (Princeton: Princeton University Press, 1952); Merlin Bowen, "*Redburn* and the Angle of Vision," *Modern Philology* 52 (1954): 100–109; William B. Dillingham, *An Artist in the Rigging: The Early Work of Herman Melville* (Athens: University of Georgia Press, 1972), 32–34. My emphasis here is on a somewhat different kind of inconsistency: the discrepancy between Redburn in the first five chapters of the book, and Redburn as a sailor on the *Highlander*. That was the inconsistency nineteenth-century reviewers noticed.

16. *Blackwood's Edinburgh Magazine*, November 1849; *Southern Quarterly Review*, April 1850. Again, I would like to acknowledge my indebtedness to the Melville Collection at the Newberry Library, which has compiled the nineteenth-century reviews.

17. In Patricia Tobin's apt phrase, the *Bildungsroman* is a "paradigmatic novel that is performed through time and pre-formed by Time." See *Time and the Novel* (Princeton: Princeton University Press, 1978), 5.

18. Lewis H. Morgan, *League of the Ho-De-No-Sau-Nee, or Iroquois* (1851; rpt. New York: Dodd, Mead & Co., 1922), 135.

19. Ihab Hassan, "The Subtracting Machine," *Critique* (1963): 4–23. Hassan here is discussing the novels of William Burroughs, but his phrase seems to me especially apt for the phenomenon I am describing.

20. *The Age of Jackson*, ed. Robert V. Remini (Columbia: South Carolina University Press, 1972), 64; Francis Parkman, *The Conspiracy of Pontiac*, 2 vols. (1851; rpt. Boston: Little Brown, 1909), 1: 3; Michael Paul Rogin, *Fathers and Children: Andrew Jackson and the Subjugation of the American Indian* (New York: Vintage, 1976), 117. Also see my discussion of this point in Chapter 1.

21. Schoolcraft, *History of the Indian Tribes of the United States: Their Present Condition and Prospects, and a Sketch of Their Ancient Status*, 6 vols. (Philadelphia: J.B. Lippincott, 1857), 6: 27, 29.

22. I differ here from James Duban, *Melville's Major Fiction*, 51–60, who sees *The Wealth of Nations* as a formative influence on *Redburn's* rhetoric of self-reliance.

23. Marc Shell, *The Economy of Literature* (Baltimore: Johns Hopkins University Press, 1978), 85.

24. H. Bruce Franklin, "Redburn's Wicked End," *Nineteenth-Century Fiction* 20 (1965): 190–94; Duban, *Melville's Major Fiction*, 47–53. For other criticisms of Redburn's conduct, see Terrence G. Lish, "Melville's *Redburn*: A Study in Dualism," *English Language Notes* 5 (1967): 113–20; Edgar A. Dryden, *Melville's Thematics of Form: The Great Art of Telling the Truth* (Baltimore: Johns Hopkins University Press, 1968), 67; John Seelye, *Melville: The Ironic Diagram* (Evanston: Northwestern University Press, 1970), 52.

25. For an extended discussion of homosexuality in *Redburn*, see Robert K. Martin, *Hero, Captain, and Stranger: Male Friendship, Social Critique, and Literary Form in the Sea Novels of Herman Melville* (Chapel Hill: University of North Carolina Press, 1986), 40–58.

26. *Blackwood's Edinburgh Magazine*, November 1849.

27. For the same reason, Redburn is not allowed to acquire any sailorly skills, for instance, reefing the topsail. See *Redburn*, 121.

28. Melville to Lemuel Shaw, 6 October 1849, in *Letters*, 92; Melville to Richard Henry Dana, Jr., 6 October 1849, in *Letters*, 93.

29. Melville to Richard Henry Dana, Jr., 6 October 1849, in *Letters*, 93.

30. *White-Jacket, or, The World in a Man-of-War* (Evanston and Chicago: Northwestern University Press and the Newberry Library, 1970), 1. All further references to this edition appear in the text.

31. As the editors of the Northwestern-Newberry edition point out, in revising the preface Melville tended "toward brevity," until finally in the American edition, the preface was so severely truncated that it became simply a "Note." For a fuller account of the history of Melville's revisions, see "Revised Fair Copy of Preface," in the "Editorial Appendix" to *White-Jacket*, 489–92.

32. See, for example, Samuel Leech's *Thirty Years From Home, or, A Voice from the Main Deck* (Boston: Charles Tappan, 1843); Nathaniel Ames, *A Mariner's Sketches* (Providence, R.I.: Cory, Marshall & Hammond, 1830); Henry James Mercier and William Gallop, *Life in a Man-of-War, or, Scenes in "Old Ironsides" during her Cruise in the Pacific* (Philadelphia: Lydia R. Bailey, 1841). For Melville's sources, see Howard Vincent, *The Tailoring of Melville's "White-Jacket"* (Evanston, Ill.: Northwestern University Press, 1970), 7; Willard Thorp, "Historical Note," in *White-Jacket* (Evanston and Chicago: Northwestern University Press and the Newberry Library, 1970), 417–24.

33. Leech, *Thirty Years From Home*, 1–33.

34. *Literary World*, 16 March 1850; *Southern Literary Messenger*, 16 April 1850.

35. For White-Jacket's aristocratic traits, see Charles Roberts Anderson, *Melville in the South Seas* (New York: Dover, 1966), 418; Larry J. Reynolds, "Antidemocratic Emphasis in *White-Jacket*," *American Literature* 48 (March 1976): 13–28; Rowland A. Sherrill, *The Prophetic Melville: Experience, Transcendence, and Tragedy* (Athens: University of Georgia Press, 1979), 62–81.

36. William Charvat, *The Profession of Authorship in America, 1800–1870*, ed. Matthew J. Bruccoli (Columbus: Ohio State University Press, 1968), 3.

37. Richard Henry Dana, Jr., *Two Years Before the Mast* (New York: Harper and Brothers, 1840), 1.

38. For a more general discussion of the relation between legibility (or visibility) and power, see Michel Foucault, *Discipline and Punish: The Birth of the Prison*, trans. Alan Sheridan (New York: Vintage, 1979). Along the same lines, Jonathan Arac discusses the relation between the nineteenth-century novel and social systems of vision and knowledge; see *Commissioned Spirits: The Shaping of Social Motion in Dickens, Carlyle, Melville, and Hawthorne* (New Brunswick: Rutgers University Press, 1979).

39. In this respect, Melville's "realistic" portrait of Jackson illustrates Leo Bersani's point that in realism, "the characters merely repeat in dialogue and action what has already been established about them in narrative summaries. Their lives mirror the expository portraits made of them at the beginning of the novel." See his *Baudelaire and Freud* (Berkeley: University of California Press, 1977), 121.

40. Maureen Quilligan has interesting passing references to the relation between allegory and "silent textual surface" in "Allegory, Allegoresis, and the Deallegorization of Language," in *Allegory, Myth, and Symbol*, ed. Morton Bloomfield (Cambridge: Harvard University Press, 1981), esp. 176–77.

41. Melville's initial account of the jacket certainly encourages the book-jacket analogy, for the jacket is made (out of a duck frock) in a most curious fashion, by "making a continuation of the slit there, open[ing] it lengthwise—much as you would cut a leaf in the last new novel" (3).

42. Vincent, *Tailoring*, 222–25.

43. Ibid., 150–53.

44. Leech, *Thirty Years From Home*, 78–79, 86, 93–94.

45. For a discussion of the connecting devices in *White-Jacket*, see Scott Giantvalley and Christina C. Stough, " 'Precedents are Against it': An Examination of *White-Jacket* as a Corrective for the 'Two *Moby-Dicks* Theory,' " *Studies in American Fiction* 8 (Autumn 1980): 165–81.

46. Anderson, *Melville in the South Seas*, 431.

47. *New York Tribune*, 5 April 1850.

48. Commodore Charles Henry Davis to Admiral Samuel Francis Dupont, 12 April 1850. See Frederick J. Kennedy and Joyce Deveau Kennedy, "Some Naval Officers React to *White-Jacket*: An Untold Story," *Melville Society Extracts* 41 (February 1980): 6.

49. Melville to Evert Duyckinck, 6 October 1850, in *Letters*, 115.

50. Here I am drawing upon Mikhail Bakhtin's useful discussion of represented utterance. See "Discourse in the Novel," in *The Dialogic Imagination*, trans. Caryl Emerson and Michael Holquist (Austin: University of Texas Press, 1981), esp. 355–66.

51. John Gerlach has also discussed this passage as "a calculated exaggeration which exposes its own foolishness" in "Messianic Nationalism in the Early Works of Herman Melville: Against Perry Miller," *Arizona Quarterly* 28 (Spring 1972): 5–26.

52. My sense of metaphor as a modality of space comes from Roman Jakobson's classic distinction between metaphor and metonymy. Jakobson sees metaphor as a mode of selection based on equivalence, and metonymy as a mode of combination based on contiguity. It would follow that metaphor selects from a group of equivalent but discontinuous terms. See "Linguistics and Poetics," in *The Structuralists From Marx to Lévi-Strauss*, ed. Richard T. De George and Fernande M. De George (Garden City, N.Y.: Anchor Books, 1972), 85–122. Reprinted from *Style and Language*, ed. Thomas A. Sebeok (Cambridge: M.I.T. Press, 1960).

53. Melville's convivial metaphors exhibit the same pattern Elaine Scarry observes in certain nomenclature for torture. Torture is referred to as "the dance" in Argentina, "the birthday party" in the Phillippines, and "hors d'oeuvres," "tea party," and "tea party with toast" in Greece. See *The Body in Pain: The Making and Unmaking of the World* (New York: Oxford University Press, 1985), 44. Scarry's complex argument has to do with the undoing of language in the infliction of acute bodily sentience. My simpler point here focuses on Melville's linguistic violence in yoking together the incongruous.

54. Leech saw "blood suddenly fly from the arm of a man stationed at our gun." He saw many other horrors besides: "One of them was struck in the leg by a large shot; he had to suffer amputation above the wound. The other had a grape or canister shot sent through his ancle. A stout Yorkshireman lifted him in his arms, and hurried him to the cockpit. He had his foot cut off, and was thus made lame for life. Two of the boys stationed on the quar-

terdeck were killed. They were both Portuguese. A man, who saw one of them killed, afterwards told me that his powder caught fire and burnt the flesh almost off his face. In this pitiable situation, the agonized boy lifted up both hands, as if imploring relief, when a passing shot instantly cut him in two. I was an eye-witness to a sight equally revolting. A man named Aldrich had one of his hands cut off by a shot, and almost at the same moment he received another shot, which tore open his bowels in a terrible manner." For these and other details, see Leech, *Thirty Years From Home*, 130–35.

55. For a discussion of the "paranoid structure of the realistic novel," see Leo Bersani, "The Subject of Power," *Diacritics* 7 (September 1977): 2–21. Bersani is referring primarily to a thematic construct—a persecutory society within the novel afflicting the protagonist. My emphasis here is more on an infratextual construct—a persecutory audience implied by the author's defensive strategies.

56. Horace Mann, "Twelfth Annual Report" (1848), in *Annual Reports on Education* (Boston: Lee and Shepard, 1872), 676.

57. *Mardi, and a Voyage Thither* (Evanston and Chicago: Northwestern University Press and the Newberry Library, 1970), 556.

Chapter 4
Blaming the Victim

1. Melville to Nathaniel Hawthorne, 17 November 1851 in *Letters*, 141.

2. *Mardi, and a Voyage Thither* (Evanston and Chicago: Northwestern University and the Newberry Library, 1970), 368.

3. The citations are from *Moby-Dick*, ed. Harrison Hayford and Hershel Parker (New York: Norton, 1967), 378–79. All further references to this edition appear in the text.

4. See *American Hieroglyphics: The Symbol of the Egyptian Hieroglyphics in the American Renaissance* (Baltimore: Johns Hopkins University Press, 1980), 305. Without disagreeing with Irwin's point that the whale embodies indeterminacy, I would like to suggest that the very notion of "indeterminacy"—especially Melville's articulation of it—should itself be contextualized and historicized. The book–whale analogy is by no means a new argument, of course. See, for example, Edgar A. Dryden, *Melville's Thematics of Form: The Great Art of Telling the Truth* (Baltimore: Johns Hopkins University Press, 1968), 83–113; and David Hirsch, *Reality and Idea in the Early American Novel* (The Hague: Mouton, 1971), esp. 199–219. For a reading of the whale as text even more determinedly deconstructive than Irwin's, see Rodolphe Gasché, "The Scene of Writing: A Deferred Outset," *Glyph* 1 (1977): 150–71. Charles Feidelson's *Symbolism and American Literature* (Chicago: University of Chicago Press, 1953) remains the best discussion of American "symbolism" as textual self-reference.

5. For an interesting account of Derridean deconstruction as a "metaphysics of the discrete"—as, indeed, "an extension of Locke's doctrine of

contiguity and the associationism that ensued"—see Charles Levin, "La Greffe du Zèle: Derrida and the Cupidity of the Text," in *The Structural Allegory: Reconstructive Encounters with the New French Thought* (Minneapolis: University of Minnesota Press, 1984), 201–27.

6. See, for example, James Guetti, *The Limits of Metaphor: A Study of Melville, Conrad, and Faulkner* (Ithaca, N.Y.: Cornell University Press, 1967), 34–41; and Richard Brodhead, *Hawthorne, Melville, and the Novel* (Chicago: University of Chicago Press, 1976), 137–38.

7. Virtually all "political" readings of *Moby-Dick* have chosen to see Ahab as villain. See, for example, C.L.R. James, *Mariners, Renegades, and Castaways: The Story of Herman Melville and the World We Live in* (London: Allison & Busby, 1953); Alan Heimert, "*Moby-Dick* and Political Symbolism," *American Literature* 15 (Winter 1963): 498–534; and, more recently, Carolyn L. Karcher, *Shadow Over the Promised Land: Slavery, Race, and Violence in Melville's America* (Baton Rouge: Louisiana State University Press, 1980); Joyce Sparer Adler, *War in Melville's Imagination* (New York: New York University Press, 1981); Michael Paul Rogin, *Subversive Genealogy: The Politics and Art of Herman Melville* (Berkeley: University of California Press, 1983); James Duban, *Melville's Major Fiction: Politics, Theology, and Imagination* (Dekalb: Northern Illinois University Press, 1983). My deepest disagreement with these critics has to do with my sense of Ahab not as villain but as victim. A new and important reading of *Moby-Dick* from this perspective is Donald Pease, "*Moby-Dick* and the Cold War," in *The American Renaissance Reconsidered: Selected Papers from the English Institute, 1982–83*, ed. Walter Benn Michaels and Donald E. Pease (Baltimore: Johns Hopkins University Press, 1985), 113–55. Pease, however, sees Ahab only as Ishmael's victim. I see Melville himself as being implicated in the process of victimization.

8. Andrew Jackson, Second Annual Message, 6 December 1830, in *The State of the Union Messages of the Presidents, 1790–1966*, 3 vols. (New York: Chelsea House, 1967), 1: 335.

9. *Massachusetts Historical Society Collections*, ser. 3, 5 (1836): 138–39. Quoted in Roy Harvey Pearce, *The Savages of America: A Study of the Indian and the Idea of Civilization* (Baltimore: Johns Hopkins University Press, 1965), 69.

10. Gillian Beer discusses the importance of the idea of "extinction" to the nineteenth-century novel in her fascinating *Darwin's Plots: Evolutionary Narrative in Darwin, George Eliot and Nineteenth-Century Fiction* (London: ARK Paperbacks, 1985), 123–48. The American context, however, makes "extinction" not so much a danger to be averted (Beer's emphasis) as a desired, perhaps even eagerly awaited, end—at least for certain groups of people.

11. Francis Parkman, *The Conspiracy of Pontiac*, 2 vols. (1851; rpt. Boston: Little Brown, 1909), 1: x, xi.

12. *White-Jacket, or, The World in a Man-of-War* (Evanston and Chicago:

Northwestern University Press and the Newberry Library, 1970), 146, 144, 150.

13. Adams's phrase is from his much cited *Oration Delivered at Plymouth* (Plymouth, Mass.: J. Avery, 1820), 17. The other three phrases are from Parkman, *Conspiracy*, 1: 234, 48, and Henry Rowe Schoolcraft, *The American Indian: Their History, Condition, and Prospects* (Rochester, N.Y.: Wanzer, Foot and Co., 1851), 150.

14. See, for example, Parkman, *Conspiracy*, 1: 191, 2: 329; Schoolcraft, *The American Indian*, 15.

15. The Indians' "ruling passions," according to Parkman, are "Ambition, revenge, envy, jealousy." See *Conspiracy*, 1: 45. Pontiac's vengeful shade is described in *Conspiracy*, 2: 329.

16. René Girard, *Violence and the Sacred*, trans. Patrick Gregory (Baltimore: Johns Hopkins University Press, 1977), 15.

17. I differ here from Michael Gilmore, who sees Ahab as being implicated in exchange. See his *American Romanticism and the Marketplace* (Chicago: University of Chicago Press, 1985), 117.

18. René Girard also relates vengeance to mimesis; see "From Mimetic Desire to Monstrous Double," in *Violence and the Sacred*, 143–68.

19. The quotation is, most appropriately, from "Circles," an essay that in many ways theorizes about what Melville is practicing in *Moby-Dick*. See *Selections from Ralph Waldo Emerson*, ed. Stephen E. Whicher (Boston: Houghton Mifflin, 1960), 176.

20. For an account of Emerson's art of discontinuity, see James Cox, "Ralph Waldo Emerson: The Circles of the Eye," in *Emerson: Prophecy, Metamorphosis, and Influence*, ed. David Levin (New York: Columbia University Press, 1975), 57–81; and, more recently, Julie Ellison, *Emerson's Romantic Style* (Princeton: Princeton University Press, 1984), 160–74. Harold Bloom stresses the importance of discontinuity to poetic freedom in *The Anxiety of Influence* (New York: Oxford University Press, 1973), 39–40. I depart from these critics in emphasizing the social function of discontinuity.

21. David Simpson also sees *Moby-Dick* as "a book about substitution on the grandest scale." See *Fetishism and Imagination: Dickens, Melville, Conrad* (Baltimore: Johns Hopkins University Press, 1982), esp. 81–82. Ramon Saldivar gives a useful (though somewhat predictable) account of Ishmael's commitment to metaphoric substitution in *Figural Language in the Novel: The Flowers of Speech from Cervantes to Joyce* (Princeton: Princeton University Press, 1984), 141–51. My own sense is that Starbuck, Ishmael, and Melville are all practitioners in metaphoric substitution, while Ahab is not.

22. *Annals of Congress*, 15th Congress, 2nd session, (1818–19): 838.

23. *Register of Debates in Congress*, 21st Congress, 1st session (1829–30): 1103.

24. *White-Jacket*, 150.

25. These astonishing phrases are collected by Sacvan Bercovitch in *The American Jeremiad* (Madison: University of Wisconsin Press, 1978), 114.

26. Emmerich de Vattel, *The Law of Nations* (New York: Samuel Campbell, 1796), 1: 94.
27. Ibid., 161.
28. *New York Morning News*, 13 October 1845. Quoted in Frederick Merk, *Manifest Destiny and Mission in American History* (New York: Knopf, 1963), 25.
29. Frank Kermode, *The Sense of an Ending: Studies in the Theory of Fiction* (New York: Oxford University Press, 1966), 86.
30. Winthrop D. Jordan, *White Over Black: American Attitudes Toward the Negro, 1550–1812* (Baltimore: Penguin, 1969), 433–34.
31. David Walker, *Appeal, to the Coloured Citizens of the World* (1829; rpt. New York: Hill and Wang, 1965), 49.
32. Ibid., 39–40.
33. This comment came, significantly enough, from the *Columbian Centinel* of Boston. See Charles M. Wiltse's, Introduction to Walker's *Appeal*, x.
34. Thomas Wentworth Higginson, "Nat Turner's Insurrection," in *Black Rebellion: A Selection from "Travellers and Outlaws"* (1889; rpt. New York: Arno, 1969), 276; "About Niggers," *Putnam's* 6 (December 1855): 608–12; William Wells Brown, *The Negro in the American Rebellion* (1867; rpt. New York: Kraus Reprint, 1969), 24, 36.
35. Jefferson, *Notes on the State of Virginia* (1787; rpt. New York: Norton, 1972), 162.
36. Stowe, *Uncle Tom's Cabin* (1852; rpt., New York: Bantam, 1981), 218.
37. Ibid., 264.
38. I am here concurring with Ramon Saldivar's observation, in *Figural Language*, 124–41, about Ahab's "reliance on action." This "reliance on action," I further suggest, has a historical context, for instance, that of slave rebellion.
39. It is no accident, surely, that—even though he is really a victim—Ahab is nevertheless given the name of a biblical aggressor doomed by his deeds of aggression.
40. *White-Jacket*, 151.
41. The statement here, marking the first time the phrase "manifest destiny" was used, appeared in the July 1845 issue of the *United States Magazine and Democratic Review*. The anonymous article was attributed to John L. O'Sullivan. See Weinberg, *Manifest Destiny*, 111–12.
42. *A Treasury of American Folklore*, ed. B. A. Botkin (New York: Crown Publishers, 1944), 276.
43. *Register of Debates in Congress*, 21st Congress, 1st session (1829–30): 1103.
44. J.G.A. Pocock's idea about time as a political category is developed in *Politics, Language and Time* (New York: Atheneum, 1971) and, more cru-

cially, in *The Machiavellian Moment: Florentine Political Thought and the At-lantic Republican Tradition* (Princeton: Princeton University Press, 1975).

45. Samuel Stanhope Smith, "Of the Natural Bravery and Fortitude of the American Indian," Appendix to *An Essay on the Causes of the Variety of Complexion and Figure in the Human Species* (1787; rpt. Cambridge: Harvard University Press, 1965), 213; Parkman, *Conspiracy,* 1: 191; Schoolcraft, *The American Indians,* 150; Parkman, *Conspiracy,* 1: 160, 48.

46. Parkman, *Conspiracy,* 1: 48.

47. The Cherokees, who had not only farms but printing presses, schools, and churches, were censured for having become *too* civilized, and accordingly dispossessed. For an account of the dumbfoundering logic presented to justify their dispossession, see Weinberg, *Manifest Destiny,* 85–89.

48. Jonathan Arac discusses an analogous process in Hawthorne's use of "character." See "The Politics of *The Scarlet Letter,*" in *Ideology and Classic American Literature,* ed. Sacvan Bercovitch and Myra Jehlen (Cambridge: Cambridge University Press, 1986), esp. 255–59.

49. My sense of personification as a vehicle of control and even a vehicle of subjection differs from Bainard Cowan's view of allegory as "a cultural activity that arises at moments of crisis in the history of a literate people," an activity that permits that culture to "recogniz[e] its necessary discontinuity with received tradition." See *Exiled Waters: Moby-Dick and the Crisis of Allegory* (Baton Rouge: Louisiana State University Press, 1982). In focusing on personification as a vehicle of dominion, I am in some sense addressing the underside of the phenomenon Cowan discusses, not the project of redemption at the moment of crisis, but the project of control.

50. Jacques Lacan, "The Mirror Stage," in *Écrits,* trans. Alan Sheridan (New York: Norton, 1977), 2.

51. My discussion of the self here uses many of the terms Sharon Cameron discusses in *The Corporeal Self: Allegories of the Body in Melville and Hawthorne* (Baltimore: Johns Hopkins University Press, 1981). My somewhat different conclusions come from my different sense of the self's status and function.

52. In virtually ignoring Ishmael, I am departing from a tradition in Melville criticism that has focused on Ishmael not only as the center of *Moby-Dick* but, in one way or another, as its figure of redemption. Important works along this line include Walter Bezanson, "*Moby-Dick:* Work of Art," in *"Moby-Dick": Centennial Essays,* ed. Tyrus Hillway and Luther S. Manfield (Dallas: Southern Methodist University Press, 1953), 30–58; Paul Brodtkorb, *Ishmael's White World* (New Haven: Yale University Press, 1976); Edgar Dryden, *Melville's Thematics of Form* (Baltimore: Johns Hopkins University Press, 1968); Warwick Wadlington, "Godly Gamesomeness: Selftaste in *Moby-Dick,*" in *The Confidence Game in American Literature* (Princeton: Princeton University Press, 1975). One important exception to this tradition is the already cited essay by Donald Pease, "*Moby-Dick* and the Cold War," whose skeptical view of Ishmael I share.

Chapter 5
Knowing the Victim

1. "Hawthorne and His Mosses," in *Moby-Dick*, ed. Harrison Hayford and Hershel Parker (New York: Norton, 1967), 536.
2. Ibid., 536.
3. Melville to Evert A. Duyckinck, 3 March 1849, in *Letters*, 78.
4. *Pierre, or The Ambiguities* (Evanston and Chicago: Northwestern University Press and the Newberry Library, 1971), 67, 11, 67. Further references to this edition are hereafter included in the text.
5. From a more Freudian perspective, Myra Jehlen has also suggested that *Pierre* is a book about individualism, in *American Incarnation: The Individual, the Nation, and the Continent* (Cambridge: Harvard University Press, 1986), 185–226.
6. See, for instance, *The Great Republic: A History of the American People*, ed. Bernard Bailyn et al. (Lexington, Mass.: D.C. Heath, 1977), 1: 425–564; *The National Experience: A History of the United States to 1877*, 4th ed., ed. John M. Blum et al. (New York: Harcourt Brace Jovanovich, 1977), 187–91, 197–201.
7. Advocates for this approach include Henry A. Murray, Richard Brodhead, Brian Higgins, and Hershel Parker. See, for example, Murray's Introduction to the Hendricks House edition of *Pierre*; Richard Brodhead, *Hawthorne, Melville, and the Novel* (Chicago: University of Chicago Press, 1976), 174–81; Hershel Parker, "Why *Pierre* Went Wrong," *Studies in the Novel* 8 (Spring 1976): 7–23; Brian Higgins and Hershel Parker, "The Flawed Grandeur of Melville's *Pierre*," in *New Perspectives on Melville*, ed. Faith Pullin (Edinburgh: Edinburgh University Press, 1978), 162–96.
8. Emerson, "Address," in *Selections from Ralph Waldo Emerson*, ed. Stephen E. Whicher (Boston: Houghton Mifflin, 1960), 113. For an account of Melville's relation to Emerson, see, for instance, Merton M. Sealts, Jr., "Melville and Emerson's Rainbow," in *Pursuing Melville: 1940–1980* (Madison: University of Wisconsin Press, 1982), 250–77.
9. Emerson, "Self-Reliance," in *Selections*, 160.
10. F. Scott Fitzgerald, *The Great Gatsby* (New York: Scribner's, 1925), 99, 97.
11. Mary P. Ryan, *The Cradle of the Middle Class: The Family in Oneida County, New York, 1790–1865* (Cambridge: Cambridge University Press, 1981), esp. chap. 4, "Privacy and the Making of the Self-made Man," 145–85, in which Ryan discusses the family as a "cradle" of self-making.
12. Melville to Nathaniel Hawthorne, 17 November 1851, in *Letters*, 143.
13. Eric Sundquist has also commented on these frontier metaphors, in *Home as Found: Authority and Genealogy in Nineteenth-Century American Literature* (Baltimore: Johns Hopkins University Press, 1979), 167–68.
14. C. B. Macpherson, *The Political Theory of Possessive Individualism:*

Hobbes to Locke (New York: Oxford University Press, 1962), 42. For an account of the importance of Hobbes to America's liberal society, see Frank M. Coleman, *Hobbes and America: Exploring the Constitutional Foundations* (Toronto: University of Toronto Press, 1977).

15. For a well-known account of knowledge and possession in James, see Laurence B. Holland, *The Expense of Vision: Essays on the Craft of Henry James* (Baltimore: Johns Hopkins University Press, 1982), 377–407. Mark Seltzer, from a Foucauldean perspective, has similarly examined knowledge and power in *The Golden Bowl* as a tutelary network, indeed, as a form of "domestic colonialism"; see his *Henry James and the Art of Power* (Ithaca: Cornell University Press, 1984), 59–95. For a discussion that specifically connects vision with appropriation, see Jean-Christophe Agnew, "The Consuming Vision of Henry James," in *The Culture of Consumption*, ed. Richard Wightman Fox and T. J. Jackson Lears (New York: Pantheon, 1983), 67–100.

16. Pierre calls his mother, for instance, "Dowager Duchess Glendinning" (14) and begs her to "give that Assyrian toss to [her] head" (15). Saddle Meadows bears "the cyphers of three Indian kings" (6), and stands as an instance of "eastern patriarchalness" (11). Its very horses are "bound in perpetual feudal fealty" (21). It is "steeped in a Hindooish haze" (11). Melville wonders that such "old and oriental-like" (10) estates should survive, "like Indian mounds" (11), in the heart of a republic.

17. My sense of Mrs. Glendinning as victim differs sharply from Ann Douglas's discussion of her as a genteel (but triumphant) female tyrant. See *The Feminization of American Culture* (New York: Knopf, 1977), 294–95, 309–13.

18. My own discussion here is informed by *Discipline and Punish*, trans. Alan Sheridan (New York: Vintage Books, 1979), esp. 135–228, where Foucault discusses the production of individuality as the production of "docile bodies" in a network of discipline and supervision. See also David Rothman, *The Discovery of the Asylum: Social Order and Disorder in the New Republic* (Boston: Little, Brown and Co., 1971), esp. chap. 4, "The Challenge of Crime," on the emerging interest in the etiology of crime and the individuality of criminals.

19. *Reports on the Course of Instruction in Yale College* (New Haven: Hezekiah Howe, 1830), in *Antebellum American Culture*, ed. David Brion Davis (Lexington, Mass.: D. C. Heath, 1979), 62.

20. "Government through the Family" is the chapter title of chapter 3 in Jacques Donzelot's well-known study, *The Policing of Families* (New York: Pantheon Books, 1979), 48–95. Here, Donzelot discusses the paradoxical situation where the "autonomization of the family" actually served as a technology of social control.

21. Heman Humphrey, *Domestic Education* (Amherst, Mass.: J. S. and C. Adams, 1840), 16.

22. Ibid., 21–23.

23. Ibid., 23.
24. Henry C. Wright, *The Empire of the Mother over the Character and Destiny of the Race* (Boston: B. Marsh, 1863); Horace Mann's phrases are from *A Few Thoughts on the Power and Duties of Women* (Syracuse, N.Y.: Hall, Mills and Co. 1853), 125, 15.
25. Mary P. Ryan, *The Empire of the Mother: American Writing about Domesticity, 1830–1860* (New York: Harrington Park Press, 1985), 39, 109–110, 107.
26. In this context, it is useful to consider Edward Said's argument that the constitution of the Orient as a knowable subject was also what facilitated colonial expropriation. See Said's *Orientalism* (New York: Vintage Books, 1979). In his account, we see yet another example of the relation between the mechanics of dominion and the attribution of identity. The first chapter of *Orientalism*, "Knowing the Oriental," to my mind directly clarifies the operations of "knowledge" in *Pierre*.
27. Samuel Goodrich, *Fireside Education* (New York: Samuel Colman, 1838), 62–63.
28. See, for example, John L. Thomas, "Romantic Reform in America, 1815–1865," *American Quarterly* 17 (Winter 1965): 656–81. Thomas sees nineteenth-century reform as a kind of "perfectionist individualism."
29. Once again, I am struck by the parallel between the model of human relations in *Pierre* and the model of human relations Foucault discerns in a disciplinary society. "In discipline," Foucault observes, "the elements are interchangeable. . . . It individualizes bodies by a location that does not give them a fixed position, but distributes them and circulates them in a network of relations" (*Discipline and Punish*, 145–46). For a related discussion of the idea of "positionality," see Rosalind Coward and John Ellis, *Language and Materialism: Developments in Semiology and the Theory of the Subject* (London: Routledge & Kegan Paul, 1977), 80–81, 126–27.
30. Emerson, *Nature*, in *Selections*, 56.
31. Plinlimmon, of course, has always been something of a centerpiece in the criticism of *Pierre*. For most critics, the issue is whether he "speaks for" Melville. Those who argue that he does include William Braswell, *Melville's Religious Thought: An Essay in Interpretation* (Durham, N.C.: Duke University Press, 1943), 81–85; Newton Arvin, *Herman Melville* (New York: William Sloane, 1950), 221–22; and James E. Miller, Jr., *A Reader's Guide to Herman Melville* (New York: Farrar, Straus, 1962), 132–38. For an opposing view, see Brian Higgins, "Chronometricals and Horologicals," in *Critical Essays on Melville's "Pierre; or, The Ambiguities,"* ed. Brian Higgins and Hershel Parker (Boston: G. K. Hall, 1983), 221–25. I would associate Plinlimmon, however, most immediately with Lucy, and, more generally, with the development of social supervision in nineteenth-century America.
32. In this context, it is useful to keep in mind John Meyer's remark about individualism, that it is the "enforcement of a disciplined cosmology," within which "freedom is compulsory." See "Myths of Socialization and of

Personality," in *Reconstructing Individualism: Autonomy, Individuality, and the Self in Western Thought*, ed. Thomas C. Heller, Morton Sosna, and David Wellbery (Stanford, Calif.: Stanford University Press, 1986), 211.

33. Here I am implicitly disagreeing with Emory Elliott's argument that Pierre fails to become an original author because of his inability "to escape the bonds of the established ideology." I would argue instead that the very idea of "originality" is itself an ideologically inscribed category, and that Pierre's commitment to that idea marks his kinship with everyone else. See Elliott, "Art, Religion, and the Problem of Authority in *Pierre*," in *Ideology and Classic American Literature*, ed. Sacvan Bercovitch and Myra Jehlen (Cambridge: Cambridge University Press, 1986), 337–51.

34. *United States Magazine and Democratic Review*, 30 January 1852. I am drawing upon the Melville Collection at the Newberry Library for these nineteenth-century reviews.

35. See, for example, Allon White, *The Uses of Obscurity: The Fiction of Early Modernism* (London: Routledge & Kegan Paul, 1981), 4–9.

36. *Boston Post*, 4 August 1852; *New York Day Book*, 7 September 1852; *Southern Quarterly Review*, October 1852.

Chapter 6
Personified Accounting

1. *The Confidence-Man: His Masquerade*, ed. Hershel Parker (New York: Norton, 1971), 162. All further references to this edition will be included in the text.

2. I am here disagreeing with Edward Mitchell's interesting observation that "the attempt to define or describe the confidence men, or their victims either for that matter, in terms of their essence is an impossibility in this novel." I would suggest instead that even though essence (or, in my vocabulary, being) is impossible to define, it is not impossible to invoke—most especially, as the ground of absolution. See Mitchell, "From Action to Essence: Some Notes on the Structure of Melville's *The Confidence-Man*," *American Literature* 40 (March 1968): 32.

3. *Pierre: or, The Ambiguities* (Evanston and Chicago: Northwestern University Press and the Newberry Library, 1971), 325.

4. Mark Winsome and his disciple Egbert have generally been taken as caricatures of Emerson and Thoreau. See, for instance, Egbert S. Oliver, "Melville's Picture of Emerson and Thoreau in *The Confidence-Man*," *College English* 8 (November 1946): 61–72; Elizabeth S. Foster, Introduction to the Hendricks House edition of *The Confidence-Man*, lxxiii–lxxxii; Hershel Parker, "Melville's Satire of Emerson and Thoreau: An Evaluation of the Evidence," *American Transcendental Quarterly* 7 (Summer 1970): 61–67.

5. *Moby-Dick*, ed. Harrison Hayford and Hershel Parker (New York: Norton, 1967), 469.

6. Walt Whitman, *Leaves of Grass and Selected Prose* (New York: Holt, Rinehart, and Winston, 1949), 76.

7. Such a reading obviously departs from the two standard interpretations of this chapter. John Shroeder and Hershel Parker both see the Indian-hater as a positive figure—for Shroeder, an evil-hater of "heroic proportions," for Parker, the ideal Christian, putting to shame the "diluted" faith most Christians practice. At the other end of the spectrum, Roy Harvey Pearce denies that the Indian-hater is any kind of hero. I agree with Parker and Shroeder in seeing the Indian-hater as a heroic figure for Melville, though not for the same reasons. See John W. Shroeder, "Sources and Symbols for Melville's *Confidence-Man*," *PMLA* 66 (June 1951): 363–80; Roy Harvey Pearce, "Melville's Indian-hater: A Note on a Meaning of *The Confidence-Man*," *PMLA* 67 (December 1952): 942–48; and Hershel Parker, "The Metaphysics of Indian-hating," *Nineteenth-Century Fiction* 18 (September 1963): 165–73.

8. Cecelia Tichi summarizes a critical consensus when she describes *The Confidence-Man* as an attack on "the immoral Wall Street spirit," in "Melville's Craft and Theme of Language Debased in *The Confidence-Man*," *ELH* 39 (1972): 639–58. One important exception to this consensus is Jean-Christophe Agnew's reading of *The Confidence-Man* as a formal and thematic enactment of the "fundamental problematic of a placeless market: the problems of identity, intentionality, accountability, transparency, and reciprocity"; see *Worlds Apart: The Market and the Theater in Anglo-American Thought, 1550–1750* (New York: Cambridge University Press, 1986), 195–203.

9. Elizabeth Fox-Genovese and Eugene D. Genovese, *Fruits of Merchant Capital: Slavery and Bourgeois Property in the Rise and Expansion of Capitalism* (New York: Oxford University Press, 1983), 344.

10. Walter Benn Michaels, "The Phenomenology of Contract," *Raritan* 4 (1985): 58. Also see Morton J. Horwitz, *The Transformation of American Law, 1780–1860* (Cambridge: Harvard University Press, 1977), 160–210. Also relevant here is Emile Durkheim's discussion of the social relations engendered by contract, in *The Division of Labor in Society*, trans. George Simpson (New York: The Free Press, 1964), 200–29.

11. *The Transformation of American Law*, 161. Peter Gabel and Brook Thomas have also drawn attention to circular reasoning in legal formalism (of which Melville's father-in-law, Lemuel Shaw, was a leading exponent). See Peter Gabel, "Reification in Legal Reasoning," *Research in Law and Sociology* 3 (1980): 25–51; and Brook Thomas, "Legal Fictions," *Critical Inquiry* 11 (September 1984): 24–51. For an interesting discussion of the "disappearance of the just," see Richard H. Weisberg, *The Failure of the Word: The Protagonist as Lawyer in Modern Fiction* (New Haven: Yale University Press, 1984), 13–23.

12. And no one, not even Bartleby, can escape the fate of becoming a contracting party. For a discussion of contract and "preferring not to," see

Walter Benn Michaels, *The Gold Standard and the Logic of Naturalism* (Berkeley: University of California Press, 1987), 19.

13. For the importance of the concept "to act otherwise" to the ideas of freedom and accountability, see, for example, A. J. Ayer, *Freedom and Morality and Other Essays* (Oxford: Oxford University Press, 1985), 1–16.

14. Jean Baudrillard, *For a Critique of the Political Economy of the Sign*, trans. Charles Levin (St. Louis: Telos Press, 1981), 143–45.

15. Karl Marx, *Capital*, trans. Samuel Moore and Edward Aveling, 3 vols. (New York: International Publishers, 1967), 1: 71–74.

16. Horwitz, *The Transformation of American Law*, 181, writes, "The development of extensive markets at the turn of the century contributed to a substantial erosion of belief in theories of objective value and just price. Markets for future delivery of goods were difficult to explain within a theory of exchange based on giving and receiving equivalents in value. Futures contracts for fungible commodities could only be understood in terms of a fluctuating conception of expected value radically different from the static notion that lay behind contracts for specific goods; a regime of markets and speculation was simply incompatible with a socially imposed standard of value. The rise of a modern law of contract, then, was an outgrowth of an essentially procommercial attack on the theory of objective value which lay at the foundation of the eighteenth century's equitable idea of contract."

17. I am aware that, in the immediate context, the "man-child" means a male child. However, since the P.I.O. man is selling this man-child as a promising article, we are entitled to use the phrase in its other sense—as a generic term for a promising individual.

18. The emergence of a "placeless market," a market free of traditional spatial boundaries, is a central argument in Jean-Christophe Agnew's *Worlds Apart*.

19. Robert Rantoul, Jr., "An Address to the Workingmen of the United States of America," first published in the *Workingmen's Library* (1833), collected in *Memoirs, Speeches, and Writings*, ed. Luther Hamilton (Boston: John P. Jewett & Co., 1854), 248.

20. Speech at Kalamazoo, Michigan, 27 August 1856, in *Collected Works of Abraham Lincoln*, ed. Roy F. Basler, 9 vols. (New Brunswick, N.J.: Rutgers University Press, 1933–35), 2: 364.

21. Rantoul, *Memoirs, Speeches, and Writings*, 250.

22. Here I follow Michael Ignatieff's discussion of the penal philosophy developed during the industrial revolution. The modern penitentiary, Ignatieff argues, operated through the "social production of guilt": it secured its legitimacy (as well as the legitimacy of the social order) by insisting on the self-punishment and self-correction of the offender. See *A Just Measure of Pain: The Penitentiary in the Industrial Revolution, 1750–1850* (New York: Columbia University Press, 1978), 44–79.

23. Judith N. Shklar, *Legalism: Law, Morals, and Political Trials* (Cambridge: Harvard University Press, 1986), 200–209. Shklar is discussing the

Moscow Trials of the 1930s that held "people responsible for the unintended, as yet unrealized, future consequences of their action." Her comments apply equally to the rationale offered for the extermination of the Indians.

24. The classic accounts of the relation between capitalism and imperialism are J. A. Hobson, *Imperialism*, and Lenin, *Imperialism: The Highest Stage of Capitalism*. For a good summary of the Hobson–Lenin thesis and critiques of it, see Michael W. Doyle, *Empires* (Ithaca, N.Y.: Cornell University, 1986), 141–61. This chapter obviously has no theoretical ambitions in that direction. I am concerned here only with a figure common both to the logic of the marketplace and the logic of nationhood in America—the figure of the autonomous self.

25. My point here parallels the argument made by Richard Sennett and Jonathan Cobb about "individuality" as a discriminatory category: "individuals exist only so long as a mass exists, a point of reference consisting of others who seem pretty much alike." See *The Hidden Injuries of Class* (New York: Vintage, 1973), 67.

26. *Fruits of Merchant Capital*, 352.

27. William Ellery Channing, *Self-Culture* (Boston: James Munroe & Co., 1839), 10.

28. "Man the Reformer," in *The Portable Emerson* (New York: Viking, 1974), 83.

29. Ibid., 69–70.

30. Robert Rantoul, Jr., "Remarks on Education," first published in the *North American Review* (October 1838), collected in *Memoirs, Speeches, and Writings*, 84.

31. Ibid., 95–96.

32. George Santayana, "The Genteel Tradition in American Philosophy," in *Selected Critical Writings of George Santayana*, 2 vols., ed. Norman Henfrey (Cambridge: Harvard University Press, 1968) 2: 91; John L. Thomas, "Romantic Reform in America, 1815–1865," *American Quarterly* 17 (Winter 1965): 656–81.

33. Paul Johnson, examining revivals and economics in Rochester, New York, writes, "A nascent industrial capitalism became attached to visions of a perfect moral order based on individual freedom and self-government." In *A Shopkeeper's Millennium: Society and Revivals in Rochester, New York, 1815–1837* (New York: Hill and Wang, 1978), esp. 95–141, Johnson makes a convincing argument for antebellum reform as entrepreneural reform.

34. Warwick Wadlington has also noted this peculiar power of the confidence man. He sees this as a benign influence, however, since self-contradiction, according to him, brings out what is good in the victim. See *The Confidence Game in American Literature* (Princton: Princeton University Press, 1975), 148–49, 159–64.

35. Ann Douglas and Warwick Wadlington have both brought up the question of Melville's "irresponsibility." See Douglas, *The Feminization of*

American Culture (New York: Knopf, 1978), 301. In his typically quizzical way, Wadlington has made a positive case for irresponsibility in *The Confidence Game*, esp. 142–43.

36. The discrepancy has been pointed out by both John G. Cawelti, "Some Notes on the Structure of *The Confidence-Man*," *American Literature* 29 (November 1957): 281; and Edgar A. Dryden, *Melville's Thematics of Form: The Great Art of Telling the Truth* (Baltimore: Johns Hopkins University Press, 1968), 154–65.

37. R.W.B. Lewis, Afterword, in *The Confidence-Man* (New York: Signet, 1968), 265. Also see Cawelti, "Some Notes," 283.

38. My point here would seem to echo an earlier observation about *Mardi*. I suggest, however, that whereas in *Mardi* one voice speaks for everyone, in *The Confidence-Man* the autonomy of language undermines even the ground for a "voice."

39. The technology of "interchangeable parts" is commonly held to be the most significant advance in mass production in the nineteenth century. Recent scholarship has challenged both the efficacy and the pervasiveness of that invention. See, for example, Robert S. Woodbury, "The Legend of Eli Whitney and Interchangeable Parts," *Technology and Culture* 1 (1960): 235–53; and David A. Hounshell, *From the American System to Mass Production, 1800–1932* (Baltimore: Johns Hopkins University Press, 1984), 15–65. It is fair to say, however, that whatever its reality, the ideal of interchangeable parts remained the foremost technological ideal in the nineteenth century.

40. Michel Foucault, *Discipline and Punish: The Birth of the Prison* (New York: Vintage, 1979), 145–46. Foucault's observation is especially important for explaining why "individuality" and "interchangeability" can coexist.

41. Here I am completely in agreement with Henry Sussman, who has similarly commented on the "self-enclosed fictive domain" in *The Confidence-Man* in "The Deconstructor as Politician," *Glyph* 4 (1978): 37.

42. Adam Smith, *An Inquiry into the Nature and Causes of the Wealth of Nations*, 2 vols., ed. Edwin Cannan (Chicago: University of Chicago Press, 1976), 2: 208, 1: 477. On the importance of Adam Smith to American political economists, see Paul K. Conkin, *Prophets of Prosperity: America's First Political Economists* (Bloomington: Indiana University Press, 1980). For the importance of the idea of "self-regulation" to economic thought, see Otto Mayr, *Authority, Liberty, and Automatic Machinery in Early Modern Europe* (Baltimore: Johns Hopkins University Press, 1986), 164–80.

43. Paul Brodtkorb, "*The Confidence-Man*: The Con-Man as Hero," *Studies in the Novel* 1 (Winter 1969): 430.

44. The phrase is Merlin Bowen's. See "Tactics of Indirection in Melville's *The Confidence-Man*," *Studies in the Novel* 1 (Winter 1969): 401–20.

Index

◆   ◆   ◆

accountability: and authorship, 206–14; in economics of selfhood, 177–81, 184–86, 198–99, 201, 203; in market economy, 188, 191–92, 194, 198–99, 205–6; and victimization, 178–80, 184–86, 200–201, 204–5

Adams, John Quincy, 26, 33, 118

agency, 81, 116–17, 128–29, 137–38, 181, 203, 208; in allegory, 25–26, 29–30, 53–57; of America, 28–30

Agnew, Jean-Christophe, 194

Ahab, 24, 114–20, 129–39, 153–55, 163, 174, 177, 180, 182, 183, 185; similarities to Indians, 115–19, 135–36

allegory: and agency, 25–26, 29–30, 53–57; of authorship, 78–79, 81, 84, 92, 114; history of, 23–24; in *Moby-Dick*, 118; and personification, 25–28, 53–54, 136; and property rights, 54–57, 68–70; as public discourse, 21–22; and time, 22–23, 25; in *White-Jacket*, 97

Anderson, Charles, 100

Anderson, Quentin, 7

authorial sovereignty, 7–9, 23–24, 50, 56–57, 63–67, 75, 76, 111–12, 114, 175; lack of, 77–78, 82. *See also* creativity

authorship, 174; and accountability, 206–14; and creativity, 44, 48–50; and historicity, 4–5; and

monarchy, 46–47, 49, 66–67; and nationhood, 9–10; and property rights, 59–60, 66–67; and selfhood, 4–5; and truth, 3, 7–8, 213. *See also* Melville, on authorship

Baudrillard, Jean, 190

Beecher, Lyman, 18, 38–39, 40

Benjamin, Walter, 22, 23, 24, 25, 54, 55, 79

Bercovitch, Sacvan, 6

Bhabha, Homi, 17

Blackstone, William: on property rights, 8, 32, 44–45, 46, 66, 148

Bolton, Harry, 88–90, 99, 107–8

Boomer, Captain, 119

Brodhead, Richard, 44, 67

Brodtkorb, Paul, 210

Brown, William Wells, 127

Brownson, Orestes, 37

California: admission to statehood, 28–29

capital: and labor, 11–12, 15–16, 19, 32

capitalism, 11–12, 15–16, 19, 31. *See also* market economy

Carey, Henry, 16

Castle, Terry, 68

Chandler, Zachariach, 19

Channing, William Ellery, 34, 39, 202

characters: in *The Confidence-Man*, 207–10; in *Mardi*, 48–54, 63–65